LF

PARTICIPATION IN POLITICS

NOMOS
XVI

N O M O S

NOMOS XVI
Yearbook of the American Society for Political and Legal Philosophy

PARTICIPATION
IN POLITICS

Edited by

J. ROLAND PENNOCK   *Swarthmore College*

and

JOHN W. CHAPMAN   *University of Pittsburgh*

L

LIEBER-ATHERTON
New York 1975

Participation in Politics: Nomos XVI
edited by J. Roland Pennock and John W. Chapman

Address all inquiries to:
Lieber-Atherton, Incorporated
1841 Broadway
New York, New York 10023

Library of Congress Catalog Number 73-83019
ISBN 0-88311-021-0
Serial Publication Number US-ISSN-0078-0979

Printed in the United States of America

PREFACE

How much participation is "feasible"—at what points and at what costs? Is political participation instrumental or an end in itself? If the former, does it contribute to better policy or to self-development or to "antialienation"? What is the significance of contemporary desires for and claims to more and greater involvements? What are the expectations of the proponents of participation, and in what theoretical perspectives are these claims and desires and expectations to be viewed? It is to questions like these, and many others, that the present volume is addressed.

If we put aside Pericles, Lenin's *State and Revolution* (which he himself repudiated), and the works of Mary Parker Follett, then the two great remaining exponents of participation are Rousseau and Marx. It is instructive to notice their differences. For Rousseau the purpose of participation is mutual clarification as to the requirements of justice. Also he believes that without personal and steady involvement men will not acquire a sense of justice. Successful participation presumes moral and intellectual independence; the participators cannot merely reflect one another's opinions. If they behave as mirrors, Rousseau's citizens risk arbitrary and damaging agreement and so produce that invalid form of consensus, a "will of all" that is not a "general will." Moreover, they must confine themselves to the discovery and enunciation of general rules, and they must leave the application of these principles to their agents, lest personal and situational considerations cloud their moral insight.

Marx appears to have expected rather more from participation, nothing less than psychological and moral transformation. In his ideal society, in which the claims of justice are rendered otiose by abundance, men become rational and free, and for the first time they are able to realize all their capacities. This goes far beyond and is far more utopian than Rousseau's vision of moral salvation through direct democracy. Indeed, Marx's conception of human possibilities quite transcends Humboldt's notion of "social union" and Mill's concern for human diversity. Marx feared that a premature attempt to achieve his ideal would result in an invalid form of consensus, "crude communism," in which agreement is based on sordid and stultifying motives like envy.

The difference between the hopes for mankind of Rousseau and Marx is the difference between salvation and transfiguration. Not many of our contemporary theorists of participation have noticed this. Nor have they expressed concern that the demand for "participatory democracy" and the acceptance of supervised efforts at personal "transparency" ("encounter groups" and the like) seem to be on the increase as autonomy and independence decline. It is possible that processes very different from those envisaged by either Marx or Rousseau are present in the modern world. If this is so, then the nature and quality and significance of the craving for participation may go beyond what they had in mind. Thus the inspiration for the morals and politics of participation in the latter part of the twentieth century may well not be confined to either the liberal or the Marxist tradition.

This book began at the annual meetings of the American Society for Political and Legal Philosophy, in New York, December 1971. They provided its foundation, in terms of six papers included among the fourteen essays presented here. (Specifically, the contributions by Bachrach, Braybrooke, Kalodner, Kateb, Mermin, and Wexler.) To the chairman of the program committee, Hugo Adam Bedau, of Tufts University, the editors owe their thanks. So also to the contributors. As this volume goes to press, it will do no harm to announce to readers that anyone who would like to propose a contribution on "Anarchism" or on "Constitutionalism" should communicate with the editors.

J. ROLAND PENNOCK
JOHN W. CHAPMAN

CONTENTS

ix

CONTRIBUTORS

PETER BACHRACH
Political Science, Temple University

DAVID BRAYBROOKE
Philosophy and Political Science, Dalhousie University

CARL J. FRIEDRICH
Political Science, Harvard University

HOWARD I. KALODNER
Law, New York University

GEORGE KATEB
Political Science, Amherst College

DONALD W. KEIM
Political Science, Baldwin-Wallace College

JOHN LADD
Philosophy, Brown University

JANE MANSBRIDGE
Political Science, University of Chicago

SAMUEL MERMIN
Law, University of Wisconsin

LISA H. NEWTON
Philosophy, Fairfield University

DAVID G. SMITH
Political Science, Swarthmore College

M. B. E. SMITH
Philosophy, Smith College

ALAN WERTHEIMER
Political Science, University of Vermont

STEPHEN WEXLER
Law, University of British Columbia

INTRODUCTION

Political participation is a very old subject with new overtones, as George Kateb remarks in his essay in this volume. Especially since the Port Huron Statement, it and the unredundant concept "participatory democracy" have been much discussed and written about. In its origin, of course, "democracy" meant what we know of as "direct democracy." In that context, to speak of "participatory democracy" *would* have been redundant. For Aristotle, to be a whole man meant to be a citizen, and the reverse was equally true. While he was by no means certain that all men (other than slaves) should be citizens, he found much to commend in that form of polity. At the same time, he appears not to have believed that democratic citizens could rise to the same level of citizenship that was attainable in a polity in which that status was reserved for the more virtuous.

With the decline of the city state, talk about popular participation in politics largely went the way of its practice. And much later, as the institution of representation developed, its theory was not, for a long time, "participatory." Of Donald Keim's three major types of participatory theory (see Chapter 1), it was the first only, "self-protection," that served as a justification for the early parliaments. As the theory was broadened to stress discussion as well as control and to insist upon equal rights to participation and consideration, as with the Levellers, it was still representatives of the people who would do the discussing and in general play the active roles in popular government. So it has remained, with certain outstanding exceptions, until comparatively recent times. Early New England and the mountain fastnesses of Switzerland apart, direct democracy has seemed out of the question and the task of governing large nation states has appeared neither feasible nor attractive from the point of view of general popular participation.

Rousseau, of course, stands out in sharp contrast to what has just been said. For him representation was anathema, while participation was the very essence of democracy. But then Rousseau spoke, once more, of the city state, and he was far from optimistic about the outlook for democracy even there. In the liberal tradition, John Stuart Mill was perhaps the first proponent of representative government to place the emphasis upon the effect of participation on the participants. And among these he included not only representatives but voters as well. The educational and moralizing effects of sharing responsibility for the government of society and the need, at least the obligation, to think about and discuss matters political and the effects of one's voting upon others—these were for Mill the crowning virtues of representative government. Yet a fully democratic regime remained for him a questionable quantity. Democracy without leadership by the elite would be doomed to mediocrity or worse.

It was Karl Marx, the other outstanding exception to the general trend discussed here, who picked up Rousseau's thought and became the inspiration for much contemporary theorizing about participatory democracy. However great our doubts may be as to what Marx foresaw as the nature and role of political processes and institutions in the ultimate stage of communism, certain things are clear. Men would share equally and fully in that process. Man could become whole, no longer alienated, only by the fullest participation in determining the conditions and conduct of communal life. He would indeed be transformed, not by the deliberate pursuit of some preconceived goal, except in the vaguest sense, but by the revolutionizing process by which old institutions were destroyed and a new society created. It is from Marx, then, rather than from Mill or Green, or even John Dewey (though he would be closer), that one finds an appropriate takeoff point for introducing the subject of political participation today.

The modern advocates of greatly increased political participation encompass in their thinking at least all of the facets of the concept that have been touched upon above. They certainly justify it by reference to all three of Donald Keim's types of justification: self-protection, self-rule, and self-realization (both subtypes). David Braybrooke's designation of their theories as multifaceted and vague, and as sometimes outcome-oriented and sometimes not, is surely correct. But anyone seeking the "new overtones" must turn his attention to the demand for activity, involvement. Mill's educational and moralizing effects of political participation pale by contrast with the kind of transformation anticipated by today's participatory democrats. By commitment and participation man becomes, for the first time, a whole person and an ever changing person. In this essentially Marxian idea (*praxis*) resides an inescapable element of irrationality. One must commit oneself to the (as yet) unknown. As Peter Bachrach remarks, men cannot "rationally calculate the costs and benefits of participation" because participation changes their interests. It is not just the external results of one's activities that are unknown but also, and even more unpredictably, the alterations in one's own personality, desires, and values. One demands to participate, on the faith that what will come out of it will be more acceptable to what one then is than present circumstances are to one's present self.

Perhaps none of this is completely new. Leaders and instigators of mass movements—whether democratic or antidemocratic—have long known that to get people to participate, especially in some emotion-filled event, is the best way to get them committed to more of the same and to the movement of which the event is a part. Anyone who has participated in a "demonstration" of one sort or another is familiar with the psychology involved.

Nor is it completely irrational. We all know that to participate in a collective project is usually a pleasurable experience in itself. It is more fun to do most things in the company of others than in solitude—especially if what we are doing is not in itself a particularly enjoyable task. But some degree of irrationality remains an inherent part of the process: the commitment to the unknown, to changes designed to alter the very self that must evaluate the outcomes.

The stress on active involvement is not all that is meant by the demand for participation. From one point of view this demand is simply an especially vigorous assertion of the demand for political equality. Equality of political (voting) and civil rights is not enough. People want equal participation in decision making, and the only way this can be made effective, it is argued, is to make it direct. Seen from this angle, the demand for participation is simply a means for making political equality substantial as well as formal. The more extreme forms of the demand for equal participation tend to be in opposition to all authority. The insistence upon individual autonomy, from which the demand for equality itself appears to spring, comes once more to the surface and tends to be more prominent than the claim for equality itself. This demand may take any of various forms. It may lead to the contention that the people may not delegate their power in any significant way. Government officials must be continuously accountable for their acts. Modern versions of initiative, referendum, and recall again come to the fore.

Even more radically, what has often been considered a corollary of political equality, majority rule, itself comes into question. Majority rule constitutes formal equality, but whether it amounts to substantial equality depends upon whether or not certain members of the group are in fact permanently excluded from the majority. Perhaps even more to the point, majority rule is directly in conflict with individual autonomy. Obviously, the rule toward which all this points is that of unanimity. Since this institution can work, if at all, only in small, face-to-face groups, its constitutional embodiment must be in the form of radical decentralization. And that in fact is the direction, or one of the directions, in which the movement for participatory democracy has moved. The sheer arithmetic of the situation pushes in the same direction.

Yet decentralization is of course subject to severe limitations as a satisfactory basis for government in a large and complicated society. Apart from its weakness as a means for dealing with the governmental problems of an industrial society, it confronts an even more fundamental problem. Some face-to-face groups can act unanimously, or nearly so, or at least without hopeless dissension; but can those that are feasible for governmental purposes do so? In the ensuing pages, serious doubts are raised on this score. Thus Jane Mansbridge warns against assuming that groups determined by geographical boundaries, even neighborhoods, will behave like voluntary associations, from which dissenters have the easy out of withdrawal. And in similar vein, Lisa Newton argues that he who would govern a community by a town meeting, or anything similar, must first find (create) a community.

To point to these difficulties of participatory democracy, fundamental and serious though they are, is not of course to deny that more political participation may both be entirely possible and highly desirable. Most principles carried to their logical conclusions encounter difficulties, and this one is no exception. One of the interesting things about it, philosophically, is that this concept, in good dialectical fashion, seems to contain within it its own problems ("contradictions"). The problems inherent in the effort to achieve a community of active equals is one with which each generation must wrestle anew. The essays in this volume do not claim to exhaust its ramifications even for the present day. Other relevant considerations will be brought to bear upon it in NOMOS XVII (*Human Nature in Politics*) and in NOMOS XIX (*Anarchism*). As a moderating influence, the by-no-means irrelevant topic of *Due Process* will be inserted as NOMOS XVIII between the last two mentioned volumes!

A few words about the essays that follow. As is customary in this series, no Procrustean plan is fastened upon (or under!) the authors. Rather they are permitted to develop their thoughts on the subject in their own way. To be sure, some of the papers were originally presented (not always in their present form) before a meeting of the American Society for Political and Legal Philosophy. Accordingly, some originally took the form of comments on other papers, some were philosophical and definitional, while others were directed more to matters of practical application.

The distinction just made forms the basis for the division of the volume into two parts. The essays in Part I tend to be the more philosophically oriented discussions. Donald Keim leads off with a classification of types of participation theory. Identifying his first type, "self-protection," with "democratic revisionism," he launches an attack upon that controversial stance. Next he discusses participation as a means of increasing control, "self-rule," before turning to what it is perhaps fair to designate as his major concern, participation as "self-realization." While his sympathies lie with some version of this type of participatory theory, he also recognizes that it seems "particularly vulnerable to utopian excess."

Bachrach, like Keim, attacks conventional (pluralist) democratic theory. It is, he urges, "the moral obligation of the democratic system to recognize and implement the individual's participatory right."

David Braybrooke, in his survey of conceptual issues, provides the reader with a richness and variety of fare that defies summary. Perhaps his most important theme, as George Kateb argues in his ensuing comments, is that even if it should turn out that the demand for participation adds up only to claims for such traditional values as liberty, equality, fraternity, and justice, great psychological value is to be derived from the use of the word "participation."

John Ladd's essay, "The Ethics of Participation," is likewise too elaborate to admit of adequate summary. The conclusion, however, is simple and straightforward: the claim to participate is the claim of an autonomous, moral being to exercise a moral responsibility, and as such it ought not to be hindered.

Part I concludes with M. B. E. Smith's frontal attack on the whole case for maximizing political participation. After contending that such a policy involves many costs and that those who assert its positive values have not supported their arguments with evidence, he goes on to a detailed consideration of whether political participation is intrinsically good. This question he answers in the negative.

The more practical bent of Part II is introduced by Samuel Mermin's survey of recent implementations of the participation principle in American law. His discussion is followed by Howard Kalodner's more detailed discussion of citizen participation as provided not only by statute but also by implementing rules and regulations. His consideration of these legal provisions and their operation leads him to conclude that formal mechanisms generally do not provide the most effective means of gaining significant citizen participation. These discussions are followed by Stephen Wexler's argument that it is a mistake to place great reliance upon experts rather than laymen. Counseling in a somewhat opposed direction is Carl Friedrich's essay, "Participation without Responsibility: Codetermination in Industry and University." Speaking particularly of workers' participation, he doubts the effectiveness of participation through a single institution.

David Smith gives a new turn to the discussion by analyzing the problems involved in professional advocacy. In the administrative process especially, professionals are increasingly relied upon, whether as staff members or as outside experts. How and to what extent is it proper for them to participate in the administrative process in ways that go beyond the skills of their own professions? In arguing against the professionals' use of their *cachet* as professionals to support positions they may hold as laymen, he is, by implication, disagreeing with the thesis advanced by Wexler.

Jane Mansbridge and Lisa Newton, in two nicely complementary essays, bring the discussion around to participation in small, face-to-face groups. It is Lisa Newton's thesis that the "maximum feasible participation" requirement of the War on Poverty program misconceived the problem. It sought to provide participation for citizens of a community when in fact the people were scarcely citizens in any significant sense and where in fact no community existed. Jane Mansbridge, on the basis of a study of nongovernmental associations, concludes that the move from small to large as well as from voluntary to nonvoluntary organizations tends to be destructive of the values that participation in voluntary face-to-face groups has. The principles of equal influence, of face-to-face democracy, and of consensus have each proved subject to serious liabilities.

In the concluding essay, Alan Wertheimer brings us back to the national scene. He defends compulsory voting as a means of increasing political participation and preventing "free riding" on the system. In the course of his argument he has occasion to criticize the arguments of various authors, including Downs and Riker and Ordeshook.

These hints at the contents of the volume are intended to be no more than that. In many instances, individual authors might feel that no reference has been made to their most important points. But if these remarks have served to pique the curiosity of some and to give guidance to those who are interested in particular points rather than the subject as a whole, they will have served their purpose.

J. ROLAND PENNOCK

PART I

1

PARTICIPATION
IN CONTEMPORARY
DEMOCRATIC THEORIES

DONALD W. KEIM

The simplest definition of democracy, rule by the people, implies participation. To rule carries the unstated condition: to take part; yet the role of participation in democracy has never been agreed upon. To conclude from its etymology that democracy implies participation by the people in the activity of ruling begins, rather than ends, the controversy. What is to be achieved by participation? What is its function? If understanding were reached in this area, it would be relatively easy to describe the forms participation might assume.

Disagreement over the function of participation provides a major focus for the contemporary debate on democratic theory, but the importance of the topic offers no assurance of clarity. Instead of considering the effects of participation, the parties are feverishly involved in establishing the democratic *bona fides* of their favorite approach by asserting its claim to the mantle of "classical democratic theory."

These efforts are surely misdirected, for the issue is not pedigree —each view can be traced back to a certified democratic theory— but function: What does participation achieve? To address this problem is to return the debate to the question of the ends of politics.

A major obstacle to any rational discussion of participation is the ambiguity the subject matter breeds. To some, participation means choosing leaders; to others, it means actually deciding policy. Nor is ambiguity reduced by cataloguing the forms of participation, from "taking an interest in political news" through "running for office," for such a listing tells something about the "what" but nothing about the "why" of participation. A fruitful discussion of the functions of participation in democratic politics requires a classification scheme that sets forth the possible forms of participation *together with* their justificatory arguments. This essay presents such a scheme in the form of a typology, constructed from the justificatory arguments for participation in contemporary democratic thought. This approach risks oversimplification since the boundaries between types are seldom as precise as the analytical constructs suggest. Moreover, because justificatory arguments often incorporate several analytically distinct positions, it is impossible to assign each argument to a separate category. The task of classification is further compounded when the justificatory arguments actually hide discrepant intentions. Therefore, it should be clearly understood that I am here not concerned with cataloguing the entire range of contemporary arguments. Merely to identify and illustrate them would require a lengthy essay. I will confine myself primarily to examining the internal logic and philosophical premises of the most typical treatments of participation found in recent democratic theory.

Examination of contemporary democratic theories reveals three types of participation, symbolized by the terms self-protection, self-rule, and self-realization.[1] Each can be identified in terms of its locus, mode, and goal. Moreover, each type is predictably associated with certain presuppositions regarding man and politics. An adequate discussion of participation must include consideration of these elements.

Most of the examples used here to illustrate the theories of participation are taken from the writings of contributors to the current debate. In response to the broad attack on democratic revisionism[2] over the past decade, all schools of democratic thought have increased their efforts to articulate their arguments. This permits the examination and comparison of theories of participation within the convenient compass of the debate itself.

I will begin with a brief treatment of democratic revisionism and its characteristic participatory principle, self-protection. This is followed by an examination of the "other side," which for the sake of convenience we shall label participatory democracy (PD). As will become apparent, PD assumes two basic forms, each of which displays its own type of participation.

DEMOCRATIC REVISIONISM

The extensive exposition and analysis democratic revisionism has been subjected to over the past two decades make a review of all facets of the new democratic orthodoxy quite superfluous. Instead, we will concentrate on the features relating directly to participation, especially as they reveal the function of participation in democratic revisionism. This function, as will be seen, depends upon the views of man and politics held by democratic revisionists.

The writings of Robert Dahl constitute the *locus classicus* of democratic revisionism. In a half dozen works Dahl has presented a comprehensive statement of this position with admirable clarity. In a small volume outlining the foundations of modern political analysis, Dahl offers what may be described as the "state of nature" argument of democratic revisionism. In a chapter dealing with "political man," Dahl confronts the empirical evidence that most men are not very involved in political activities. As he puts it, "obviously man is not instinctively a political animal."[3] He then goes on, in highly revealing terms, to account for the lack of involvement on the part of most citizens.

The explanation no doubt, turns on the fact that man is not by instinct a reasonable, reasoning civic-minded being. Many of his most imperious desires and the source of many of his most powerful gratifications can be traced to ancient and persistent biological and physiological drives, needs, and wants. Organized political life arrived late in man's evolution; today man learns how to behave as a political man with the aid and often with the hindrance of instinctive equipment that is the product of a long prior development. To avoid pain, discomfort, and hunger; to satisfy drives for sexual gratification, love, security, and respect—these needs are insistent and primordial. The means of satisfying them quickly and concretely generally lie outside political life.[4]

There may be times when the rewards of political involvement are sufficient to induce participation. Usually this will occur when direct, nonpolitical sources of instinctual gratification are infringed on, or blocked, by specific political developments. Under such conditions the opportunity costs of involvement are lowered sufficiently to prompt the citizen to pursue an indirect, political strategy aimed at removing the obstacle to direct gratification.[5] Having exploited political artifice to attain his goal, he will then return to the pursuit of more immediate and direct strategies for instinctual satisfaction.

The ghost of Hobbes is clearly visible. Dahl's citizen, *homo civicus,* is a creature of "imperious desires" who discovers rather late an organized political life that may be used to enhance his more immediate instinctual preoccupations under certain circumstances, e.g., when the actions or inactions of government threaten his primary goals. Politics is regarded primarily as an instrumental artifice brought into play upon the calculation that the probabilities of gaining the rewards sought will at least balance the costs of involvement.[6]

The Hobbesian parallel may be extended. Dahl uses the language of instincts, drives, and desires to describe *homo civicus,* but behind the fashionable terms lurks the familiar figure of the utilitarian calculator. Dahl merely restates the traditional liberal notion of man in psychological jargon when he writes of "ancient and persistent biological and physiological drives, needs, and wants." For these drives, needs, and wants assume political saliency when transformed into demands, that is, articulated preferences. And, as a host of commentators have noted, revisionists, Dahl included, have treated preferences as the only satisfactory indicators of men's interests.[7] The identification of demands (articulated preferences) with interests has spawned the comfortable conclusion that when all demands have been heard all interests have been represented.

The representation of interests is thus the function of participation for the revisionists, and democratic politics is a process in which, to use Dahl's phrasing, all active and legitimate groups (i.e., all articulated preferences) receive a hearing at some crucial stage in the process of decision.[8] Dahl adds that in the "normal" American political process there is a "high probability" that this will in fact occur.[9]

The task of the political process then becomes the accommodation of the conflicting demands of individuals (singly or in groups) who have achieved access to the decision-making forum. Bargaining is the dominant mechanism in this process because it offers mutual satisfactions while at the same time acknowledging the claims of intensely held interests.[10] In sum, bargaining, along with elections, comprises the matrix of "polyarchy."

Inevitably the polyarchal model rivets attention on policy outputs. This relegates political participation to an instrumental role, a means to desired policy outputs.

"Slack" Power and Participation

Ostensibly, revisionism constitutes a systematic statement of the empirical evidence on contemporary political behavior. Its persuasiveness rests in no small measure on this claim. Yet, the irony of the contemporary debate is that few persons dispute the accumulated evidence on which the case for revisionism rests. It is not the evidence but the implications drawn therefrom that have been criticized. One such implication is the notion of "slack" power put forward by Dahl in *Who Governs?*[11] By glancing briefly at this notion we will be able to draw several conclusions regarding the function of participation in revisionist theory.

"Slack" power is one of a cluster of notions revisionists have advanced to solve the paradox between the traditional understanding of democracy as self-governing individuals who decide public issues and the reality of a citizenry that normally displays low levels of political interest, information, and involvement and that delegates the day-to-day formulation of public policy to a corps of political activists. In Dahl's formulation, limited citizen involvement actually creates the condition for popular control over political leaders by providing a degree of "slack" in the system. Although not continually engaged in political activity, *homo civicus* possesses sufficient resources to exercise influence when he is motivated to do so. There is, in other words, a large store of potential influence which may be brought to bear on political activists if *homo civicus* becomes dissatisfied with their performance. Of course, most of the time this potential need not be mobilized because the law of anticipated reactions suffices to motivate the activists to act on behalf of the interests of *homo civicus*. The system's "slack" is the key mechanism by which popular control is exercised over political leaders. "Slack" power carries a bonus, also, in that it permits assessment of the saliency of issues to citizen interests, since one can presume that "inertia" signals contentment with policy outputs of the political process; otherwise the "slack" would be taken up and the interests of *homo civicus* would be expressed by means of increased involvement.

As presented, the notion of "slack" power offers a plausible explanation of the mechanism of popular control in modern society. It has a common-sense appeal that borders on self-evidence. However, this patina of self-evident common sense derives from a prior assumption: politics is at best an instrumental activity. *Homo civicus* will participate if and only if politics will serve him as a means of achieving goals otherwise unobtainable by more direct means.

And yet, consider what would follow from a view of participation as something other than an instrumental activity, i.e., something valuable in itself: "slack" power could no longer appear as an opportunity for registering preferences but as the absence of something intrinsically valuable; not an advantage but a shortcoming. Furthermore, because politics is assumed to be an instrumental strategy pursued for specific, concrete rewards, any notion of participation as fulfilling in itself, without regard to policy goals, is excluded from consideration. The notion of participation as a mode of existence in which men may realize certain aspects of their humanity is rejected a priori on the basis of the presupposed nature of man as a creature of passions and instrumental rationality. Instead, participation is utilized in the service of the "interests" that comprise the essential nature of (occasionally) political man.

Participation as Self-protection

Several conclusions may be drawn from this discussion. For revisionism, the function of participation is the representation of interests. This derives from a set of presuppositions concerning man and politics. *Homo civicus* is a creature of imperious desires who occasionally seeks indirect political means for gratifying his biological and physiological drives, needs, and wants. Whether called drives, demands, or preferences, these features constitute the politically relevant nature of man, his interests.

The purpose of political participation is thus to maximize these interests. When his interests are threatened, i.e., when direct attainment of gratification is thwarted, *homo civicus* will seek political means to attain his goals. Political participation therefore constitutes an effort to protect threatened interests, i.e., to make possible direct gratification by removing external hinderances. Even when *homo civicus* is bestirred to advance his interests, he does so only to maximize the opportunity of protecting his self-defined interests from interference by his antagonistic fellows who, likewise, seek to maximize their gratifications. In other words, the political actors, whether they be individuals or groups of individuals, are defined (for political purposes) as utility seekers. When threatened, these actors will seek to protect their interests, and success will be measured by the concordance of policy with their interest-defined preferences.

This situation holds in both the voting booth and the committee hearing room, the primary loci of participation in revisionist theory. *Homo civicus* is constrained to a mode of participation characterized by the binomic "yes" or "no." Participation is effectively reduced to the approval or disapproval of the performance of elected official and lobbyist. Finally, therefore, to revisionists, the goal of participation is limited to the protection of interests, defined primarily in terms of the gratifications of one's private life.

Even this brief analysis should demonstrate that the real issue is the *purpose* of participation. As I have sought to show, the crux of the democratic debate lies not in the empirical evidence but in the interpretations of the evidence. These interpretations rest in turn on the respective views of the nature of man and politics. The real, albeit invisible, dialogue is among these differing conceptions.

I will continue to concentrate on these matters as I turn to participatory democracy.

PARTICIPATORY DEMOCRACY, TYPE I

"Participatory democracy" conjures up a vision of town-
meeting democracy. Decisions affecting the whole community are
made by the members in plenary session. The image is one of direct involvement in community decision making.

This view is by no means restricted to laymen. The editors of a
recent reader on participatory democracy offer the following definition: "Participatory democracy connotes decentralization of power for direct involvement of amateurs in authoritative decision making." [12] According to their understanding, the two components of
participatory democracy are the dispersion of authoritative decision
making and the direct involvement of nonelites or amateurs. This
definition has serious shortcomings, but it does render faithfully
one of the thrusts of participatory democracy. Consider Community Action Programs. They represented an effort to provide "maximum feasible participation" in the belief that the persons who are
most immediately affected by governmental programs should have
a say in determining the direction and operation of the program.
More recently, former President Nixon announced plans for a
"New American Revolution," to be affected by "giving power back
to the people." Colloquial language says it best: The aim is to offer
as many people as possible a "piece of the action." Both schemes
feature decentralization and direct involvement—two familiar democratic themes. But why suddenly their renewed prominence? An
answer to this question will reveal much about participatory democracy.

The explanation must begin with the realization that even among
individuals critical of governmental actions it was long assumed that
the government can and does respond to citizens' needs that are vigorously and vocally pressed. Critics and defenders alike took faith
in the maxim: "The squeaky wheel gets the oil." Dissatisfaction
with government policies at home and abroad led numerous individuals to put this belief to the test. When, despite vocal demonstration of people's preferences, policies were slow to change, many
looked for ways of explaining the lack of responsiveness. The problems were quickly identified—the distance of citizens from centers

of decision and the obstacles to access to decision-making forums thrown up by the defenders of the status quo. The prescribed remedy for both problems was to "give the government back to the people." Two possible approaches to this task emerged. One would bring the decisions closer to home, either by decentralization or by some plebiscitary scheme such as national television referenda. The second approach would involve citizens directly in decisions by easing access to decision-making forums. Both approaches were praised for increasing popular involvement in decisions that have widespread impact on society.[13] These efforts to encourage the direct involvement of citizens, with the intention of increasing their control over decisions, we shall refer to as Participatory Democracy, Type I (PD-I). Its justificatory principle we shall call self-rule.

As revisionism has shown, having a direct hand in decision making is not a necessary ingredient in democratic theory. The task of the citizen in revisionist theory is to assess regime performance and to register preferences. This is generally accomplished by indirect means, but even on the rare occasions when citizens speak with a clear voice on issues, not they but their representatives actually make the decisions.

Yet there is a current in democratic theory that gives prominence to direct involvement. Two developments provided catalysts for its emergence. First, the traditional notion of "consent" became associated with the equal right of each individual to share in the establishment and exercise of power.[14] Second, the liberal view of political freedom as the absence of heteronomy (control by others) acquired positive expression as submission to self-imposed laws (moral autonomy).[15] The result was a trend in democratic thinking that emphasized equal and direct participation not simply for purposes of self-protection or self-advancement but because only in so doing would the individual be an autonomous human being. This "radical" or Rousseauist democratic tradition, of which PD-I is a contemporary expression, stems from a political anthropology different from the one leading to revisionism. We shall discover below the consequences of PD-I for the function of participation.

In his many writings Peter Bachrach has strongly affirmed the aspirations encompassed in PD-I.[16] He has charged revisionism with contributing to the widespread feeling of "powerlessness" by defining out of existence a basic component of democratic theory, namely, the emphasis on political involvement as a means of ex-

ercising control over one's own life. "For democratic theory, especially classical democratic theory, conceives the public interest in
terms of both results and process. Thus public interest is measured
by the soundness of the decision reached in the light of the needs
of the community *and* by the scope of public participation in reaching them." [17]

Bachrach is fully aware of the arguments concerning the size and
complexity of contemporary government; in fact, he is willing to
concede that major policies will be made by a relatively small number of activists and experts. But despite the impossibility of realizing government by the people, strictly interpreted, widespread
public participation in the political process is perhaps still possible
if the scope of the "political" is extended to cover so-called private
governments, such as corporations, unions, and similar institutions. [18]
If these "private governments" are treated as "political" on the
ground that they often make decisions that have widespread and
significant impact upon citizens' lives, [19] then, despite the impossibility of attaining an equality of power in regard to the major decisions of public policy, participation in the political process
may still be realized within the "small systems" of the body politic. [20] Bachrach blames the revisionist preoccupation with the re-
cruitment of and control over political elites for diverting attention
from the democratic ideal of equality of power.

> The crucial issue of democracy is not the composition of the
> elite. . . . Instead the issue is whether democracy can diffuse pow-
> er sufficiently throughout society to inculcate among people of
> all walks of life a justifiable feeling that they have the power
> to participate in decisions which affect themselves and the com-
> mon life of the community, especially the immediate commu-
> nity in which they work and spend most of their waking hours
> and energy. [21]

The substance of Bachrach's proposal is obvious: Participation
should be introduced into the board room and work places of industry. Thus the decisions of industry would be more closely attuned to the needs of the community (greater responsiveness),
while, at the same time, participants would increase their sense of
political efficacy and thereby gain in self-esteem—both vital aspects of a sound theory of democracy. [22]

However, when discussing how these results might be achieved, Bachrach blurs apparent distinctions between them, thereby over-looking the possibility that they may not always be coincidental or even compatible. For example, as a presumptive solution to the widespread feeling of "powerlessness," he recommends increased participation. Having a voice in making decisions that immediately affect them will enhance the citizens' sense of autonomy and there-by increase their self-esteem.[23] One cannot help but wonder, how-ever, whether Bachrach's solution does not vitiate his goal of in-creased control by citizens over decisions that affect their lives. We know that he is concerned with the inequalities of power in society and that he expects increased participation to reduce those inequal-ities. But now we are told that the crucial issue is not "who gov-erns?" but "whether democracy can diffuse power sufficiently ... to inculcate among the people ... a justifiable feeling that they have the power to participate. ..." Has not Bachrach himself point-ed out that political elites may provide nonelites with opportunities to participate in ostensibly significant but carefully circumscribed areas of decision making in order to convey the impression of con-trol where no such situation obtains?[24] One must wonder whether Bachrach has not inadvertently substituted a therapeutic placebo in the form of (empty?) self-esteem for authentic self-rule.

Extending the Scope of Politics

The casual slide from self-government to self-esteem, while by no means trivial, does not completely destroy Bachrach's argument. More damaging is the misconception that emerges when he attempts to redefine the political to embrace what he calls "small systems" or "private government."[25] Bachrach offers as the defini-tional criterion the extent of the impact on society of the allocation of values made by a decision making body.[26] Unfortunately, broad-ening the notion of the political in this fashion results, at the same time, in its being made trivial.

According to Bachrach any decision that allocates values (are there any that do not?) qualifies as political if its impact is suf-ficiently extensive. Moreover, the decisions that have the greatest and most direct impact upon a person are often those that affect him in his workplace. It would seem, then, that by politicizing pri-vate centers of power, "powerlessness" would be transformed into self-control *and* self-esteem.[27]

However, in applying this solution to contemporary society Bachrach readily concedes that to many individuals the political issues and decisions that shape their lives "appear either trivial or remote and beyond the reach of their influence."[28] Fortunately of a different magnitude are those issues and decisions that directly affect individuals in their place of work, "issues which are comparatively trivial, yet are overlaid with tensions and emotions that often infuriate and try men's souls."[29] The answer to "powerlessness," then, is to exercise control over these decisions.

Again it appears that the effort to broaden the scope of participation through a redefinition of the political may result in the worst of both worlds. By including any issue that significantly affects individuals, political participation is reduced from a means of controlling one's destiny to a means of lessening the tensions and antagonisms that arise from the domination of man by man. Destiny-shaping decisions remain "either trivial or remote and beyond the reach of [men's] influence"[30] while the *feeling* of powerlessness is lessened by means of participation in decision making processes with results that have *immediate* impact on men's lives.

The intention here is not to deny concerns such as "powerlessness," which have recently received widespread attention, but to question the facile identification of participation in decisions that significantly *affect* one's destiny with participation in decisions that immediately *touch* one's life. Objective control and the subjective sense of political efficacy may be related, but the latter is not an adequate substitute for the former. Yet it is precisely this ersatz that Bachrach and other proponents of PD-I seem to be offering.

These observations also apply *mutatis mutandis* to any decentralization scheme proposed as a means for achieving greater self-rule. Obviously there is no automatic correspondence between proximity and significance. Decentralization may or may not provide increased control, but if it does, it will not be the result simply of participation in decisions that are closer to home. Significance and (more broadly) self-rule are not simple linear functions of distance.

It may be argued that this critique does not meet the thrust of Bachrach's most recent writings, in which the emphasis has shifted from individual control over one's destiny to individual self-awareness of one's "real" interests.[31] Through participation the individual grows in the understanding of his manifold interests; he learns to translate vague moods into articulate demands while simultaneously enhancing his sense of moral or civic responsibility toward himself and others. Bachrach seems to suggest that participation in pedestrian affairs may do for today's citizen what John Stuart Mill expected jury duty and parish office to do for the newly enfranchised citizen of the last century.[32]

I have no quarrel with the proposition that participation may increase self-awareness or bring about attitudinal and value changes. What continues to be problematical in Bachrach's formulation is the presumption that any and every form of direct participation will lead to the kind of self-awareness he has in mind. Consider: (1) If participation in any decision will contribute to the growth of self-awareness, there is no reason for Bachrach to plump for an expansion of the scope of the political. Any set of decisions should suffice. (2) If the subject matter of the decisions is decisive, then it becomes important to know what issues will enhance self-awareness. Here the salience of the trivialization of the political emerges. Is every issue "public" that touches large numbers of people? Or is there some other *differentia?* The problem comes back to the notion of the political. Is it a matter of making decisions, or the subject matter of the decisions? If the former, then self-awareness becomes a function of the number of decisions in which one is involved. If the character of the decisions is important, then Bachrach's argument stands or falls on his notion of the political.

This is not the place for an evaluation of Bachrach's conception of the political beyond that offered above.[33] What I wish to point out is the dependence of Bachrach's argument for increased participation upon his presupposition regarding the nature of the political. This is true regardless of whether direct involvement is recommended for the sake of enhancing self-awareness or one's "real" interests.

What happens, then, when we compare the conceptions of politics offered by PD-I and revisionism? Both schools view politics as decision making. This parallel is confirmed, despite Bachrach's desire to contrast(!) his version of PD-I with revisionism (Bachrach: "elitism"), in a table drawn near the end of *The Theory of Democratic Elitism.* Under a column marked "political" he describes the revisionist position as "governmental decision making and that which relates to it."[34] He describes his position as "decision making which significantly affects societal values."[35] In both cases political is taken to mean *decision making;* the only distinction is the scope of the decisional processes covered by the term "political." In practice the difference between revisionism and PD-I is often about the width of a disagreement over preferred policy outcomes.

On the other hand, there is an identifiable and irreducible difference between PD-I and revisionism with respect to their justificatory principles, which may in turn be reflected in programmatic demands. This difference can be illustrated by the following situation. Imagine an individual who is by all accounts without grievance—all preferences honored, all needs met, all desires fulfilled, in other words, all interests satisfied. Yet this individual demands the opportunity to participate in making decisions that affect him on the grounds that only through participation will he continue to exist as an autonomous human being. How are we to explain his demand?

It might be argued that the demand is a matter of prudence: He has no grievance today, but one may arise tomorrow if he does not remain vigilant. Let us, however, stipulate that there is no foreseeable reason for him to be apprehensive; indeed, to avoid a canvass of extraneous arguments, let us stipulate that there are no utilitarian grounds for participating. How could we then explain the demand? More important, would we want to do so?

If we are to give any warrant to political experience, the answer is that we would want to explain the demand, and to do so we must attend to the purposes for which the demand was made. Consider a well-known passage from the "Port Huron Statement." Commenting on the recommendation that "the goal of man and society should be human independence," the authors explain that "the object is not to have one's way so much as it is to have a way that is one's own."[36] While the phrasing is too facile to be self-explanatory, it is obvious that the authors wish to distinguish between the attainment of a preferred outcome and the condition that surrounds the process of attainment. Specifically this condition is characterized by independence (or autonomy). Although anarchic connotations can be read in the notion of "having a way that is one's own," it can also be read as a plea for return to the venerable democratic idea of self-government. Whatever construction is put on it, without the distinction suggested by the Port Huron Statement passage, the demands for participation in the absence of grievance are inexplicable.

Hence we are obliged to consider self-rule as an ambiguous but distinct participatory type, sharing revisionism's view of politics yet differing in implicit conceptions of man.

PARTICIPATORY DEMOCRACY, TYPE II

Throughout its recent revival, PD has continued to wear the faded gown of anachronism. After all, who can seriously challenge the argument from practicality? "Direct participation is impossible in a country of 200 million people."

The obvious limits of scale for PD have persuaded many that it should be laid aside as largely irrelevant to the present age. However, there are those participatory democrats who dispute this judgment on the grounds that it reflects the revisionist fallacy of equating politics with policy making. These theorists reject this utilitarian conception as the *sole* content of democratic politics. Politics is more than decision making; it is (or can be) a *mode of activity* the goal of which is *not the satisfaction of wants but the realization of self.*[37] In his now classic critique of "the neo-elitist theory of democracy," Jack Walker outlined the difference:

> Although the classical [democratic] theorists accepted the basic framework of Lockean democracy, with its emphasis on limited government, they were *not* primarily concerned with the *policies* which might be produced in a democracy; above all else they were concerned with human development, the opportunities which existed in political activity to realize the untapped potentials of men and to create the foundations of a genuine human community.[38]

The revisionists have ignored the developmental consequences of participation and as a result insufficient attention has been paid to participatory forms that promote self-realization rather than self-protection or self-rule.

There are two versions of PD-II, both of which have won increasing attention during the course of the democratic theory debate. Examination will show that both versions involve presuppositions substantially different from those of revisionism and PD-I. Because the first version is reasonably familiar it will receive only the attention necessary to indicate its major thrust. This will permit us to concentrate on the second version, which is less familiar but contains the necessary materials for a direct confrontation with revisionism. It is hoped in this way to channel the democratic theory debate in a potentially rewarding direction.

Developing the Potentialities

The first form of PD-II is directed at *self-realization of human potentialities*. Basic to this form is a conception of man as a composite of faculties that require exercise for their full development. This conception is typically associated with a criticism of society as stunting human development. Marx's description of the alienating effects of the division of labor in *The German Ideology* and his vision of a "well-rounded individual," fishing, herding, criticizing at will, exemplifies this perspective. John Stuart Mill offers a similar view in *Representative Government* when he praises the moral instruction afforded by participation in public functions.[39]

A contemporary version is offered by Henry Kariel. In numerous writings he has deplored the stultifying effects of contemporary conceptions of political action. In his most outspoken statement, *Open Systems,* Kariel decries the tendency to close off avenues of self-development prematurely. Using a theatrical metaphor, he calls for the playing of alternative roles as a means of testing and expanding the boundaries of the self. Politics too must assume the spontaneous quality of play. Action *for its own sake*— simply to test the boundaries of one's identity—must be recognized as the essence of political action.[40]

Although critics sympathetic to the development of the so-called counter culture have found the notion of role playing too stereotypic to convey the spontaneity involved, the general intention of both Kariel and his would-be critics is clear. The self, conceived as an array of latent potentialities, requires exercise in order to be realized. Without political activity certain faculties remain dormant, resulting in a truncated self. Political participation is thus regarded as an activity valuable without regard to eventual policy results. Moreover, participation as here envisioned entails more than the periodic expression of preferences; it must involve continuous interaction between the participant and his environment (including, of course, other participants). In the final analysis it is a creative activity.

The Citizen Reborn

The second subtype of the participatory principle of self-realization I will label *self-realization of citizenhood.*[41] From time to time political theorists have voiced concern over the apparent disappearance of active citizens on the model of their Greek antecedents. In recent decades several writers have issued pleas for the return of an engaged citizenry.[42] These appeals have not rested simply on the grounds of popular control but see the loss of active citizenship as bringing about the demise of a distinctive mode of human existence.

This concern carries us to the heart of the distinction between self-realization of citizenhood and all other principles of participation. We are dealing not only with a distinctive form of participation but also with an almost forgotten conception of political life. As will be seen, this type of participation presupposes conceptions of political man and political activity that directly challenge the conceptions that dominate revisionist thought.

Robert Pranger is the most vocal exponent of this position. His starting point is the familiar critique of revisionist politics. He is appalled by the quality of political life today. The democratic vision of an active citizenry participating in the adventure of self-government has acquired a ghostly pallor. The citizen as key participator in creating political life has been replaced by apathetic, mindless "nonelites" who at best vote occasionally and "orient" themselves to increasingly distant political objects and "elites."[43] Politics has become a spectator sport in which the citizen intervenes only when his interests are directly threatened. When the danger passes, he returns to his seat on the sidelines and reverts to nonpolitical strategies for attaining his primary goals.[44]

This childlike behavior Pranger attributes to the paucity of spontaneous civic experience in contemporary American society. What revisionists see as sloth and indifference, spiced with emotional vendettas in times of anxiety, Pranger sees as feedback from the prevailing political culture. "What is sometimes taken as a *cause* of the politics of power, the unpolitical nature of ordinary citizens, turns out to be an effect of the politics of power. . . ."[45] And the only way to recapture the political virtues of active citizenhood, in

Pranger's estimation, is to regain awareness of the political dimension of man's existence.

Pranger's proposal for a revitalized "politics of citizenship" involves reconsideration of the citizen's role, along with a clarified understanding of the nature of political existence. "The citizen's primary role is to create a politics, not to function as an appendage, or mere participant, for the structure of power."[46] One must understand the citizen's role as a creator of political life from the standpoint of a conception of man as *animal symbolicum,* a being who actively appropriates environmental phenomena and transforms them into an "existence" that has meaning for him.[47] Seen thus, the citizen creates a "political dimension" of existence, the locus of which we may call "political space." "In political space lives political man, the citizen, as contrasted to biological man, psychological man, and so forth."[48] This "political space" may be conceived as a common ground, created by the common involvements of citizens, and demarcated physically and mentally from other "spaces" by the lineaments of social tension.[49] Because the objects in "political space" are products of a common involvement, they carry common meanings for the citizens, making common (as contrasted to aggregative) actions possible.

Technically, "political space" is a symbolic realm, but this does not mean that the symbols merely stand for "concrete" things. It is precisely Pranger's point that such putative positivism misses the entire significance of man's symbolizing capacity. The symbolic realm—"political space"—is "real," just as "real" as the realm of necessity in which man *qua* biological organism strives for self-preservation. To see the former realm as nothing more than a mirror of the latter is to flatten man's existence and to ignore his distinctly human capacity to act as a political being in "political space."

We are presented here with the materials for a conception of participation which differs radically from those of revisionism and PD-I. However, these very differences impose difficulties for adequate understanding since we must become attuned to a different vocabulary, indeed, to a different conceptual framework. Therefore it will be necessary to explore in somewhat greater detail the basic components of this conception of participation. We begin with the nature of political man and then move to a consideration of the nature of the political.

Political Action and the Public Realm

A revitalization of political participation such as Pranger envisions implies that the revisionists are myopic in their analysis of *homo civicus*. Pranger has sought, with help from the writing of Hannah Arendt, to substantiate this conclusion. In so doing he has simultaneously articulated the PD-II conceptions of man and politics.

If man *qua* political being is distinguishable from biological man, psychological man, economic man, etc., as the participatory democrats maintain, then there must be a *differentia*. The antique Greek conception of action serves this function. By action is meant the capacity to begin something wholly new, to initiate.[50] In the time of Homer this unique capacity of man was seen as the doing of great deeds and the speaking of great words. When Aristotle sought to describe the realm of human affairs he chose action and speech as the activities of man which distinguished the truly human life from the life of necessity.[51] Through action and speech men distinguish themselves from the otherness of the remaining objects of the universe; they are the media through which human beings appear to one another, not as physical objects but as men.[52]

This formulation is important because it directs attention to the contextual ground of actions. The Homeric deed is meaningful only if undertaken in the presence of men. "Action . . . is never possible in isolation; to be isolated is to be deprived of the capacity to act."[53] In this way action assumes a revelatory character; the self is revealed through action.

This self-revealing process requires for completion the concomitant of speech. Through speech a union is created between the facticity of the deed, the self of the actor, and the audience of other men who immortalize the deed through their deeds and speeches.

Shedding the antique terminology, the humanity of action derives from the creation of a common ground in which men reveal themselves to others (and to themselves) through their participation in this process of creation. Men are revealed to be participators in this common enterprise. Indeed, part of what it means to be a human being is to take part in, *and* to be a part of, this common enterprise. This is not to deny the other facets of the human being; to the contrary, the thrust of this argument is an em-

phasis on the multidimensional nature of man. The intent of the
participatory democrats is to expose the revisionists' view as myopic, as failing to consider the manifold possibilities of being
human.

Thus far we have followed Pranger/Arendt to the conclusion that
political man is man as he engages in action. It remains for us to
clarify the notion of the political. As the previous paragraphs suggest, what distinguishes an action as political is its context, not
some physical characteristic of the activity. This view requires that
political life be understood as a mode of existence rather than as
a type of activity. Frequently this is interpreted as meaning that,
because men create a common ground through action, the "public realm" (as Pranger and Arendt call "political space" in its concrete form) is a product of the sociability of men. Political life
would then be an expression of human gregariousness. Such an interpretation would account for man's social but not his political
nature.[54] As the Greeks knew, sociability is a trait of many animals and relates to biological life. The political realm is characterized by a qualitatively different relationship.

If sociability does not account for political life, what does? The
answer lies in the substance of the public realm. Men, as they in-
teract with one another, are often concerned with the worldly things
that physically lie between them and out of which arise their specific, objective, worldly interests.[55] These interests relate men to
one another as a table links together the people who sit around it.
Most of the time the actions and speeches of men are concerned
with this "in-between," which means that most words and deeds
are about some objective reality. However, any intercourse concerning this "in-between" will involve at one and the same time its
tangible contents and the intangible overlay of action and speech.
Though intangible, this "in-between" is no less real than the world
of things men visibly have in common.[56]

Thus, the public realm is composed of the tangible and intangible objects that link men in a common enterprise. The realm
is symbolic in the important sense that the objects carry common
meanings for those linked together by them. It makes possible the
mutual revelation of that aspect of human nature that sets men
apart from other animals.

Here the nexus among action, public, and the political is brought
into full relief. Action is the mode of activity characteristic of the

political realm. The public quality of the political realm originates in its condition as an "in-between." In turn this "in-between" provides the locus for activity that can properly be called *political action*. Without a public realm action is impossible. Human action that takes place in the public realm is political.

Relocating the Boundaries of Politics

The PD-II conceptions of man and the political outlined above form the basis for a distinction between political participation that is undertaken for its own sake, i.e., for benefits that flow from the experience itself, and participation that is an input, a means to some particular policy-end or output. A renewed awareness of this distinction can be a valuable contribution to the democratic debate, but only if its central premise is not misconstrued. Too often the crux of the distinction, the qualitative character of the activity, is overlooked in favor of its locus, the public realm. There is much debate over what constitutes the boundaries of the public realm, but insufficient attention is given to the mode of activity that characterizes it.

Pranger himself provides an example of this in his effort to work out an explanation of the political which would resolve the difficulties encountered by Bachrach and other advocates of PD-I in redefining the boundaries of politics. Like Bachrach, he believes the traditional boundaries between private and public realms that have stood since the advent of liberalism are today anachronistic. However, the problem is not the scope of impact, as Bachrach argues, but a loss of certainty with respect to private and public expectations. The source of difficulty Pranger traces to "the increasing density of life."[57] Urbanization, global communications, mass transportation, and other factors have generated greater tensions as the individual suffers more and more incursions into his life-space. Areas previously considered private are opened to the visibility of other persons.[58] Concomitantly, tensions increase between public and private roles. As the lines between them are blurred, the citizen's duties, public and private, likewise lose definition. The result is a shifting of the ground beneath the citizen with increased potential for conflict matched by increased uncertainty as regards public and private expectations.

Given this definition of the problem, Pranger looks for help in readjusting the boundaries in accordance with the realities of increased density. He turns first to John Dewey to seek clarification of the scope of public and private realm. Dewey's operational distinction hinges on the commonplace observation that human acts have consequences. "The line between private and public is to be drawn on the basis of the extent and scope of the consequences of acts which are so important as to need control, whether by inhibition or by promotion."[59] Borrowing this distinction, Pranger makes the *scope of consequences* a key to his notion of "public."

To this notion Pranger juxtaposes the "noninstrumental" notion of "public" he has borrowed from Arendt. The public realm is an "in-between," a world of tangible artifacts and intangible relationships which extends beyond the necessities instrumental to men's private lives.[60] Then, in a feat of intellectual graftmanship, Pranger slips Dewey's "public" into Arendt's framework, so producing a "public" that "has wider ramifications, encompassing more 'others' than do private relationships, and establishing simultaneously common or shared relationships."[61] This amalgamation is necessary, Pranger concludes, because Arendt's noninstrumental notion of "public" does not cover areas like business, whose ostensibly private concerns have widespread consequences. With the addition of Dewey's operational criterion of "scope of consequences," activities until now considered private become amenable to public appraisal.

It would seem, however, that Pranger's scheme is not only wrongheaded but self-defeating. To achieve a broadened public realm that will subject certain private activities to public values, Pranger proposes to delineate "public" in terms of the scope of consequences. To do so leads to one of two results. First, debate will center on the location of the threshold—two persons, a dozen, a hundred, a thousand? This permits consideration of decisions that affect large numbers of people, but at the same time it undermines Pranger's original purpose in introducing Arendt's noninstrumental notion of "public," i.e., to show that political life is a qualitatively different mode of existence from that envisioned by revisionism. By imposing a quantitative measure Pranger vitiates his own distinction. Second, the adoption of Dewey's definition of "public" inevitably leads back to the revisionist view of politics as a decision making process that produces "outputs" with wider-ranging consequences.

Pranger encounters a similar difficulty when he attempts to capture the interplay between public and private in a world of increasing density by conceptualizing politics as focal tension: "Focal tensions and attempts to control the violence associated with such tensions appear to be the most significant phenomena of political nature."[62] Here Pranger has two sets of phenomena in mind: the tensions between self and others that derive from scarcity, and tension between one's private self and one's public (citizen) self. Therefore "political space" must stretch beyond the "ordinary public institutions and activities commonly associated with [politics]; it is particularly clear that 'politics' appears, latently at least, in most social groups."[63] On the other hand, while "everything is potential politics," societal tensions become political when they acquire the character of common concerns.[64] In other words, politics is equated with common focal tensions.

Yet the proposition that everything is potential politics turns out to be either tautological or mistaken. If it refers to the process of symbolization into common headings, then whatever constitutes an "in-between" (in this case symbols) is political inasmuch as it is precisely the "in-between" that is the locus of political existence. Moreover, these symbolized relationships are the content of the political realm. However, if one finds potential politics wherever the potential for societal tensions exist, then Pranger is in error since this situation is the equivalent of the equation: tension=politics. If this were so, then wherever tension existed the public realm would be present; we are back with the revisionist vision of politics as conflict. The public realm would then be the space where, one might hope, the clash of private interests would be ameliorated.

Nor can one escape from the dilemma by saying, as Pranger seems to do, that issues become "public" when they are placed on the agenda of public controversy.[65] To consider as "political" whatever issues are "public," and to consider as "public" whatever issues reach the agenda of public controversy, is to remain hostage to the anachronistic notion of "public" that Pranger is trying to transcend. "Public" remains what people think should be matters of mutual concern. Yet this is the present problem exactly. To specify that issues involving the adjustment of individual interests with the common interest are proper items for the agenda[66] does not solve Pranger's problem either; it merely forces him back into the orbit of revisionism (Politics=interests).

A One-Dimensional View of Politics

The confusions and contradictions in Pranger's writings, coming from one who has devoted so much attention to the conceptual issues involved, cast doubt on the entire participatory democratic perspective. Before dismissing the enterprise as hopelessly flawed, however, we may profitably ponder where the argument for participatory democracy has gone awry.[67]

The major difficulty arises with the critical redefinition of politics. Both Bachrach and Pranger, as spokesmen for the two schools of PD, have called attention to the narrow conception of politics held by revisionists. By understanding politics to be a utilitarian device for the accommodation of conflicting interests, the revisionists have circumscribed politics in two ways. Proponents of PD-I object because the decisions of corporate America are removed from public scrutiny on the ground that they involve "private" matters, despite their manifest impact upon the lives of persons not party to the decisions. Proponents of PD-II object because attention is diverted from the consequences of participation for the individual in aspects other than the protection of interests.

Yet, in spite of the acuity of their criticisms, the participatory democrats have been unable to present an alternative conception of politics free from debilitating inconsistencies. The source of this failure lies in the manner in which the issues are posed. In criticizing the revisionists' narrow conception of politics, Bachrach and Pranger continued to restrict man to a one-dimensional existence.[68] No doubt they do so in their anxiety to challenge the revisionist conception. The result, nonetheless, has been to paralyze their arguments with contradictions. We must understand why this has occurred.

Imagine the world of *homo civicus* as a flat plane fenced off into sectors. Each sector represents a particular means of achieving personal gratifications. Within each sector *homo civicus* practices a particular type of instrumental activity: economic, familial, aesthetic, political. Traditionally *homo civicus* erects the highest fence between the political sector and the other, private, sectors. Behind this fence, with the security it provides, he pursues those private activities of work and leisure that maintain self and family.

On occasion he will step into the public realm to pursue his private satisfactions through indirect political means.

The participatory democrats have sought in effect to move the political fence to take account of conflicts and decisions hidden until now in private sectors. Yet, having done so, they still are left with a one-dimensional existence dominated by an instrumental notion of politics. This results from their use of the *scope of impact* as a bench mark for relocating the public/private boundary. The upshot is that (a) the activity remains instrumental insofar as policy consequences determine placement, and (b) the quality of politicalness is determined by where the activity takes place and not by what it is.

These results are not unexpected in the case of PD-I since it has frequently succumbed to revisionist presuppositions, but it runs contrary to Pranger's efforts to construct a different, noninstrumental conception of politics.

The Political Dimension

Although participatory democrats have not been able to offer a coherent redefinition of politics, the outlines of such an argument are present in Pranger's work. This material can be utilized to reformulate the PD-II position in a manner that constitutes a direct challenge to the revisionist view of participation. At this stage my intention is not to generate a new theory of participation but to set forth the major elements of PD-II in a fashion that permits comparison with other theories of participation. There are four points in the argument.

1. Political action is noninstrumental, i.e., it falls outside means/ends categories.[69] The ground for this claim may be expressed by recalling an Aristotelian distinction. Aristotle applied the term *energeia* to activities that do not pursue an end but exhaust their full meaning or actuality in the performance itself. When Aristotle described the "work" of politics as "to live well," he sought to indicate that political life represented in its actuality the "work of man," that it lay outside the category of means and ends, and that its full meaning was imbedded in the activity itself. Politics was the mode of existence of men *qua* men.[70]

2. Political action is common action. Each actor partakes in a common activity, not as tasks are shared in the division of labor,

but in the sense that a common ground is both created by and composed of noninstrumental political actions. Political action is therefore the activity of men when they are engaged in the joint human enterprise of creating a common matrix of political life.

3. The political or public realm is where political action takes place. Its boundaries are defined not by the scope but by the type of activity undertaken. At stake ultimately is the character of political life. Will political experience be plotted by the latitude of impact and the longitude of tension or will it be judged by the facets of the human being that are quickened to action?

4. Political life is one of the modes of existence available to man. As a political being man creates a world of common objects and meanings in "political space." This "in-between" does not minister to him so much as it provides a ground on which he can realize that aspect of his nature which can only be fulfilled through common involvement with his fellows. This means that politics is not simply a technical instrument to be picked up and put down for the sake of achieving some primary, i.e., private, goal. Instead, politics as an enterprise of common involvements is itself a primary (but not private) experience in which the end—fulfilling an aspect of one's nature—is realized in the enterprise itself. Its meaning is carried in the doing: political man is a doer. At the same time, he is a particular kind of doer, a doer of common enterprises. To do something alone is to diminish man's existence since it means that he does not realize that aspect of his nature which carries him beyond his self and into the *community* of men.

Fundamental to this conception is the proposition that part of what it means to be a human being is to partake in the affairs of the community. It is not something done when all other means of achieving one's goals have been exhausted. Rather it is something that is necessary if one's full nature as a human being is to be realized.

This vision animates Pranger's critique of the revisionist understanding of participation. Revisionism forecloses the possibility of realizing the political dimension of man's nature. It does so not by the weight of empirical evidence, as is so often claimed, but by presupposing utilitarian man in a one-dimensional world. Pranger's claim is not that the revisionist conception of man is "wrong" but that it is incomplete: man is a multifaceted being who lives a multidimensional existence. He is a political being as well as an economic, aesthetic, or moral being insofar as he participates in the experiences embodied in political, economic, aesthetic, or moral life. Moreover, these dimensions are coexistent so that the exercise of one in no way diminishes the others.

When PD-II is reformulated as above, it take on a radical appearance. It goes beyond piecemeal reform of decision-making processes, proposing instead a new (or ancient) way of looking at political life which runs counter to some of the deepest convictions of liberalism.

Whether anything enduring will come from PD-II it is far too soon to know. Yet it has already made several contributions to the contemporary debate. It has helped call attention to the philosophical roots of revisionism, particularly with regard to its conceptions of man and the political. By asking some new questions, it has encouraged re-examination of democratic theory at a time when conventional wisdom appears to be losing credibility.

On the other hand, the self-realization version of participatory democracy seems particularly vulnerable to utopian excess. When it becomes enfolded in "counter culture" rhetoric, PD-II sounds like nothing so much as a messianic voice assuring us that, in participatory democracy, all things are new.

Yet, as we shall argue in the next section, the radical appearance of the PD-II argument may be more a function of viewpoint than of intrinsic character. We shall withhold judgment on this matter until we have reviewed the major conclusions of this essay.

CONCLUSION

It is a cliché of political philosophy that the foundation of a political theory is its anthropology. This is evident in democratic revisionism where the scene is dominated by utilitarian man. *Homo civicus* looks upon political participation as a strategy by which his interests may be served. He uses participation as a means of holding decision-making elites accountable. In this way he *protects* his interests from exploitation by political activists. At the same time, through the electoral process, *homo civicus* registers his preferences, usually retrospectively, for alternative system outputs. From this standpoint participation is an input medium, part of the authoritative decision-making process of society.

Broadly speaking, in this context politics becomes the equivalent of decision making. The inevitable conflicts over scarce resources and rewards are structured in a decision-making framework. Politics therefore has two faces. The experiential face is that of conflict and associated techniques for its control; the second, substantive, face of politics encompasses the outputs of the decision-making processes by which values and resources are allocated. Regardless of its aspect, politics is understood by revisionism as a means of achieving gratification.

The recent upsurge of participatory democracy has assumed several forms, the most popular of which is shaped by the principle of self-rule. The emphasis of PD-I has been on increasing the control that individuals have over decisions that significantly affect them. To this end recommendations have been made for structural changes that are to enlarge the decision-making forum and simultaneously broaden the scope of the decisions made. The changes contemplated include decentralization, intended to bring the forum closer to those affected and to increase the opportunities of having salient voices heard. Changes in the conventional boundary between private and public concerns have also been recommended on the ground that many decisions that directly impinge upon men's lives are reserved to decision makers whose policies are not subject to public accounting despite their obvious impact upon the life-chances of uncounted men.

The autonomy of the individual is the ostensible moral impetus for many of the claims on behalf of PD-I. Supporters maintain that this essential element of democratic theory and politics has been overlooked by revisionists. Nevertheless, PD-I theorists are equivocal about *what* should be autonomous. Often it appears that interests, not individuals, are the real actors.[71] Decentralization proposals that stipulate the representation of all salient community interests illustrate this point.[72] At other times autonomy becomes a subjective feeling rather than an objective condition. Frequently it is unclear whether one is confronting a distinct type of participatory theory or a desperate rationalization for a change in the power structure.

The second type of participatory democracy (self-realization) diverges markedly from both revisionism and PD-I. It eschews policy disputes for ontological disputations, counters studies of political behavior with arguments for multidimensional conceptions of man. This of course makes PD-II exciting as well as suspect. Whether it constitutes a momentary aberration or a new direction remains to be seen.

Self-realization has long been an important theme in democratic thought, most notably as part of the "radical" or "Rousseauist" tradition.[73] Until the "model democrat," the putative backbone of democratic government, was defined out of existence by revisionism,[74] self-realization comprised a vital element in the conventional defense of democracy.

Popular though it may have been, self-realization rested uncomfortably with the other aspects of democratic theory. In spirit it reached back to ancient Greece for its foundation. Along with his somatic and psychic natures, man possesses a political nature; he is among other things a political being. Part of what it means to be a complete human being is to participate with one's fellow men in the creation of a "political space" where men may display their humanity as doers of deeds and speakers of words. Deprived of this experience men lose that quality which separates them from other living organisms. When men choose to create a public realm in which they are inexorably linked by common bonds of joint enterprise, they actualize their natures as political beings. This concept requires that political activity be viewed not as an instrument for achieving private satisfactions but as an activity whose reward is (political) being itself.

The instrumentalist view of politics has dominated recent democratic theory. It has contributed to the development of a political culture that minimizes the value of citizen involvement while belaboring citizen incompetence. The pattern will remain until the citizen reclaims his role in democratic politics. Glimmerings of this reclamation are visible in the increasing attention given to the effect of institutions and systems on individuals—i.e., not only what they do *for* men but *to* them.

This idea can be stated in terms of continua. If we apply this scheme to democratic theory, we can say that recent democratic theory has accommodated politics on a single continuum. Imagine a polity evaluated in terms of the extent to which it maximizes the limiting criteria of a democratic system. Does the citizen have an opportunity of proselytizing in behalf of a point of view? Do the preferences of the greatest number prevail? Etc., etc. A given polity is located on the continuum according to the degree to which the democratic criteria are realized.

What is called for by the perspective of the participatory democrats is the inclusion of another continuum which bisects the first.
On this second continuum would be measured the consequences for
the individual of a polity's performance. Does it deliver the material goods? Does it provide for popular control over important
decisions? Does it contribute to the self-realization of man as a
political being? Or does it threaten central values, life, security, or
self-esteem? If both sets of criteria were used in evaluating a political system, topics such as apathy, "powerlessness," and citizenship
might become central issues for political science.

To date, participatory democrats have offered little more than
criticisms and generalities. Their positive recommendations have
been conspicuously infrequent; few have canvassed alternatives by
which men might regain the participatory experience; fewer still
have sketched the empirical results to be expected. Hence, whatever significance participatory democracy, particularly PD-II, may
have is not to be found in operationally framed manifestos. We
must look elsewhere for the full significance of the PD upsurge.

The Tensions of Democratic Theory

The contemporary debate between revisionists and participatory democrats[75] has not been notable for its degree of interaction. Both sides have carried on monologues, making little effort
to speak to the issues raised by the other side. Self-assurance accounts for some of this, but more interesting is the communication
failure that results from the radically divergent conceptions of politics each side maintains. Assertions are made about political reality; evidence is marshaled in support. The dispute is not about the
evidence, however, but about how the evidence can be fitted together. "Slack power" is read as rational behavior by revisionists
and social pathology by participatory democrats. But both readings are in large measure functions of the presuppositions. In fact,
the crux of the debate is not empirical but theoretical, or even
metaphysical.

This is not to say that the ostensible grounds of controversy are
all a misunderstanding or mistake, that when political scientists
thought they were tapping political attitudes they were actually
engaged in metaphysical disputation. The point is a simpler one.
Opportunities for genuine dialogue have been lost because those

involved have misunderstood what real communication entails. Political scientists today recognize not only that empirical theories have normative implications but also that "facts" do not speak for themselves. Data configurations are shaped by presuppositions. Yet the tendency remains to evaluate theories in terms of their internal consistency rather than in terms of the resonance of their accounts of political experience. Resonance, however, is more complex than a positivist "correspondence with reality." At the minimum it must include investigation of presuppositions and other theory components with an eye toward what is omitted as well as included.

Admittedly, such investigation, even on the modest scale undertaken in this study, risks compounding the obstacles to dialogue. Presuppositions could become matters of arbitrary choice—*de gustibus non est disputandum*—thereby reducing the debate between revisionism and participatory democracy to a process of choosing the "right" presuppositions, i.e., the presuppositions one "believes in," and then defending them against contrary opinions.

This approach must be rejected if more than ideological victory is sought. The issue must be whether revisionism and participatory democracy adequately capture and communicate political experience on both empirical and conceptual levels. The question ceases to be whether revisionism is "right" and participatory democracy "wrong," or vice versa. The question is how much of the variegated experience of political man is captured by either theory.

The beginnings of progress toward fruitful dialogue will be marked by the acceptance of the fact that no single notion captures all of political experience, i.e., that no single democratic theory of participation can be defended to the exclusion of others. Once this stipulation is accepted, the contributions of participatory democracy to the democratic debate become readily apparent.

1. By emphasizing the multidimensionality of existence, participatory democracy encourages consideration of democratic theories as proximate symbolizations of aspects of experience rather than as revealed truth.

2. More directly, participatory democracy can provide a counterpoint to the revisionist account of political experience. The animus of many recent critiques of revisionism has arisen out of concern over the manner in which revisionism has seemingly swept the field of rival interpretations of political experience. In

the process it has sapped the democratic heritage of much of its vigor. The experiences, values, and perspectives emphasized in the democratic tradition of Rousseau, J. S. Mill, Green, Cole, et al., have been all but forgotten. The result has been the effective removal of that component of the democratic heritage which calls upon the citizen to take responsibility for the common weal even as he pursues his private interests.

3. The most enduring claim of participatory democracy, therefore, may be that it restores the tension between the two democratic traditions and thereby reminds us that democratic politics remains in the end a moral enterprise of high purpose.

THE ARGUMENT FROM PRACTICALITY

If the democratic debate is to progress, a number of important issues must be clarified. In particular, the controlling relationships between presuppositions and participatory principles demand greater attention than they have received to date. Thus, by way of illustrating some of the points raised in this study, I will close with a brief examination of one important example.

The problem of size is among the more vexing issues of participation in a democracy. Can one realistically expect widespread participation in a country of more than 200 million people? There are many answers to this question, but one of them—"the argument from practicality"—has assumed a prominent role in the revisionist theory of participation.

In popular discussion the argument usually runs as follows: "Government is too big, too complex, too distant to be understood by the average person. Of course, direct democracy is the ideal, but it's impossible these days because there are simply too many people. Town meetings are no longer practical. Instead we have representative government. And it's not a bad arrangement if we can find good representatives who will look after our interests."

These arguments—size, numbers, expertise—can be translated for present purposes into what Dahl in his recent book, *After the Revolution?*, has called the "Criterion of Economy." [76] Economy or utility is calculated in terms of opportunity costs. Participation is "profitable" if the ratio between rewards and costs is positive. [77] The "Criterion of Economy" thus requires that payoffs from participating must outweigh the opportunity costs.

As stated, this proposition is unobjectionable—*if* the "Criterion of Economy" is understood as an effort to describe the rational behavior of a citizen. But the reassuring image of rationality should not lull one into supposing that all salient questions have been thereby laid to rest. Consider for example the manner in which Dahl phrases the conditions under which it is advantageous to participate. With but one exception—"enjoyment"—the value of participating is measured in terms of the results to be gained by influencing the "decisions of an association." [78] Participation is treated as a utilitarian instrument.

Here the focus of debate grows sharper. The revisionists correctly maintain that these propositions are unexceptionable. Moreover, it is possible in principle to calculate the marginal utilities of any set of participatory forms, including those proposed by participatory democrats. Dahl's "Criterion of Economy" could then indicate what goods may be rationally pursued by what participatory modes.

The critics respond to this suggestion by charging that the utilitarian formulation will in itself prejudice the evaluation because it presupposes an instrumental notion of participation. They point to Dahl's criticism of participatory democrats as an example of the prejudicial process at work. Dahl professes amazement that anyone could ignore the stiff costs of time participation exacts. He exclaims, "how many speakers I have heard of late who talk as if people are willing to participate in decisions without any regard for the costs of time: as if time had no value, as if attending meetings had no costs." [79] But surely Dahl's comment misses the whole point, for participatory democrats do not claim participation is costless, but that its rewards are worth the cost.

Dahl overlooks this possibility not because he intentionally seeks to discredit participatory democracy through obfuscation but because his utilitarian framework militates against the inclusion of the kinds of rewards that are imaginable if one entertains the possibility of noninstrumental participation. His utilitarian criticism of the costs of participation assumes that revisionism is the only meal in town. This is the equivalent of saying to someone who wishes lobster for dinner that when ordering prime rib it should be ordered "rare" rather than "well done." Fine, but what about the lobster? That topic is never broached; it is assumed that roast beef is the only item on the menu. Perhaps this is the case, but we may then wish to question the menu selection, the purchasing practices of the food manager, or the costs of fresh lobster. These are issues different from the best way of enjoying roast beef. In effect, revisionist theory is preoccupied with the choice between "rare" and "well done."

The consequences stretch beyond matters of taste. Robert Pranger is at least half right when he accuses democratic revisionism of having confused cause with effect in regard to the apoliticalness of *homo civicus*. Can we say with reasonable certainty that *homo civicus* does not spend time on public matters because he is apolitical? Or can it be that he is apolitical because he does not spend the time? That is, it seems equally plausible to argue that *homo civicus* is apolitical because he believes (or has been led to believe?) that the payoffs of political participation are marginal given the present range of goods included in his table of preferences. But has *homo civicus* confronted the full range of possible alternatives? Would he remain apolitical if he discovered that certain goods associated with public life increased the rewards of participation? We see no evidence that these possibilities have been confronted as yet by democratic theorists. Nor can they be, as long as the debate continues without taking into account the substantial differences between revisionist and participatory democratic presuppositions.

To remove this oversight would require accepting the possibility of a noninstrumental participatory experience. This the revisionist conception of man will not permit. To assume with Dahl that "*homo civicus* is not, by nature, a political animal," [80] that his primary goals are private and nonpolitical, implies that these goals are logically prior to his political strategies. They are nonpolitical while politics is instrumental. In this framework, the major premise of the participatory democrats' argument evaporates. Man as a self-actualizing political being is denied a priori, and with this conception goes the possibility of a noninstrumental notion of participation. Thus, a definitional fiat sunders the participatory tradition from contemporary democratic thought, without debate or reflection, depriving democratic politics of the tension between systemic and individual concerns which has been its strength.

NOTES AND REFERENCES

1. The generation of the categories used in the typology, along with extended historical analyses of the major participatory forms, may be found in Donald W. Keim, "Political Participation: Paradigms and Prospects" (unpublished Ph.D. dissertation, University of Michigan, 1970).

2. This term (more briefly, revisionism) is used in this study in an effort to avoid dispute over the connotations associated with such labels as "democratic elitism," "neo-elitist theory of democracy," and "pluralist democracy." To dispute labels obscures the important issues.

3. Robert A. Dahl, *Modern Political Analysis* (Englewood Cliffs, N.J.: Prentice-Hall, 1963), p. 59.

4. *Ibid.*, pp. 60-61.

5. *Ibid.*, pp. 60ff.

6. *Ibid.*, p. 61.

7. Nelson Polsby provides a classic example of the revisionist position when he writes "people participate in those areas they care about the most. Their values, eloquently expressed by their participation, cannot, it seems to me, be more effectively 'objectified' " ("The Sociology of Power," *Social Forces,* 37 [March 1959], 235). This quotation was brought to my attention by Professor William Connolly in an unpublished paper, "On 'Interests' in Politics," which he has allowed me to read. For examples of other studies of interests which speak to the point raised here, see Robert Paul Wolff, *The Poverty of Liberalism* (Boston: Beacon Press, 1968), chap. ii; Isaac Balbus, "The Concept of Interest in Pluralist and Marxian Analysis," *Politics and Society,* 1 (February 1971), 151-178; and Christian Bay, "Politics and Pseudopolitics," *American Political Science Review,* 59 (March 1965), 39-51.

8. Robert A. Dahl, *A Preface to Democratic Theory* (Chicago: University of Chicago Press, 1956), p. 137.

9. *Ibid.*, p. 145. In *Who Governs?* "high probability" becomes for Dahl a virtual certainty ([New Haven: Yale University Press, 1961], p. 93).

10. Dahl, *A Preface to Democratic Theory,* p. 150. See also Robert A. Dahl and Charles E. Lindblom, *Politics, Economics and Welfare* (New York: Harper Torchbooks, 1953), chaps. xii-xiii.

11. Dahl, *Who Governs?,* p. 305 and *passim.* See also David Ricci, *Community Power and Democratic Theory* (New York: Random House, 1971), pp. 137-138. Ricci's term, "slack" power, has been adopted in this discussion as shorthand for "potential power" and/or "indirect influence." Precision does not seem imperative in this context.

12. Terrence E. Cook and Patrick M. Morgan, eds., *Participatory Democracy* (San Francisco: Canfield Press, 1971), p. 4.

13. There is an irony in recent decentralization proposals. Decentralization is seen as a means of improving the responsiveness of government by bringing the decisions closer to the people. Historically, centralization has been used to improve responsiveness by removing decisions from the hands of local oligarchies. The irony will be appreciated but not enjoyed by liberal proponents of "busing."

14. Alexander Passerin d'Entrèves, *The Notion of the State* (London: Oxford University Press, 1967), p. 197.

15. Rousseau is generally cited in this context.

16. In addition to his essay in this volume, see *The Theory of Democratic Elitism: A Critique* (Boston: Little, Brown, 1967); and, with Morton Baratz, *Power and Poverty* (New York: Oxford University Press, 1970),

which builds upon their earlier articles, "Two Faces of Power," *American Political Science Review*, 56 (December 1962), 947-952, and "Decisions and Nondecisions," *APSR*, 57 (September 1963), 641-651.

17. Bachrach, *Democratic Elitism*, p. 3.

18. *Ibid.*, p. 6. It should be made clear that not all participatory democrats would agree that "government by the people" is impossible today. For example, the 1962 Port Huron Statement of the Students for a Democratic Society called for "the establishment of a democracy of individual participation" (reprinted in *The New Left: A Documentary History*, Massimo Teodori, ed. [Indianapolis: Bobbs-Merrill, 1969], p. 167). Nonetheless, I have used Bachrach as the prime example of PD-I because I believe he articulates the major underlying presuppositions, which are a major concern to this study.

19. Bachrach, *Democratic Elitism*, pp. 77-81.

20. *Ibid.*, p. 87.

21. *Ibid.*, p. 92.

22. *Ibid.*, p. 101.

23. *Ibid.*, chap. vii, especially p. 101.

24. *Power and Poverty*, pp. 44-45.

25. *Democratic Elitism*, pp. 87-88, 93-106.

26. *Ibid., pp.* 77-81, 87-88.

27. *Ibid.*, pp. 101-103.

28. *Ibid.*, p. 103.

29. *Ibid.*

30. *Ibid.*

31. See in particular Bachrach's essay in this volume. I am indebted to John Chapman for calling attention to this matter in his comments on an earlier version of the present essay.

32. See chapter iii of Mill's *Considerations on Representative Government*.

33. The arguments offered by proponents of PD-II (discussed below) may be read as an implicit critique of Bachrach's conception.

34. *Democratic Elitism*, p. 100.

35. *Ibid.*

36. Teodori, *New Left*, p. 167.

37. The obstacles to be overcome before this perspective is even granted a hearing are illustrated by the anthology on participatory democracy by Cook and Morgan (note 12, *supra*). As we have seen, in their Introduction the authors offer a definition and typology of participatory democracy which emphasize the structure of decision making. Even when they deal with "the case for participatory democracy," they see "the beneficial learning experience of the very process of participation" as a subject of justificatory arguments for a particular structural configuration (pp. 6-7). No indication is given (beyond implicit skepticism on p. 11) that participation can be divorced, existentially or conceptually, from decentralized structures.

38. "A critique of the Elitist Theory of Democracy," *American Political Science Review*, 60 (June 1966), 288.

39. The "educative" aspects of participation have long enjoyed an important place in democratic theory, as Carole Pateman has recently reminded us (*Participation and Democratic Theory* [Cambridge: Cambridge University Press, 1970], chap. ii). The essays of Bachrach and Braybrooke in the present volume call attention to a recent version: Participation aids men in discovering and articulating their interests; some might even say it helps educate men to their "real" interests.

To avoid increasing the complexity of the discussion, the "political education" version of participation has been subsumed under "developing the potentialities," of which it is a subtype.

40. Henry Kariel, *Open Systems: Arenas for Political Action* (Itasca, Ill.: Peacock, 1969), pp. 7-8.

41. "Citizenhood" is preferred to the more familiar "citizenship" because the latter carries distracting connotations. Citizenship conjures up an image of well-behaved individuals undertaking obligations out of civic duty. Citizenhood, on the other hand, brings out the idea that man, as a member of a political order, is (or may be) in a specific existential condition.

42. See for example H. Mark Roelofs, *The Tension of Citizenship* (New York: Rinehart, 1957); Joseph Tussman, *Obligation and the Body Politic* (New York: Oxford University Press, 1960); and Robert Pranger, *The Eclipse of Citizenship* (New York: Holt, Rinehart and Winston, 1968).

43. Pranger, *Eclipse,* pp. 10-11.

44. Robert Dahl, *Who Governs?,* pp. 223-225.

45. Pranger, *Eclipse,* p. 52.

46. *Ibid.,* p. 89.

47. Pranger, *Action, Symbolism, and Order* (Nashville, Tenn.: Vanderbilt University Press), pp. 152ff., especially pp. 157, 183.

48. *Ibid.,* p. 43.

49. *Ibid.,* p. 44; Pranger, *Eclipse,* p. 93.

50. Hannah Arendt, *The Human Condition* (Garden City, N.Y.: Anchor Books, 1959), chaps. i-ii.

51. *Ibid.,* p. 25.

52. *Ibid.,* p. 156.

53. *Ibid.,* p. 167.

54. *Ibid.,* p. 24.

55. *Ibid.,* p. 162.

56. *Ibid.,* p. 163.

57. *Action,* pp. 107-108.

58. *Ibid.,* pp. 109-110.

59. John Dewey, *The Public and Its Problems* (Chicago: Gateway Books, 1946), p. 15, quoted *ibid.,* p. 99.

60. *Ibid.,* p. 100.

61. *Ibid.*

62. *Ibid.,* p. 44.

63. *Ibid.*

64. *Ibid.,* p. 50.

65. *Ibid.,* pp. 51-52.

66. *Ibid.,* p. 51.

67. To avoid misunderstanding, it must be repeated that this essay is concerned with the theoretical aspects of participation only. The practical problems of participation are left to others to discuss.

68. The notion of one-dimensionality has achieved a degree of popularity through the writings of Herbert Marcuse. It is used here, however, without regard to Marcusean connotations.

69. To describe political action as noninstrumental is not to deny the many instrumental aspects of politics; in this revisionism is unsurpassed. What is at issue is whether political activity is everywhere and always instrumental, or whether one can legitimately suppose that there are other kinds of activities which involve man as a political being but which are

not directed toward the achievement of self-interested ends.

70. For extensive elaboration of this point see Arendt, *Human Condition,*
    p. 135.

71. The fact that an individual may "carry" or represent interests does not
    eliminate the equivocation, because the moral force of the argument
    rests upon man's condition as an autonomous being, free from control
    by others as part of his humanity. Interest arguments, whether expressed
    in economic or psychological terminology, construe individuals as re-
    sponding or reacting to some prior stimulus.

72. See the elaborate analysis of Community Action Programs and their
    rationales in Theodore Lowi, *The End of Liberalism* (New York:
    W. W. Norton, 1969), pp. 233-349.

73. Pateman, *Participation and Democratic Theory,* chap. ii; C. B. Macpher-
    son, "The Maximization of Democracy," in *Philosophy, Politics and
    Society,* Peter Laslett and W. G. Runciman, eds., Third Series (New
    York: Barnes and Noble, 1967), pp. 83-103; T. H. Green, *Lectures on
    the Principles of Political Obligation* (Ann Arbor: University of Michi-
    gan Press, 1967); Isaiah Berlin, *The Two Concepts of Liberty* (Oxford:
    Oxford University Press, 1958); J. L. Talmon, *The Rise of Totalitarian
    Democracy* (New York: Praeger, 1960); and George Sabine, "The Two
    Democratic Traditions," *Philosophical Review,* 61 (December 1952),
    451-474.

74. For a classic example of definitional homicide see Gabriel Almond and
    Sidney Verba, *The Civic Culture,* abridged ed. (Boston: Little, Brown,
    1965), p. 338.

75. When the term "participatory democracy" is used in the balance of this
    essay, it should be understood as referring to the second, self-realization,
    type unless otherwise indicated or obvious from the context.

76. Robert Dahl, *After the Revolution?* (New Haven, Conn.: Yale Univer-
    sity Press, 1970), p. 40.

77. *Ibid.,* pp. 45-46.

78. *Ibid.,* pp. 46-47.

79. *Ibid.,* p. 44.

80. *Who Governs?,* p. 225.

2

INTEREST, PARTICIPATION, AND DEMOCRATIC THEORY

PETER BACHRACH

Defenders of representative democracy persist in posing the wrong question. The fundamental issue is not whether the few rule in the interest of the many or in their own interest. It is rather that they rule and thereby deprive the many of their freedom. This denial, I contend, stems principally from a misconception of "political interest" in democratic theory.[1]

Writers as diverse as Plato and Marx or Burke and Marcuse distinguish between real and apparent interest, true and false consciousness, or true and false needs, holding that the individual cannot necessarily ascertain what is in his own best interest. Avoiding the elitist implication of this position, democratic theorists have traditionally rejected a dualist interpretation of interest.[2] An individual's political interest, they insist, is simply what he says it is. As A. D. Lindsay contended, no one is in a better position to know where the shoe pinches than the wearer. In this view, then, interest may be defined as "articulated preference." [3]

These apparently mutually inconsistent interpretations are not on closer examination wholly incompatible. Undoubtedly, in a democracy, articulated preferences—especially over a long run—are the only legitimate basis for formulating public policy. This basis, however, can be valid only insofar as the rules and procedures of the democratic process are not violated. A departure from the rules raises doubt about whether expressed choice made by the people reflect their real interests. For example, General Thieu's victory in the last presidential election in South Vietnam was judged illegitimate by democrats throughout the world because a free election had not taken place. Not only was the range of alternatives restricted, but also the opportunity to hear views fundamentally opposed to the government's position. Thus legitimacy was withheld despite the fact that the people recorded their "articulated preferences."

In effect the democrat is saying that since democratic norms were violated, there was no assurance that the articulated interests of the people actually reflect their *real* interests. Put differently, a principal function of constitutional and democratic institutions is to ensure a reasonably close convergence between expressed and actual interest.

It is the central contention of this paper that a dual concept of political interest, which recognizes that not all expressed wants reflect real needs, is an essential concept for determining the degree to which a political system is democratic. In terms of this concept, a system is democratic to the extent that it recognizes and enforces the right of the individual to participate in making decisions that significantly affect him and his community. Such participation is an essential means for the individual to discover his real needs through the intervening discovery of himself as a social human being.

This concept of a duality of interest gives substance to the argument that the political system in the United States is, at best, only partially democratic. It has failed to construct channels and institutions to facilitate and encourage people from the lower strata to articulate their interests. Further, it has failed to provide participatorial structures to afford working men and women an opportunity to determine who they are and what it is they really want. These deficiencies cast serious doubt as to whether the political system, in responding to articulated preferences, is responsive to the real interests of a large group of the electorate.

This paper does not intend to present an alternative interpretation of democracy that may be accepted or rejected depending upon one's political predilections. Rather, it is meant to demonstrate that acknowledgment of the right to participate is an integral and essential part of a political system that purports to be democratic. Democratic participation, for purposes of this paper, is a process in which persons formulate, discuss, and decide public issues that are important to them and directly affect their lives. It is a process that is more or less continuous, conducted on a face-to-face basis in which participants have roughly an equal say in all stages, from formulation of issues to the determination of policies.[4] From this definition it follows that demonstrations, sit-ins, confrontations, and pressure group bargaining on the one hand, and voting, speech making, and campaigning on the other, do not, singly or together, constitute democratic participation. All these forms of political action are legitimate and essential attributes of a democratic polity, and some are important if not vital means to the realization of democratic participation. However, among other things, none of them affords the individual the opportunity to engage in the decision making process on a regular face-to-face basis. Hence they must be distinguished from the concept of democratic participation as used here.

I

Democratic pluralism, the leading theory supportive of ongoing political institutions in the United States, is predicated on two major assumptions. Like classical liberal thought, it assumes, first, that most men acquire firmly identifiable political interests in their social and organizational involvement, and that their expectations, as well as their fulfillments and frustrations, are transferable from the social to the political realm. Assuming that social wants can be translated into articulated political demands within the social framework, it is understandable that for purposes of the political system, political preferences or demands are considered as givens. More specifically, the outer parameter of the political system on the input side is placed at the point where political demands are articulated as the basis for policy formulation.[5] Viewed in this way, the democratic system cannot be charged with the responsibility of fostering the conversion of personal feeling into political preferences, since this conversion process occurs beyond its input border.

The justification for excluding this conversion process is based upon the untenable premise that, in society, individuals naturally acquire the ability to perform this task themselves. The evidence that this is not the case for a significant segment of the population is quite conclusive. We know that a predominant number of individuals in the lower socioeconomic strata are politically apathetic and ignorant. We also know that there is a positive correlation between social status and political participation—that the level of citizen participation and the distribution of organizational resources vary according to the shape of the stratification system.[6]

These findings graphically demonstrate the need for a dualist concept of political interest. Failure to delineate the real from the articulated interest of lower strata individuals implies that their political apathy reflects the relative absence of personal concerns. Such a conclusion repudiates what we know to be true: people consumed by the hardship of everyday life—those enmeshed in the "prison on their aloneness," to use Erich Fromm's phrase—possess neither the energy nor the capacity to transform moods of bitterness and futility into articulated preferences.

Thus the issue becomes one of determining the extent to which the democratic system is responsible for their disfranchisement. The system is not exonerated from this responsibility by the usual explanation that the underclasses have an equal opportunity—at least constitutionally—to participate in all aspects of political life and that their propensity for political passivity is largely an outgrowth of severe social and economic deprivation, not political repression. Admittedly, the source of the problem lies in inequality in wealth and power within the economic system. This fact, however, does not make the political system any less undemocratic. Nor does it imply that further democratization of the political system must await basic reform within the economic sector. Political reform could well be the first step toward reducing the basic inequalities in both sectors.

The primary challenge for the student of democracy, however, is to explore how the democratic system itself can be reformed to combat its own deficiencies. To do so, a difficult question must be confronted at the outset: if indeed a large number of people have real but unexpressed political demands, how can a democratic system respond to such demands?

Certainly democratic theory provides no justification for political elites to determine where the shoe pinches as well as how the pinch should be eased. (Democratic principles aside, if the past is any indication, elites have neither the commitment nor the insight to do this job.) In a democracy, the task of determining the latent interests of the inarticulate rests exclusively with the inarticulate themselves. If the underlying assumption of this paper is sound—that a man becomes aware of his political interests only as he becomes a communicative being—this cycle can be broken only if the polity as a whole develops democratic structures that facilitate political reflection and action by people from all groups in society.

In other words, the time has come for the underbelly of society to acquire the democratic and constitutional protection upper parts of the social body have traditionally enjoyed. For example, freedom of speech is indeed an inviolable right, but a right exercised only by those who can express opinions and who have the opportunity for discussion and dialogue. How can this basic right be made relevant and useful to individuals who have no opinions? That is the problem.

Persons who in their everyday life—in their clubs, professional organizations, and social activity—have the opportunity of formulating and honing their opinions are in a position to determine where their interests lie. It is the political equivalent of these organizational structures and activities, lacking in the lower-class subculture, that the political sector must provide. It is not until socially disadvantaged groups become involved in structuring their own channels of communication and their own decision-making forums that they will begin to gain self-awareness. And it is only through self-awareness that they can identify their political interests. In short, political participation plays a dual role: it not only catalyzes opinion but also creates it.

In this context, the Office of Economic Opportunity (OEO) antipoverty program was instrumental. As the now-famous "maximum feasible participation" principle was implemented and took effect, inarticulate and passive representatives of the poor, sitting on various boards and commissions, were invariably transformed into angry, articulate, and concerned individuals. By its very nature, their participation, contrary to the anticipation of most government officials, was destined to "get out of control" as it evolved from a cooptative instrumentality to genuine involvement.[7]

Given the deep-seated grievances of the poor, the participatory process could hardly have developed otherwise. Daniel P. Moynihan was right: participation by the poor did disrupt the delivery of services and benefits to ghetto residents.[8] However, he overlooked the significance of the government's experiment, albeit on a small scale, in giving people an incentive and an opportunity to participate in open discussion and, in the process, to become aware of their interests.

This experience does not suggest that government should launch a massive program to build political structures for the dispossessed and the powerless. At this stage—especially in light of OEO's demise as a political force—such an idea is utopian. Rather, the experience demonstrates a moral imperative: in a democracy, each individual should have the right to participate in making decisions that significantly and directly affect his life. In the absence of this right and its effective exercise, the political system cannot be considered democratic: without them, the system cannot respond to the real interests of the people. In other words, when the boundaries between the social and the political sectors are set at a place that prevents the political system from facilitating the political development of all its citizens, then only those who have the private resources for this kind of development can articulate their real interest and cross the boundary into the political. A significant number are thus blocked from making the conversion from feelings and moods to articulated preferences.

Not to relinquish the assumption, which is deeply rooted in the philosophy of liberalism, that man is fully-formed prior to acting politically, and that he enters into the public sphere only after becoming whole and autonomous in the private sphere, is to perpetuate a political system that is profoundly class bound. Formally the system does indeed provide equal rights of participation to all citizens irrespective of class. But are not these rights quite empty when, in actuality, they are unable to be taken advantage of by an entire segment of the population?

It is ironic that in other pursuits—economic, educational, athletic, etc.—the idea of equality of opportunity implies the right of individuals to develop their capacities free from external impediments to enable them to compete on an equal basis. In politics it is a different matter. Here the linkage between man's right to participate and his right to develop a capacity to participate is seldom recognized. If it were, more thought would be given to how these interdependent rights could be implemented.

II

The second assumption underlying pluralist theory is that the American political system is essentially an open one—that political demands, spearheaded by legitimate groups, are convertible into issues that are seriously considered in an appropriate decision-making arena.[9] With this assumption, one can focus on the process by which issues are converted into public policy. Evidence of vigorous competition and a dispersion of power among political elites, directly or indirectly participating in the decision-making process, will permit the pluralist to conclude that the democratic system is alive and well.

An important inference can be drawn from the pluralist interpretation of the democratic process. Not only is the system responsive to the articulated interests of the people, but the responsiveness is elicited by minimum exertion on the people's part. To exercise control over the leaders and to insure their continuing responsiveness, it is essential that a significant portion of the electorate vote. Also, to protect their private interest, they must occasionally air their views to their appropriate representative. In this view, democracy is conceived as a method that affords maximum output (policy decision) from leaders with minimum input (participation) on the citizens' part.

Pluralists fail to consider the possibility that all political systems, including democracies, are shaped by the interests of the constellations of elites that regularly share power within the polity.[10] The exclusion of this possibility prevents pluralists from examining the extent of the power and influence elites exercise to sustain the biased system. The hard fact is that the unorganized, the poor, and the weak are more or less excluded from the political system.[11] Even when they mount a political protest, they usually cannot generate a conflict of sufficient magnitude to influence decision makers. Their failure to convert demands into issues is, to a considerable degree, a function of their powerlessness.[12] But it also has been shown that their failure has been perpetuated through the exercise of power by elites intent upon keeping them outside the political system.[13]

Demands for community control and decentralization in decision making are clearly a reaction to the malfunctioning of the democratic system. Barred by gatekeepers from established political channels, the excluded have begun to construct their own decision-making forums. Again, practice has outpaced theory. Despite the difficult, and as yet unresolved, problems that this movement has created for democratic theorists,[14] it is essential on democratic grounds that it be legitimated and nurtured in its growth. Although decentralization is not equivalent to democracy—indeed, it is not an unreceptive structure to breeding small tyrannies[15]— it can nonetheless be an effective means for opening and vitalizing the system as a whole. As a potential vehicle for the dispersion of power and the erosion of non-decision-making capacities of established elites,[16] its growth would very probably precipitate the emergence of new issues within the system—issues stemming from the demands of the lower classes.

In any polity, power is not primarily exercised by decision makers in the usual sense of that term; instead it is primarily wielded by those who determine what issues will or will not be considered for decision. As the elites' non-decision-making capacities become weakened, the system becomes more open. Within this context, the claim that persons have a right to participate in making decisions that directly affect them and their community is to a considerable degree a strategy for the redistribution of power. This strategy does not make the claim any less legitimate, for a key index of democracy is the extent to which each individual is valued as a human being, equally with all other human beings. Translated politically, the polity is democratic to the extent that citizens share power equally. The probability of a convergence of real and articulated interests becomes greater, therefore, as the dispersion of political power is broadened. Ultimately, it is the moral obligation of the democratic system to recognize and implement the individual's participatory right. The first step toward this goal is the incorporation of this right within contemporary democratic theory.

III

With their growing disenchantment with the working class as a force for social change, many liberal intellectuals no longer accept the traditional democratic doctrine of majority rule. Legitimacy is questioned on the ground that the majority mandate no longer reflects the "real" interest of the people; that owing to the elite-mass nature of society, a false consciousness, especially among the working class, has taken hold.

The essential difficulty with this contention, it could be argued, is the lack of supportive evidence. Even assuming that evidence could be marshaled in support of the young Marx's thesis that the capitalist system of production alienates the worker, there is no basis for presuming that alienation significantly impairs the worker's ability to make rational political choices. Even on the assumption that working-class people lack self-awareness, there is no other democratic option but to accept what they consider to be their interests as a basis for formulating policy. It is hardly tenable to assume, it is argued, that if workers expressed their real interests they would be supportive of radical social change. To the contrary, it may be that their rational self interest is basically in accord with the status quo, that the worker, in deriving pleasure in his leisure hours from consumptive activities and occasional indulgence in invidious comparison at the expense of his fellow man, is reasonably content with the system. Against this line of argument, I contend that there is a prima facie justification for doubting whether workers' articulated political preferences reflect their real interests.

There is no serious challenge among scholars today to the view that gargantuan multinational corporations are political institutions in the strictest sense of the term; that oligarchical self-perpetuating heads of these leviathans "authoritatively allocate values" that affect millions of people, both within and without the corporate constituency; and that not infrequently the vast power resources of the oligarchies are drawn upon to compel compliance of potential recalcitrants.

Within this relatively large and important political arena, work-ers are disfranchised. While they have an indirect voice through their unions on issues relating to wages, hours, and working con-ditions, they are barred from participation in determining the whole range of policies related to what they produce and their relation-ship to fellow workers, their employers, customers, and the gen-eral public. Denied this right to participate, the worker has no basis upon which to form intelligent opinions, to articulate his in-terests, to gain insights that could well add positively to his work environment and give his life meaning as a contributing member of society.

Like ghetto residents, workers lack the essential ingredients for effective participation in the political sector that is most crucial to them. It is doubtful, therefore, that in those political exercises in which they do participate, their articulated preferences actually reflect their more deep-seated concerns. It is my contention that these concerns would emerge and become focused if workers were to participate actively in shaping policy within their work place. An experience of this kind—whether it intensified feelings of bit-terness toward the corporation or fostered a sense of purpose and self-esteem—cannot help but raise the level of workers' conscious-ness of national issues. There is some evidence to support this as-sertion. We do know, for instance, that as persons from lower classes become active within organizations, they become more ac-tive in politics.[17]

This evidence suggests that as structures for participation for nonelites develop, so does the greater possibility for political change. There is certainly no reason to doubt that if corporate hierarchical structures were reassembled to accommodate worker participation in decision making, profound political change would most likely follow because principal sources of elite power would be materially diminished while worker participation would generate new issues for discussion and decision. Once again, this process demonstrates the relationship between the right to participate and non-decision making; as the right is actually acquired, it undermines the elite power to control the agenda—to determine what issues will be con-sidered.

Clearly, then, the legitimacy of the majority rule principle, as ap-plied to national elections, is questionable as long as large numbers of people within the industrial sector of the political system are denied the right to participate in making decisions, within their place of work, that significantly affect their relationship to the work they are engaged in and to their fellow workers, and that ultimately affect their self-awareness and outlook on life. The absence of this right to participate, in fact, casts serious doubt on the political system as a whole: in responding to articulated preferences, is it receptive to the real needs of the people?

IV

In his recent *After the Revolution?* [18] Robert Dahl has propounded a strong, pragmatic case for the decentralization and democratization of the corporate structure. He believes that large corporations are political oligarchies and that owing to their vast power and minimal external constraints, they have become disruptive forces in a democracy. Pragmatically, Dahl has transcended the structural confinement of pluralist theory. Theoretically, however, Dahl's position has not departed in any major respect from the narrowly drawn pluralist concept of interest.

Dahl establishes three criteria for democratic authority that must be met if decisions are to be legitimated. He then shows that his proposal for workers' self-management meets these criteria and is therefore legitimate. In regard to his first criterion, Personal Choice, Dahl states that an individual has the right to gain his own ends—his "rational self-interest"—providing others have an "opportunity to pursue their ends on an equal basis." Decisions, therefore, "must be made in such a way as to give equal weight to the personal choices of everyone." [19] Second, his criterion of Competence legitimates a decision, if it is made "by a person who is particularly qualified by his knowledge or skill to render a correct judgment." [20] Third, the criterion of Economy requires that the polity, in establishing its decision-making process, consider the time a citizen spends in political participation as a "cost." Hence, it follows "that if the gains exceed the costs it is rational for the citizens to participate." Conversely, "if the rewards do not exceed the costs, it is foolish for the citizen to participate at all." [21]

I believe these criteria are too egocentric and drastically undervalue the use of participation in a democratic polity. Furthermore, they are open to several other criticisms. First, Dahl, like other liberal theorists, assumes that the individual knows his rational self-interest before discussion of alternatives. In other words, Dahl views participation solely as an instrumentality to gain a "benefit," failing to recognize the value of participation as a means of understanding one's own position. Second, in order to define political interest as "rational self-interest"—interest directed to "gain my own ends"—he presupposes that man is incapable of holding a social interest that conflicts with his self-interest.[22] This premise ignores the choices between self and social interests with which people are often confronted. For example, one often chooses to participate in discussions, despite the personal sacrifice, because of a moral obligation to do so—a belief that such participation may contribute, in the course of the discussion, to the well-being of the polity.

Third, the criteria preclude unanticipated benefits to self that participation may bring with it, benefits derived from participation as process and independent of the results of participation. Thus Dahl fails to conceive of political participation two-dimensionally: as instrumentality to obtain end results *and* as a process that affords the opportunity to gain a greater sense of purpose and pride and a greater awareness of community. In Rousseauian terms, Dahl has failed to consider participation as a process through which man can become master of himself. On the basis of his reasoning, the less the individual has to participate in politics to protect or augment his own self-interest, the better off he is. For the less he participates, the more time he has to engage in other profitable or enjoyable pursuits.

The elitist implications in this concept of participation are clear. With rare exceptions, elites are available to represent the nonelites' interest in the decision-making process. By occasionally attending a meeting and casting a ballot, nonelites can support elites who have yielded high returns.

Fourth, the criteria are based on a static conception of political interest. They presuppose that the rational man will maintain the same set of interests that he had prior to the discussion throughout the participatory process. Without this assumption, he could not rationally calculate the costs and benefits of participation, for the calculation would be based on maximizing preconceived interests— interests that might in fact be radically changed in the course of participation. Changes in interest might occur not only because of the force of the argument presented at the forum but also because of a personal involvement in the participatory process which may significantly change one's attitude, perspective, and value priorities. This is likely to occur over a considerable period of time. If one chooses not to participate in the short run—owing to the results of a cost-benefit calculation—then potential personality and value changes derived from participation during the long run would be aborted at the outset.

Finally, in focusing on self-interest, the criteria obliterate from consideration the potential in direct impact of widespread democratic participation upon societal values—especially attitudes toward authority, equality, and community. For example, our limited experience with participation in governmental programs and in communities suggests that participation helped to undermine the invidious distinctions of social class rooted in American society. To people who have not made their mark in other walks of life, participatory forms have provided the experience of exercising political power in the shaping of community policy. More important, in stripping away the artificial differences among individuals—at least during discussions and decision making—participation has fostered an interchange of ideas among people who live and think differently. Equality of opportunity has traditionally been a cherished value in American society. As consciousness of the right to participate widens, the idea of equality of power may also emerge as a significant value.

The demand by nonelites for greater democratic participation has seriously challenged the traditional view of authority, a view that bestows upon those who possess merit, as evidenced by high rank in the hierarchy, a natural right to make the important decisions.[23] Usually administrators exercise this right by responding to pressures from below by instituting policy changes *they* consider to be just and reasonable. Viewing reform as properly emanating from above, elites are invariably shocked when nonelites react to benevolent action with criticism, if not hostility. Elites often overlook the issue here: the legitimacy of their authority. In focusing on the substantive policy issue, elites ignore, until confronted by those from below, more fundamental questions relating to power and the right to participation.

Participation also leads to a challenge of the expert's role. The tendency of the professional to link his ability to perform services with an obligation to make value judgments as to how the services should be rendered and for what purpose, has been challenged by the view that this linkage is illegitimate: value questions relating to the nature of professional service, as well as its goals, should best be left to the recipients of the service.[24]

This type of change in attitudes and values, which indirectly flows from expanded participation, cannot be evaluated by criteria designed to maximize the self-interest of individuals. My objections to these criteria—criteria that are implicitly the value basis of contemporary democratic theory—are aimed specifically at the notion on which they rest: that democratic participation is merely an instrumental value, to be implemented when net gains for the individual can be maximized and to be dispensed with when his time is better used in pursuit of preferences in private life or when the value choice can best be made by experts. Participation cannot be equated with sailing, money making, or theater going; this means that it cannot be fitted into Bentham's frame which supposedly enables one to choose rationally between alternative pleasures. To engage in the participatory process, in the late Arnold Kaufman's words, "enriches the lives of men not only by what it does *for* them but by what it does *to* them." [25] The unperceived effects of participation—upon individuals' outlook and personality, and upon their development into social beings—make the cost-benefit calculus for self-interest inappropriate.

The *real* interest of man is freedom: the freedom to discover himself and, beyond that, the freedom to develop into a socially conscious human being. For this reason, democratic participation must be recognized as an integral moral value of contemporary democratic theory.

NOTES AND REFERENCES

1. Despite major disagreements with the position taken by Isaac D. Balbus and William Connolly in their papers on the concept of political interest, I have been very much influenced by them. See Isaac D. Balbus, "The Concept of Interest in Pluralist and Marxian Analysis," *Politics and Society* (1971), 151-177; and William E. Connolly, "On 'Interests' in Politics," unpublished paper, July 1971.
2. For example, in reply to C. Wright Mills' position that "false consciousness" is "the lack of awareness of and identification with one's objective interest," Nelson Polsby argues that "people participate in those areas they care about the most. Their values, eloquently expressed by their participation, cannot, it seems to me, be more effectively 'objectified.' "

("The Sociology of Community Power," *Social Forces* [1959], quoted in Connolly, "On 'Interests,' " p. 3.)

3. For an analysis of the diverse ways the concept of interest has been defined in political science literature, see Richard Flathman, *The Public Interest* (New York, 1966), chap. 2. Also see David Easton, *A Framework for Political Analysis* (Englewood Cliffs, N.J., 1965), p. 120; Isaac D. Balbus, "Concept of Interest"; and Connolly, "On 'Interests.' "

4. I am aware that this definition leaves much to be desired. Notably it fails to define participation with sufficient precision to be useful in distinguishing between genuine and pseudo or cooptative participation. The formula "issues that are important to them and directly affect their lives" is both too narrow and broad at the same time. Too broad because almost anything that is "political" affects our lives; too narrow because elites can permit participation involving issues that appear to affect our lives in important ways, but only to the extent that they do not affect the basic parameters of privileges and inequality in the system. I would argue, in fact, that elites have encouraged "participation" in the United States precisely to the extent that bureaucratic control mechanisms have declined in effectiveness—primarily in the ghettos, the universities, and the political parties—and to the extent that they are faced with a "crisis" of legitimacy. Thus, democratic participation as I have defined it above may not always be liberating; it may be repressive to the degree that it promotes a false sense of well-being among participants who are absorbed in decision making on marginal issues.

The problem is not resolved by the stipulation in the definition that participants must have roughly an equal say in all stages in the decision-making process, for this requirement could be met without interfering with the crucial power of elites to prevent issues that are potentially threatening to them from being raised and considered.

This difficulty could be theoretically overcome by including in the definition the requirement that all participants in the formulation of issues and in the decision-making process possess approximately an equal amount of power resources. Although this requirement would clearly distinguish between genuine and pseudo participation, in practice it would be almost an impossible standard to meet. It would especially rule out emerging situations in which nonelites are in the process of gaining a greater share of power in the political process. Perhaps the following standards would be helpful in judging the dynamics of the participatory process:

1. Whether new issues important to nonelites succeed in reaching the decision-making agenda and are debated and seriously considered.
2. Whether the pattern of decisions manifests a shift in the structure of power in the subpolity in favor of nonelites.
3. Whether the pattern of policy outputs reflects a more equitable allocation of values between established elites and nonelites.

5. For a brilliant analysis of this point, see Balbus, "Concept of Interest," pp. 162-164.

6. Norman H. Nie, G. Bingham Powell, Jr., and Kenneth Prewitt, "Social Structure and Political Participation: Developmental Relationship," *American Political Science Review* (1969), 819.

7. See Peter Bachrach and Morton Baratz, *Power and Poverty* (New York, 1970).

8. Daniel P. Moynihan, *Maximum Feasible Misunderstanding* (New York, 1969).

9. See Robert Dahl, *A Preface to Democratic Theory* (Chicago, 1956).

10. As E. E. Schattschneider has so admirably put it, "All forms of political organization have a bias in favor of the exploitation of some kinds of conflict and the suppression of others because organization is the mobilization of bias. Some issues are organized into politics while others are organized out" (*The Semi-Sovereign People* [New York, 1960], p. 71).

11. Michael Parenti, "Power and Pluralism: A View from the Bottom," *Journal of Politics* (1970), 501-531.

12. Bachrach and Baratz, *Power and Poverty*, chaps. 5-7.

13. Michael Lipsky, "Protest as a Political Resource," *American Political Science Review* (1968), 1144-1158.

14. For example, what principles or guidelines are applicable for determining the *legitimacy* of a particular claim for decentralization of decision making? Further, if decentralization is decided upon, what guidelines are appropriate for determining the jurisdiction of the decision-making arena? Is power, in Hobbesian fashion, to be the sole determinant in answering these questions?

    A corollary problem is one of establishing concurrent authority between decentralized and central decision-making agencies involving policy issues that significantly affect several publics or the general public. This problem is made more difficult by the tendency of people to interpret the right to participate in community decisions as an exclusionary right —one which precludes others who have vital but indirect interests from a voice in the policy determination. Today, for example, lower-income black groups who are deeply although indirectly affected by housing decisions, made "democratically" by suburban neighborhood organizations, have been locked out of the decision-making process.

    On the philosophical side, the concept of freedom embodied in the theory of participatory democracy is in fundamental conflict with the theory of representative democracy and the latter's application of the majority rule principle. Nonetheless, there is no escape from the fact that democratic participation can function only on a wide scale within a majoritarian representative framework. The impurities of the theory, therefore, must be realistically accepted rather than ignored. Thus, the basic problem or challenge that the theory presents is, given its inherent restrictions: How can democratic participation be maximized?

15. See Theodore Lowi, *The Politics of Disorder* (New York, 1971); and Grant McConnell, *Private Power and American Democracy* (New York, 1966). Their thesis, that small units which are conducive to popular participation are also vulnerable to elite manipulation and domination, has considerable force. However, this danger primarily applies to participatory groups that are outside large bureaucracies. Since the constituencies of large corporations and universities, for example, are composed of a wide range of interests, there should not be great difficulty in establishing decision-making units along functional lines that are reasonably small, to facilitate rank-and-file participation, yet are sufficiently heterogeneous to prevent pressure of conformity from overwhelming those sharing in the decision-making process. There are also other reasons which support the view that participatory democracy can best be established within rather than outside bureaucracies. One of these reasons is discussed in the next part of this paper.

16. A nondecision is a decision that results in suppression or thwarting of a

latent or manifest challenge to the values or interests of the decision maker. See Bachrach and Baratz, *Power and Poverty,* p. 45.

17. Nie, Powell, and Prewitt, "Social Structure," pp. 821-827.
18. New Haven, Conn., 1970.
19. *Ibid.,* p. 12.
20. *Ibid.,* p. 28.
21. *Ibid.,* p. 46.
22. For a discussion of this issue, see Robert Paul Wolff, *The Poverty of Liberalism* (Boston, 1968).
23. For a superb essay on the elitist implications of the doctrine of equality of opportunity, see John Schaar, "Equality of Opportunity and Beyond," in J. Roland Pennock and John W. Chapman, eds., *Equality,* Nomos IX (New York, 1967), pp. 228-249.
24. S. M. Miller and Martin Rein, "Participation, Poverty and Administration," *Public Administration Review* (1969), 21.
25. Quoted in Arnold S. Kaufman, *The Radical Liberal* (New York, 1968), p. 56.

3

THE MEANING OF PARTICIPATION
AND OF DEMANDS FOR IT:
A PRELIMINARY SURVEY
OF THE CONCEPTUAL ISSUES

DAVID BRAYBROOKE

I

For a time, I thought I might begin with a paradox: Participating is not the same thing as having and playing a recognized role in a joint human activity; yet demanding to participate is the same thing as demanding such a role to play. Alas! the paradox all too quickly bursts out of bounds and leads to a real contradiction. It is true that when there is a special word for the recognized role (as there is, much more often than not, if the role is an established and familiar one), the existence of that word presents a substantial obstacle to speaking of the role as "participating." We might properly hesitate to say that a judge

PUBLISHER'S NOTE: At the author's request this contribution was neither edited nor copyedited by our staff except for punctuation.

participates in a trial, any more than a bride or a bridegroom participates in a wedding. The word "participate" seems to be at home with formal ceremonies. Weddings, though formal ceremonies, are perhaps not pompous enough, however, for anyone to be said to "participate" in them; but even the colloquial approximations to the sense of "participate" with which I shall mainly be concerned are unsuitable. Neither the priest nor the best man, much less the bride or bridegroom, "takes part" or "has a part" in the wedding. "Takes part" suggests a special initiative, without which an enterprise would have turned out differently. "Has a part," which might perhaps do for an usher or a page, grossly understates the case for the bride and bridegroom.

The obstacle to speaking of "participating" is not insuperable, however. There is a generic sense of "participate" always within reach, which can be called in to get over the obstacle. Suppose we asked what arrangements a certain society (maybe our own) had for dealing with crimes or disputes about property; it would be perfectly in order to go on to ask which members of the society participated in these arrangements and on what terms. The answer might be that a few people participated as judges, appointed for life; many people (though perhaps no blacks and no working-class people) participated for brief periods by serving on juries; other people participated as lawyers, advocates for one side or the other.

The demand to participate is often, I think normally, put forward on the generic level. It is met, if it *is* met, by opening up one or more of the established roles (so that, for example, blacks begin serving on juries, receiving briefs as counsel, obtaining appointments as judges) or by creating new roles (as when, for example, voters begin choosing party candidates in primary elections as well as choosing, at general elections, between the candidates of different parties). Normally, when there is a special word for the recognized role newly obtained, the word displaces "participate"; thus, once the demand has been met, we no longer readily speak of participating, perhaps because to do so suggests something less than the facts about the roles and their institutionalization. But it is a contradiction, not merely a paradox, to admit that a person has a recognized role which falls under the generic concept of participation and to deny that he participates (though one may deny that he merely participates).

To demand to participate is, I repeat, to demand to play a recognized role in a joint human activity. The chief ways of not being recognized appear to be: being defied, with the defiance directed against a would-be participant with equal or superior power and evident willingness to use the power; being interdicted, whether by ecclesiastical pronouncement or by statute, as in apartheid laws; and, less formally, being ignored, which has many varieties—not being received, not being allotted time to speak, not being listened to (even to the extent of formal pretense), never being heeded, not being given credit. Recognition itself varies greatly in degree of formality and is accorded in one degree or another to all sorts of roles, ranging from roles recognized only *pro tempore* (for example, speaking to a legislative body when one is not a member, not even normally present), through permanent roles without much formal elaboration, some of them very simple roles (like running for exercise with a group of people who run in the park every Sunday), some of them very complicated and variable (like being a member of the executive committee of a society agitating for prison reform). At the other extreme, there are recognized roles both permanent and very elaborately defined, with many attendant formalities (for example, the role of a judge, especially a judge in one of the higher courts). The recognition in question is always recognition by other participants, understood as such on both sides; I do not mean to treat roles imputed by sociologists, on whatever good grounds in theory or observation, if they are not roles known and recognized as such by the people concerned.

Can one participate without playing a recognized role? Certainly one can force one's way into an activity; the present participants may not dare show defiance; their defiance, even if they dare show it, may not succeed. But I think such cases can be treated as cases of forced recognition. Whatever the intruder accomplishes with force, he will not have achieved participation unless he has achieved recognition. He may seize a place in the starting line-up; he may even compel the judges to give him the prize if he comes in first; but he will not have taken part in the race if the other runners ignore him—if they do not, whether cheerfully or under duress, race against him. So he must force them to race against him, and with that, he obtains recognition, however grudgingly granted.

Can one play a recognized role without participating? I think not, but it must be granted that a role may be recognized, even invested with formal elaboration, and yet not count for much in the joint human activity in which it figures. A herald, a sergeant-at-arms, the chaplain of the Senate, all have recognized roles, but they are roles which I shall pass over to deal with more substantial participation.

One way of making sure that the participation is sufficiently substantial to be worth treating—and worth demanding—is to relate it to the *outcome* of the joint activity. I now proceed to do so, by saying that at least to begin with I shall be treating only recognized roles that consist of an opportunity for action or a duty, in either case one capable of making a significant difference to the outcome of the joint activity.

There is, I expect, little need to explain how it is that people, when they demand to participate in a joint human activity, are often understood to be demanding an opportunity to act in ways capable of making a significant difference to the outcome. Very often the outcome in question is one that is likely to affect the interests of the people who demand to participate: they want to participate in order to protect what is at stake for them in the outcome (lower taxes, an end to conscription, a cleaner environment) and in giving this reason they make the motivation behind their demand intelligible.

The alternative interpretation, sometimes called for, of a demand to participate as a demand to be given a duty capable of affecting the outcome, may not be so easily countenanced. Can it stand alone? Do people ever demand chances of affecting the outcome through duties assigned them, when they do not regard the duties as opportunities to protect their stake in the outcome?

I think they do. Moreover, when this alternative interpretation, relying on the notion of a duty, does stand alone, it can serve to draw attention to another sort of reason for the demand to participate, for when the duty interpretation stands alone it connects with this sort of reason only. (Whereas the opportunity interpretation can stand alone with or without such a connection.) Reasons of this sort relate participation to outcomes, but not by way of supposing that the participation will aim directly at affecting the distribution of rewards embodied in the outcome or associated with it. Imagine a city in which a great project is started up—say, of rebuilding the city center with profits extracted from colonies overseas. It will be by far the greatest thing done in the city during a generation, perhaps during several generations. It will call for a variety of efforts and talents. Not all citizens may demand to take part; some may not wish to. However, might not a citizen quite understandably make such a demand and justifiably object to being left out of all the assignments, whether to skilled work in the quarries or on the center site, or to one of the committees for design and supervision, and object even if no question arose of his being harmed in respect to life or livelihood or freedom?

It might be said that he objects because he has a stake (an interest) in leading as significant a life as possible; he will lose a chance to live more significantly if he is excluded from the most significant joint activity in his time and vicinity; he may also lose standing with his fellow citizens. There are genuine rewards to be had in these connections; and, no doubt, "stake" can be extended to cover the possibility of obtaining them; but only at some risk of obscuring the different relation to the outcome. It is not so much the impact that the outcome will make upon the person making the demand that counts for him on this interpretation, but the impact that he can make upon the outcome, in respect, say, to its physical content or durability or beauty. He wants to be able to say, "If it had not been for me, one of the horses prancing in the frieze of the Parthenon would have been left out of the design," or "put in facing the other way," or "cut from defective stone," or "finished less carefully." He wants, in other words, a genuine, certifiable share of the glory, and to have that share he must beforehand have a share of the responsibility.[1]

Both a duty to be performed and an opportunity for action are modes of "participation" in the sense that I am mainly concerned with, the "taking part" sense. But both also invite the application of "participate" in quite a different sense—a sense neatly expressed, both in partnership with "taking part" and in opposition to it, by the verb "partake."[2] In this sense one participates in a "get-rich-quick" scheme and its proceeds, in the profits of a firm (if one is stockholder), in the fruits—and the glory—of victory in the field or triumph in the arts. There is some crudity, a sign perhaps of excessive stress on outcomes, about assimilating "glory" to "proceeds." Besides "glory," moreover, we must consider humbler parallels, like the appreciation of one's family and friends for a duty conscientiously performed. Are such rewards to be treated on the same footing as a share of the profits from some possibly ignoble enterprise? But participation in rewards associated with the outcome has already been implied in the reasons for demanding either a duty or an opportunity that will affect the outcome, and I think I can give due honor to the "partaking" sense of "participate" without suggesting that the rewards to be participated in appeal only to ignoble motives like greed. Continuing for the time being to treat participation as related to the outcome of a joint human activity, I shall assume that a substantial demand to participate embraces among other things a demand to be given at least a chance of partaking in whatever benefits result from the activity or from sharing in the responsibility for its outcome. I speak of "a chance of partaking" rather than of "partaking" to allow for the possibility that the activity may fail or that what one tries to do as a participant may not be accommodated in the outcome.[3]

A number of theorists have carefully fostered consideration for educative aspects of participation.[4] The scheme that I have just outlined can be adjusted so as to make sure of keeping such aspects in view. People can learn through participating in a given activity to identify the benefits which the activity and others of its kind offer, actually or potentially; simultaneously, people advance in understanding how these benefits answer to their own known interests. But they may also advance in defining and articulating interests which they were not previously aware of: interests that they have as individual persons, and, besides, interests that they have as members of groups with common dangers and common opportunities.[5] Thus Marx supposed the workers would awaken to class consciousness and simultaneously to conceptions of fuller personal lives. My scheme can be stretched to count advances in knowledge in all these respects as rewards associated with the outcomes of current activities.

Such rewards are less closely associated with outcomes than glory, to be sure, since they may be substantial when the outcomes are humiliating, even shameful. However, like glory, they could be included in outcomes, if "outcome" were used in a comprehensive sense, to include all the effects and consequences of a joint activity; and like glory, they are assets that can be carried forward. If they do not lead immediately, for the participants who acquire them, to impacts of the sorts they seek, including on occasion impacts directly upon the distribution of rewards, they may yield success on these points later on. Suppose, however, that a person fails continually in having the impact on outcomes that he aims for, whether his aims are self-interested, or public-spirited, or inspired by a thirst for fame; by learning, through participation, to address himself in a larger way to the pursuit of any of these aims, he may yet have learned to lead a larger and richer life.

II

People not only demand participation for themselves; they also demand participation by others. I have a hypothesis about this second sort of demand. It is that there are two distinct alternatives to participating and yet that both are condemned over the same range of activities. One of the alternatives to participating is being excluded (the varieties of which I surveyed earlier, in surveying the ways of not being recognized); the other alternative to participating is remaining aloof. Both imply nonparticipation, but they are independent and mutually exclusive conditions. If I do not participate through aloofness, then I am not excluded from participation. If I do not participate because I am excluded, the question of my aloofness does not arise. (Pretending that I do not care about being excluded is not the same thing.)

The part about the two alternatives being condemned over the same range of activities is the more controversial part of the hypothesis. There are in fact a variety of counterexamples, and while some of these do not seem to reach the heart of the matter, others have enough force to bring this part of the hypothesis down from speaking categorically to speaking of a strong tendency, which can be found in a number of cultures very different in other ways.

In many cases we might resist any move to take away someone's right to take part in a certain activity, and so oppose his being excluded, when because he was sick or away he was in fact not going to take part; but then his not taking part would not amount to aloofness, and, besides, the question of his not taking part arises in respect to the present stage of the activity while the question of his exclusion relates to stages present and future. It is equally easy to allow for another sort of objection: some activities are multiform, and a person may be supported against being excluded from a multiform activity—a sports program offered by a neighborhood club, for example—and yet not condemned for standing aside, once he has been admitted, from a given branch of the activity. He may not wish to play tennis or volleyball, and no one may reproach him for passing them up; but in that case it might be supposed there would be some alternative branch of activity in which he would engage: he would play his part in the sports program by, say, joining the swimming team.

A distinctly more unsettling objection lies in the possibility of campaigning against the exclusion of certain people in the hope that once they are admitted they will bring the activity to an end.[6] For may not one way of bringing it to an end be to pack the group that is supposed to carry it on with people who will remain aloof from it? Imagine a beauty pageant, which some people might object to both because it excluded black girls and because it degraded the female sex. Suppose the campaign against exclusion is won; black girls enter in great numbers, but then ostentatiously refuse to cooperate with the proceedings. The same people might applaud their conduct who had condemned their exclusion. I think this example must be met by qualifying the hypothesis: exclusion is condemned by the same people over the same range of activities as aloofness with the possible exception of certain activities which those very people disapprove of.

Even with this qualified reformulation, however, the hypothesis looks vulnerable to the most important objection of all: some people do condemn a person's being excluded from participation in politics and yet tolerate, even approve of, his being aloof in many cases, at least to the extent of actually taking very little part. Thus Berelson and others have reconciled themselves to most voters' being apathetic about politics. If these voters were more active they would be more partisan; by being less partisan they exert a moderating influence on the competition between parties and candidates.[7] This particular version of the objection can be fielded in part by pointing out that in effect these writers are distinguishing between activities; and no one supposes that approving general participation in one activity (voting) implies approving general participation in other activities. Other writers have held, by contrast with Berelson, that it is best for ignorant and apathetic voters not to exercise their admitted right to vote; and this version of the objection can be dealt with by pointing out that the same writers would very likely hold it even better for these voters to learn enough and care enough to exercise their right properly. Again, however, the objection is met only in part; a residue of this version of the objection and of the first appears again in a third version, in which the right to vote is looked upon as a potential recourse that every sane grown person should have, but it is simply denied that everyone with the right has an obligation to exercise it continually. This version of the objection embodies a certain laissez-faire attitude toward political activity, though I do not propose to ascribe it to classical laissez-faire liberals, much less suggest that it is characteristic of them. The attitude is one that both Plato and Aristotle were ready to adopt —Plato, accepting Socrates' inhibitions about taking part in the politics of an imperfect society;[8] Aristotle, in unqualified praise for a self-absorbed life of contemplative activity.[9]

How much weight is to be given to the attitude? The attitude exists, but it is not, I think, prevalent with us. The grounds for condemning aloofness are too strong, and though they are largely distinct from the grounds for condemning exclusion, I expect they suffice, for most people in our culture, to make the condemnation of aloofness go hand in hand almost the whole distance with the condemnation of exclusion.

Exclusion is condemned on the same grounds that a person demands to participate: expressed in relation to the outcome of the joint activity, these are, as canvassed earlier, the chance to benefit or to suffer from the impact of the outcome and the desire to share in the achievement. Thus, excluding a person jeopardizes his own well-being; at the very least, he stands to lose something in the way of a chance to lead a life that he regards as significant. There is some linkage with the grounds for condemning aloofness. If we take the educative aspects of participation seriously, we should accept as one ground for condemning aloofness the failure of the person in question to improve himself. Moreover, one ground for condemning exclusion is that it deprives (just as aloofness would) the other people carrying on the activity of the skills and wisdom which the person excluded might bring with him. Yet the grounds for condemning aloofness are weighted, as the grounds for condemning exclusion are not, on the side of the effects (through the outcome) on other people. The main ground for condemning aloofness is typically that everyone stands to lose if the outcome is diminished by the failure of even one of the people eligible to participate to make his contribution, indeed the best contribution that he is capable of (taking into account his other responsibilities).

To make this ground cogent the joint activity is conceived as a common task; it may be, a task the success of which hangs by a thread even if everyone works his heart out. At first sight, this conception may not seem to apply very readily to activities that consist chiefly in voting on who shall hold office or on what shall be done with the surplus left at the end of the financial year. Applied to governments, it suits best governments under siege, which claim to be reconstructing the whole of social life—against desperate odds, encircled by hostile powers; but it is just under such governments, of course, that any sign of aloofness is most fiercely condemned.

The task-conception, however, if not quite so intensely exploited, is almost as potent elsewhere. Americans are brought up within a web of voluntary associations, many of them—for reasons set forth by Downs[10] and Olson[11]—running with less support from their members than would guarantee their effectiveness or even their survival. Exhortations against aloofness, that is to say, against depriving a group of our contribution to the common task, are as familiar as our daily bread. These exhortations encompass government, which in this connection is still looked upon as something like a voluntary association, not because of any recollection of contractarian ideas, perhaps, but simply with our history of (mainly) voluntary immigration in mind—hence "America: love it or leave it." Applied to the tasks of government, the task-conception finally succeeds in getting a purchase on voting. The means becomes the end; the task, to keep up the practice of democratic government. According to Downs,[12] a conscientious citizen can have rational grounds for not remaining aloof—for voting—in his contribution to this task, even if he does not expect to have a significant effect upon the benefits that he receives from the outcome of any one vote.

Whatever Plato and Aristotle came to think afterwards, Athenians too, in the summertime of their democracy, were evidently ready to insist on participation by every citizen. Speaking for them, in an address that also evokes the beauty of their public buildings, like those on the reconstructed Acropolis, Pericles says, "We differ from other states in regarding the man who holds aloof from public life not as 'quiet' but as useless." [13]

III

I have been treating both demands to participate and demands for the participation of others as relating various persons to the outcomes of joint human activities. But which persons and which activities? Surely it is not sensible to demand of anyone that he participate in every joint human activity; it is hardly more sensible for anyone to demand himself to participate in every activity, or even in all that he fancies of those that he hears of. Can anything useful be said about general principles for matching people with appropriate activities?

The general situation, let us say, is one in which a person N demands to participate in a joint activity A of a group G; the activity will have one or more outcomes representable (by propositions describing the state of the world in part) as P_1 or P_2 or P_3 ... or P_n.[14] A demand to participate is fully intelligible (as to content) if the person N making the demand, the group G, and the joint activity A are all identified (with the outcome set described in as much detail as necessary to identify the activity).

The demand may nonetheless be absurd if the necessary conditions are not met, first, of N's not being so wholly committed to other activities (in the vicinity or elsewhere) as to be unable to be physically present to the extent required for participation; and, second, given our present insistence on keeping always in view activities in relation to outcomes, of N's at least believing that he would (if he participated in A) have some chance of having a significant effect upon outcomes current or future. Putting aside cases in which the demand is raised simply as a distraction or vexation, if either of these conditions failed, the demand to participate could not be assigned an intelligible motivation. We might understand what was being demanded, but we would not understand why the demand was being made.

Not all intelligible motivations deserve respect, however, or will obtain a serious hearing for a demand to participate. The demand must not be intrusive. Suppose N is not a member of a group G and has no claim to be a member of the group and no claim to the resources that G is using in A and its other activities. He may nevertheless conceive, quite accurately, that if he participated in A he could shape the outcome in some way profitable to himself. The family next door has bought a boat; if he could take part in making the decisions about using it he could get it several days a month to go fishing. But it would be outrageous presumption for him to demand to participate.

What is the principle that rules out intrusive demands? It is not a principle that depends on the existence of private property in things like boats; or even on the existence of private family households. G is a group of young musicians rehearsing a wind serenade. N, not a member of the group, or anyone with authority over it, would prefer to have them play "Preussens Gloria," his favorite march-tune. N knows that if he were given a chance to take part in deciding what the group would play, he could make himself so obstructive (or so ingratiating) as to persuade them away from the wind serenade. N's demand to participate is still intrusive and will not normally be entertained for that reason.

The principle seems to be one that presupposes social provisions sufficient by current standards to guarantee N's opportunities to gain a livelihood; protect himself from serious harm, whether in the way of physical injury or of disgrace or otherwise; and amuse himself in a reasonably full way; and sufficient to cover these opportunities without contemplating that N would be a member of G, which is part of or a consequence of the provisions for other people. These presuppositions are disputable in particular cases, but when they are accepted, N cannot be said to be harmed by being kept out of G (since he is covered otherwise by social provisions); his demand to participate may amount to nothing more than a purely selfish effort to increase his pleasures, an effort with which other people may legitimately refuse to co-operate.

Yet there are demands to participate that are not merely efforts at aggrandizing one's pleasures; on the contrary, they represent desperate attempts to protect one's vital interests in the absence (acknowledged on all sides) of sufficient social provisions; they are nevertheless properly not entertained. Consider a mother-in-law observing her son's wife attempting a reconciliation with her son. The mother-in-law may correctly apprehend that if the reconciliation occurs, her son will move away (at the wife's insistence) and neglect her. She may in fact need her son much more than the wife does. She nevertheless does not have the standing necessary to obtain a serious hearing for a demand to participate.

The same difficulty besets (in the eyes of stockholders) workers' demands to participate in decisions about the location of a company's factories. If the proposal, heard from time to time, to let only the young men who will have to do the fighting vote upon declarations of war were accepted, the same difficulty would beset the demands of other citizens, who would have some stake in the issue even if the war was not going to be brought home to them.

In each of these examples, there are two classes of people, defined not by their stakes in the outcomes of the activities in question, but by age or property rights or relations of kinship; and in each of them, the stake of one class is given precedence over the stake of the other, sometimes evidently because as a rule the stake of one class taken as a whole is greater than the stake of the other, but in other cases—in the stockholders' case—for obscurer reasons. I suspect that deep questions about justice would have to be gone into before the difficulties raised by these examples could be laid to rest. I shall deal with them here by extending the other provisions principle so that it runs, "A demand to participate shall be seriously entertained only if there are not provisions other than belonging to G and taking part in A minimally sufficient for N's well-being; or in the absence of such provisions, N belongs to at least one class of people outside G, whose stake in the outcome of A is held to be at least as deserving of attention as the stake of another class of people, i.e., those who currently belong to G." This formula, by begging some of the right questions, points to considerations that are known to be frequently crucial in disputes about demands to participate.

There are two exceptions to the operation of the other provisions principle as a necessary condition. One, which might be called the *non de trop* exception, obtains when N can join G and take part in A without in any way threatening to diminish the benefits of A to those already in G, if it is only by getting in the way or straining the chain of communication. The second arises when N's demand to participate is taken as implying a proposal to improve on existing arrangements; granting that these make minimally sufficient provisions for him, N may claim that by reorganizing G, perhaps taking him in as an additional member, perhaps letting him change places with someone now in the group, he or some other people will be better off and no one will be worse off.[15]

To accommodate another familiar set of considerations that are frequently crucial in disputes about demands to participate, we may join to the other provisions principle the principle of ability: N's demand to participate in an activity A shall be seriously entertained only if N has at least as much ability to participate as is required for successful participation in some capacity. One can imagine grotesque discrepancies between N's ability and the capabilities required by activity A. N has never studied mathematics and has no native talent for calculation; A is the activity of calculating the size and shape of our galaxy from radioastronomical data. Very often, of course, the discrepancies are hard to make out, especially when one inquires into them seriously. Management does not rely entirely on the property rights of stockholders as an argument against workers' participation; it invokes conventional assumptions about the activity of management being too intellectual or at least too specialized for workers to carry on competently. Yet these assumptions are at least disputable. Here and elsewhere, in fact, the whole issue of participation is likely to be joined in disputes about ability. So it has been in disputes about the participation of ordinary citizens in effective choices of government policies; so it has been in current disputes about the participation of students in university government.

Again, the operation of the principle is complicated by the possibility that what is being demanded is at bottom not participation in A as the activity is now organized, but participation in a reorganized activity, which might allow for different capacities. Then the ability that is held to be a necessary qualification for participation must be defined and reckoned in relation to the reorganized activity. Whether N has the ability will still be a question of fact, which is not best settled by enthusiasm; the answer as to the facts may not favor him, since every form of reorganization that might accommodate him might sacrifice too many other advantages.

Even after it has met all the conditions that I have listed, N's demand to participate may still not be accepted, though I think reasonable people will give it a serious hearing, and disputes about N's ability or the sufficiency of other provisions for him will, once started, sometimes end only with a decision to comply with the demand. Whether or not the demand is accepted in the end will depend, sometimes, on peremptory considerations about the legitimacy of the activity or the consistency of N's participation with his (other) duties; sometimes, on meliorative considerations about the consistency of N's participation with more productive rather than less productive assignments of people to groups and of groups to activities. N's demand to participate may deserve consideration but be rejected finally because the outcome for everyone concerned is likely to be better if he does not participate in A but does something else—work, play, or contemplate. It may even turn out that, examined closely in the course of giving N's demand to participate a serious hearing, neither activity A nor group G would figure under better arrangements within reach. N's demand to participate would be rejected, but his making the demand might have as a consequence,—surprising to N perhaps and perhaps gratifying, perhaps not, a social reorganization abolishing both the activity in question and the group.

IV

Participation has degrees, at least with respect to activities defined in familiar ways: one can take part more or less fully in the sports program or in the campaign for the Senate. A useful notion of minimum provisions for participation can be defined with the help of an analogy with the process of social choice. In that special case, a person N could be said to be permitted to participate provided that he was permitted to express his preference at least for the single outcome which he most favored and provided that there was at least one possible combination of expressions of preference by other participants such that N's expression of his preference would resolve the choice of outcome in favor of the outcome which he preferred. For example, if all the other participants were indifferent between outcomes, N's preference would prevail; or it would prevail if the others were equally divided pro and con. For the general case the minimum provisions for participation would then be that N would be permitted to act (whether by expressing a preference or a judgment or by actually intervening physically, say by taking up the chisel himself to cut part of the frieze) so as to affect the outcome at least tentatively and that there would be at least one possible combination of actions by other participants such that N's action would be allowed to stand and would have some part of its intended effect on the outcome. I say "some part of its intended effect" to allow for the possibility that N, intending to contribute a certain feature to the outcome, might mistakenly expect the other participants to make congruent contributions; as things turn out, N's contribution will not fit in, or add to the beauty and grace of the outcome. In accordance with earlier remarks, I add that the action and the effect must fall within a recognized role associated with the activity in question.

Clearly, N may get precious little chance to participate from such minimum provisions. The amount of participation allowed him, under a system of single-ballot simple majority voting, might be reckoned as the reciprocal $(1/v)$ of the number of voters.[16] Obviously this measure of participation will have a vanishingly small value if the number of voters is very large—on the order, say, of the number of voters in Canada, over 10 million, to say nothing of the number of voters in the United States. Even then, he may vote on the losing side on any given issue and hence not see his desires or talents reflected in the outcome even to the extent of a share of one ten-millionth, or partake of the benefits in any degree at all. Evidently the most that he can expect is that, win or lose on subsequent issues, some of the benefits will be generalized enough for him to partake of them; or that the winning and losing sides will be reassorted sufficiently from time to time for him to be occasionally on the winning side. But even then his impact will be negligible, both in appearance and in reality.

The difficulty is just as formidable, apart from voting, in the general case. According to Simmel, modern organizations are incomparably more efficient than those which they have superseded, and have become so by "the uniform and purposive regulation of every smallest part"—the individual member—"by one single idea and reciprocal determination between each element and every other";[17] but they have also become "too extensive and complex" to allow any of their members more than "mechanical significance," poignantly incomplete in personal meaning.[18] Not only does the individual member count for very little; very little of the individual member, in purpose and potentiality, is asked for, in subordinating him to the single idea of serving the purposes of the organization.

It does not follow that increased provisions for participation ought to be granted him. Perhaps some members could participate more only if others participated less. Perhaps (though this argument generally deserves a skeptical inquiry) increased participation would jeopardize the particular benefits now being produced. It is no wonder, however, that demands for increased provisions for participation are very common, indeed so common that demands formulated otherwise, simply as demands to participate, can often be regarded as demands for increased provisions for participation. Workers may feel that if collective bargaining does not extend to questions about the location of the company's factories they have no participation at all; it does not matter (at least for the moment) that they may have a recognized role in reaching other sorts of decisions by the company, or that they can petition or demonstrate against moving the factory, with some account being taken of their protests. Students were sometimes listened to before they were given seats in university senates, and listened to more systematically afterwards, when they made use of their seats. Some of them have felt, however, that the representation is only token and the participation is less than genuine; so the inclination to demand to participate has recurred.

There are a number of ways of increasing the provisions for N's participation. The two basic ways are increasing N's power over the outcome of a given activity A and increasing the number of activities in which he has a given amount of power to exercise. But the provisions may also be increased by expanding or otherwise changing the assortment in the outcome-set of an activity—the agenda P_1 or P_2 or P_3 ... or P_n; and in a way not simply reducible to increasing the number of activities, by increasing the number of groups to which N belongs. Furthermore, these increases in provisions, like the minimum provisions that may have existed before, can be safeguarded and perpetuated through successive repetitions of the activities in question by formal stipulation of one sort or another, and gaining these safeguards may be counted as a way of increasing participation. It is certainly a frequent and important object of demands to participate.

All these ways of increasing provisions may be looked upon as means of increasing N's chances of obtaining outcomes that answer to his needs or desires; and it is perhaps idle to contemplate measuring increases in any of the provisions independently of their connections with such chances. If the outcome is to be determined by a vote, then N's power to determine it increases in a certain sense as the proportion of votes required to carry any one proposal P_1 varies over the range between simple majority to unanimity, for thus N comes ever closer to having the power of veto. Unfortunately, he also may run a greater risk of not obtaining the one outcome that he most wants or needs, and perhaps a substantial risk not only of diminishing the benefits to be expected from the activity but also of there being no outcome at all. The group may even dissolve for failure to decide on one, which may be worse than having the worst of the originally envisaged outcomes.[19]

The connection with wants or needs is equally impossible to ignore if we consider increasing the number of activities in which N has a certain power. If we count repetitions (tokens) of a certain type of activity separately, there is the difficulty that some of those repetitions—perhaps just one—may be crucial in a person's life and the others too early or too late to make much difference to him. The value of the activities has to be balanced against their number even in this case; obviously it must be so balanced when increases of activities of different types are brought into question. Likewise, additions to the outcome-set which a given group in a given activity may act upon will not please N and his friends very much if they are all trivial additions. A neighborhood school committee might not consider that the provisions for its participation had increased very much if enlarged in number and variety of outcomes though the agenda might have become, it still did not embrace the possibility of dismissing or transferring teachers. All these sorts of provisions require, each sort within itself as well as all sorts together, at least in the end a comparison and evaluation of combinations: a greater increase in participation and in the provisions for it may be brought about by increasing provisions in fewer ways but more important ones.

Increasing the number of groups to which N belongs is no exception to this requirement of economic evaluation, but I would like to single out this sort of provision for a moment's attention in another regard. It does not reduce simply to increasing the number of activities in which N takes part: it has a claim to separate consideration, because holding an activity A and its outcome-set constant, the number of subgroups involved may be greater or smaller, as may the number of such subgroups to which N belongs. In other words, under this provision a given activity may be reorganized to allow N multiple opportunities (or duties) of participation, working through as many subgroups. The procedure may be looked upon as a specially intensive version of a technique for increasing participation by "decentralizing" authority and reducing organizational dependence on hierarchy. The technique is the one used to increase workers' participation in an industrial process by devolving responsibilities for subprocesses upon different "teams" or "gangs." [20] In this intensive version, the same worker would belong to more than one such team, and thus might simultaneously have a role to play at the design stage, during assembly, and (say) in testing. Some of the industrial arrangements in Yugoslavia may approximate multiple participation of this kind, and may accord to some degree with Marxist expectations that such participation would help remedy alienation by inducing in workers more adequate conceptions of the overall activity and a well-founded sense of purpose in contributing to it.

V

Does it appear by this time that demands to participate raise too many diverse considerations to be manageable? It may seem also that most, maybe all of the considerations can be raised under other, more familiar heads. Is participation a redundant criterion for judging institutions, groups, activities, as well as a polymorphously vague one?

The repertory of democratic criteria is already redundant: what people ask for under the heading of equality, for example, can in most cases be asked for under the heading of welfare; and the heading of rights, extended to include rights proposed as well as rights established, will cover any discrepancy. The considerations that we have just canvassed regarding participation give some foundation for thinking that invoking it simply increases the redundancy of the repertory, for they seem to be reminiscent of one or another head long familiar elsewhere in the repertory. Direct consideration of other heads confirms this impression. Denials of participation offend against freedom or equality or justice or fraternity; moreover, such denials often violate rights, acknowledged or commonly advocated. The demand for majority rule implies a demand to participate at least in respect to information and effective voting, and thus far makes it unnecessary to demand participation separately. The demand for a decent standard of living (under the heading of human welfare) is much the same thing as the demand to partake of the benefits of a joint activity—here, perhaps, the over-all joint activity of carrying on a society with all its concurrent productive processes. Even the objections to lack of participation by others appear to be covered under the heads of equality and fraternity and justice. When they are directed against aloofness, for example, may they not be said to amount to holding that a person remaining aloof is in an *unbrotherly* way refusing *unjustly* to do his *equal* reciprocating share of contributing to the success of common tasks?

Even if participation were, as this evidence may suggest, a logically redundant criterion in every respect, there might still be some psychological point to the fashion of invoking it. People may feel that other terms are worn out, whether or not the criteria which the terms stand for have been satisfied, or that the criteria have been satisfied according to the historic programs for satisfying them, but in ways that turn out to be in many respects mere formalities. If these feelings are to any extent well founded, a shift to stress on "participation" can be justified as a means of rekindling hope and action.

However, there is far from being sufficient warrant for saying that participation is a redundant criterion. At least four considerations tell against there being such a warrant. The first is little more than a cautionary suggestion, and the other three, though somewhat more substantial, are inconclusive. But inconclusiveness on this subject is unavoidable, in the absence of an exhaustive inventory of criteria in the democratic repertory with a complete synchronic account of the distinctive semantic conditions for the use of each[21]—something which I am in no position to supply. I am not even sure that the project of supplying it is feasible, in the sense of producing results precise enough to establish a conclusive answer to the question of redundancy, though one might

sensibly hope that work on the project would get farther than my
present suggestions toward indicating that "participation" would
figure nonredundantly in a plausible idealized model of the repertory.

I suggest, by way of caution, that stress on participation may
change the distribution of emphasis placed on various other criteria for democracy, in a way not readily expressed, if it can be
expressed at all, merely by invoking those other criteria in combination. The very obscurity of this notion of a distribution of
emphasis may obtain some weight for it at this juncture. If we concede that there is likely to be some truth to the suggestion that
stress on participation changes the distribution of emphasis, and
just what this change might amount to is obscure, we should at
least refrain from hurrying to the conclusion that participation is
a redundant criterion. If stress on it increases the weight given to
fraternity, for example, relative to the weight given to constitutionally entrenched rights to property or to a livelihood, then it
would hardly be a redundant criterion in every important sense,
even if everything asked for under it could be asked for under
some other head or heads already present in the repertory.

Of the three more substantial considerations telling against the
suspicion of redundancy, one merges with another. The demand
to participate often comes from outside group G; indeed, if there
are people already participating in the way demanded, and G is
defined so as to take in only these people, the demand can always be understood as coming from outside. The familiar criteria
other than participation take no special account of this division
between insiders and outsiders: both freedom and fraternity, for
example, are looked upon as indefinitely extensible, not stopping
until all mankind has been embraced; or (as is all too often the
case in practice) they are treated as matters of concern only when
they affect members of the same caste or race or nation.

An analogue or variant of the division also occurs within a
given group G. Everyone may acknowledge that the people demanding to participate are members of G; their demand to participate as much as members placed hierarchically above them
might be pursued under the heading of equality. Yet equality may
be sought and won without seeking or winning a recognized role
in any joint human activity; separate facilities need not logically
be unequal facilities, though they might still be obnoxious on other

grounds. Moreover, equality may be more than what is wanted. The demand to participate is often directed against hierarchical organization without intending to do away with hierarchy entirely; what is wanted is a more responsive hierarchy, which can often be realized by diluting the existing hierarchy with other techniques of social control.[22]

Many people would ascribe the current stress on participation to alienation from organizations run by hierarchies remote and unresponsive by their very complexity.[23] The demand to participate seems in fact to be paired a good deal of the time with feelings of alienation, and this relation to alienation constitutes the third reason for thinking that participation is not a redundant criterion. For over part at least of its range—where it concerns alienation from work, for example—alienation raises issues that the traditional criteria in the democratic repertory did not anticipate; and the pairing with participation occurs in such connections, too, as its invocation by Marx as a remedy for alienation illustrates.

Moreover, participation pairs with alienation both in sometimes being outcome-oriented and in sometimes not being. As we shall see in a moment, demands to participate are sometimes wholly or in part demands to be accepted in roles without reference to outcomes. Other criteria seem to operate mainly or exclusively on one side of the orientation distinction or the other; welfare, on the outcome-oriented side; fraternity, on the other. Those criteria that do operate on both sides are clearly distinct from participation: equality, in ways already mentioned; freedom, because freedom might logically be increased in most cases by by-passing any joint activity, whereas there is no participation without a joint activity to participate in. (The freedom to participate cannot be increased by by-passing, but then it cannot be defined without the help of the concept of participation.)

The vagueness of the concept has to be conceded, and put up with, along with some obscurity about its nonredundancy. It is not only vague, it is polymorphously vague, afflicted with both the sorts of vagueness most often noticed, multiple-criteria vagueness and degree vagueness.[24] The forms of participation vary so enormously that the features which some forms have in common with each other are less important in constituting them than the features which they share with forms of nonparticipation: com-

pare playing offensive fullback for the Chicago Bears with observing two minutes of silence on Remembrance Day. Furthermore,
the various forms severally admit "intensification and remission
of degrees," both at the means stage (as with the approximation
to veto power when the voting rule is varied from requiring a
simple majority to requiring unanimous consent) and, in the end,
in effect on the outcome.

This vagueness, however, no more prevents us from using the
concept of participation effectively, especially in the initiation of
discussions, than it prevents us from using effectively the concept, say, of traveling, which is polymorphously vague too, as are
many other useful concepts. Moreover, vagueness is indispensable
to demands to participate, using that term, as they are commonly
intended; to be properly expressed, the demands require a vague
term. People want more say, or more to do; but they often do
not know specifically just what say, or what to do, or when, or
in what capacity. The demand to participate is thus a demand
that groups and activities be reorganized to give people recognized roles which they do not now have and which they may
not be able, at this point in time, to specify. The absence of this
specification, when it is absent, does not make the demand any
less serious.

The absence—at times inevitable absence—of specification also
vindicates in part the inclination, which I struggled with at the
beginning of this paper, to find a paradox in the comparison between demands to participate and the description of the roles that
might be held to satisfy the demands or to anticipate them. When
an appropriate role in a joint human activity A has been established and recognized, the need to speak of participation tends to
disappear, along with the demand for it, for it has a special name.
(I say only "tends" because sometimes, as for example in connection with conversations, especially diplomatic conversations,
the word "participate" does survive as the name of the role.)
Moreover, the more clearly the role that is wanted is known and
defined in advance, the greater (I conjecture) is the tendency to
substitute for "participate" a special name for the role. People
demand the right to vote, rather than the right to participate in
politics, if voting is exactly the role they want to play; or they
demand to serve on juries. If they use the word "participate" instead, or as well, is that not normally a sign that they have not

made up their minds about voting or serving on juries being the whole of what they want? Demanding "to participate in the judicial process" then expresses a demand both to serve on juries and possibly to play some unspecified role or roles beyond.

VI

The role demanded is liable to be unspecified at least in part even when the demand to participate has in view a firmly institutionalized activity of a familiar group. So cases of this kind too partly bear out the abortive paradox about demands to participate being satisfied under some other name or names. But such cases not only have this feature: they have an arguable claim to being logically paramount. Can there be a fully intelligible demand to participate without there being at least a specific group G in view, and also a specific joint activity A carried on by that group? Without such specific targets, can the demand be logically complete? I gave earlier, as a sufficient condition for full intelligibility in a demand to participate, the identification simultaneously of N, the person making the demand; G, the group in view; and A, the joint activity in question.[25] Might this condition also be reckoned a necessary one, most surely met when the identifications are made by specifications expressed in expressing the demand itself?

It would seem, moving in the ambit of these suggestions, that demands to participate are in at least one important respect inherently conservative demands. In presupposing groups and activities that already exist, they appear to accept existing institutions and to call for no more than roles in these institutions, to be given people at present excluded from such roles.

It is important to realize that demands to participate may be conservative in this respect. One might wonder whether the current vogue does not reflect mainly a widespread and somewhat defeatist assumption that the large bureaucratic organizations in which we are all involved cannot be done away with and that the most that can be done with them is to try to make them more congenial in detail by diluting their hierarchical features. The tendency to consider a demand to participate as logically complete only if it has in view a specific group and a specific activity may thus work hand in hand with a pervasive compound fact about political attitudes: existing institutions are easiest to specify and considered very difficult to abolish.

Nevertheless, the fact does not stand alone, and the tendency, even if one gives way to it, does not conclusively favor existing groups. The groups specified, and the activities, need not be existing ones, or familiar ones, or even ones easy to comprehend on first, advance description; they may in principle involve drastic and far-reaching reorganizations of present institutions, or wholesale substitutions for these. Even if the inevitability of bureaucratic organizations is accepted, the present bureaucracies may not be. Those demanding to participate may insist that the sorts of recognized roles which they want, with what would in their eyes be significantly increased participation, can only be obtained from new organizations. Furthermore, organizations less bureaucratic may be envisaged, with provisions for decentralization and multiple participation.[26]

At the limit, the form of organization specified in specifying the group and the activity and the expected character of the participants may be radically different from what now obtain. I am not thinking only of the new men and women who are to live under Communism-the-final-stage. I am thinking, for example, that the demand for full participation by students in university government is not necessarily defeated by demonstrating (if indeed it can be demonstrated) that the present students would not be competent to participate fully in running universities of the present kind. Those who make the demand may believe, or come to believe, that, to obtain participation, universities should be turned into institutions devoted chiefly to long-term adult education and university students into adults returning from time to time to the universities with the competence gained in a variety of careers.

Demands to participate thus vary from being quite conservative in their attachment to existing institutions—more conservative than lots of political demands coming forward under other heads —to being maximally radical.

The vagueness of the concept does, however, foster a tendency for the demands, once started, even under conservative assumptions, to increase continually and to become more radical in becoming larger. Any form or degree of participation short of predominance is subject to being repudiated as merely "token" participation—"genuine" participation, it continually appears, would carry with it much more power and scope.

Such moves are easily, but wrongly, dismissed a priori as instances of cynical tactics. People demanding to participate have no monopoly on cynical tactics in this connection. Such moves are to be expected, moreover, even when there is perfect good will on both sides. The concept of participation is more useful for initiating discussions than it is for bringing them to an end. There are no standard indications, helpful for either side, of satisfactory stopping places short of predominance. These are left by the concept to be worked out on an *ad hoc* basis suitable to each particular case. But this arrangement is a precarious one; the conceptual vagueness on which it depends is bound to cause uneasiness in those who use the concept. When the uneasiness rises to the point of inviting closure, the people who demand to participate are likely to effect closure by applying the most familiar conception of legitimate power ready to hand, which will almost always be majority rule; and no more imaginative about appropriate arrangements than the advocates of participation, the people on the other side are not likely to have an alternative answer, or at any rate any answer that is not subject in their own minds to undermining by their own sentiments in favor of majority rule. Yet in many cases affording participation without jeopardizing outcomes must, I suspect, require very subtle and imaginative efforts of sociological engineering in defining and redefining roles and activities; though this suspicion, like all the other considerations affecting demands to participate, is liable to be abused by people who do not want to meet the demands.

VII

Up to this point in my discussion of demands to participate I have continually kept in view the relation of such demands to the *outcomes* of joint human activities. I have tried to avoid giving undue prominence to the outcomes of decision-making activities; I have meant to make no more of voting, for instance, than it deserves as a special case of a joint activity that often has important outcomes and as the source of helpful analogies respecting certain dimensions of participation. But I have given preeminent attention to outcomes of one sort or another and I have reckoned the dimensions of participation in terms of those outcomes. I have done no more than hint from time to time that there is another perspective on participation, in which the relation to outcomes is not of prime importance, and which ought not to be entirely subordinated to the perspective in which it is.

In this other perspective, people can be seen to demand to participate not because, or not just because they want to affect outcomes; but because they want to be treated as persons by people who have been ignoring them and perhaps in the course of ignoring them treating them as objects to be exploited without regard to their claims as persons. Among those claims are claims bearing not upon outcomes but upon the relations of mutual recognition and reciprocity that constitute (or should constitute) the activity itself. People demand to participate sometimes mainly, sometimes simply, because they want to be joked with, gossiped with, applauded, teased, argued with, striven with, reassured—in short, to count in the others' eyes as friends or possible friends, as teammates, or as worthy rivals—perhaps as all three at once.

The attention that I have given to participation in relation to outcomes is perhaps not objectionable if it disavows any pretense to exclusive rights over the subject. For outcomes still matter, even if they are not the only things that matter. The demands to participate in our time most familiar, urgent, sustained, and widespread are demands related to outcomes. Workers demand to participate in management in order to affect outcomes with respect to their conditions of work and training, and outcomes having to do with the disposition of profits, investment, and the location of industry.[27] French-Canadians in Quebec demand increased participation in making economic policy; they want to be "maîtres chez nous" so that they can make sure that the outcome of economic policy will strengthen and preserve their cultural community. Blacks, whether they are still willing to participate alongside whites or not, want to affect outcomes regarding schools, jobs, and places to live. Women will count themselves liberated only when they participate fully enough in activities now carried on chiefly by men to make sure of outcomes more favorable to themselves, for example, in salaries and offers of part-time work. Less organized than any of these movements, but no less articulate, are renewed demands for bringing technological change under control, so that (for example) the outcomes are less unfavorable to human ecology; broader participation, if not universal participation, and broader agendas for economic policy are demanded as techniques for achieving such outcomes.

The demands to participate just surveyed are, then, all outcome-oriented (and notably they are all demands aimed at affecting sorts of outcomes reached through decision-making processes). The prominence that I have given to the relation to outcomes is so far justified, by the prominence given to it by people actually making specific demands to participate. Nevertheless, they as well as I may be thinking of participation too much in terms imposed upon us by the commercial and technological biases of our present culture. The language of outcomes runs all too close to the language of outputs; indeed, after some decades of experience, practical and metaphorical, with computers, the word "output" is now as much at home in the discussion of decision-making processes as it is in the discussion of material production.

We need to recall that not all joint human activities are activities designed to have outputs or outcomes beyond themselves; not all are decision-making activities; not all are productive, or meant to be productive. Those people running together in the park may be using benefits to their health merely as a pretext: what they are really there for are simply the current enjoyments of exercise, fresh air, and comradeship. Or consider parties and conversations among friends: what outcome need a party or a conversation have? The jointness of such activities is not the jointness of collaboration in producing anything beyond themselves; it consists rather in people accepting and welcoming each other's presence and in their rejoicing at each other's present happiness.

A life-ideal proposed by Dr. Johnson comes close to being an adequate illustration: "If . . . I had no duties, and no reference to futurity, I would spend my life in driving briskly in a post-chaise with a pretty woman; but she should be one who could understand me, and would add something to the conversation."[28] A "be-in" illustrates the point no more vividly perhaps, but at least on a larger scale: "There are . . . rituals," Theodore Roszak says, "in which men participate democratically for the purpose of freeing the imagination and exploring self-expression. . . ." Such are the "rites" that

> our hippies improvise for themselves out of potted anthropology and sheer inspiration. . . . The tribalized young gather in

gay costume on a high hill in the public park to salute the mid-summer sun in its rising and setting. They dance, they sing, they make love as each feels moved, without order or plan. . . . All have equal access to the event; no one is misled or manipulated. Neither kingdom, nor power, nor glory is desperately at stake. Maybe, in the course of things, some even discover in the commonplace sun and the ordinary advent of the summer the inexpressible grandeur that is really there and which makes those who find it more authentically human.[29]

I am not sure I understand Roszak's further suggestion that this sort of activity might be "the ultimate expression and safeguard of a participative democracy, without which the popular control of institutions might always be corrupted by partisan interest or deference to expertise";[30] but I agree that he has illustrated participation in a way that poses a moving challenge to the outcome or output orientation of most current demands to participate, and to the would-be progressive spirit in which they are put forward. The hippies' demand to participate goes deeper than a demand to have a part in controlling the bustle of production and technological change; it is a demand for a different sort of activity and it implies a protest against the bustle itself.

Participation could not go further in not being outcome-oriented, since the joint human activity could not go further. Participation that is not outcome-oriented can also be present, however, in activities that are; and the demand to participate may be concurrently outcome-oriented and something else besides. Suppose in a certain city a seat on the library board goes for the first time to a black man; he has proposals to make and they are all accepted unanimously, so that his desires with respect to outcomes are wholly fulfilled. But the other members of the board never really listen to him; they never seek his advice; they give him no sign that they value his presence and cooperation. Would he not rightly think that the participation afforded him fell far short of what he might reasonably demand? The very speed with which his proposals were accepted would add to the insult and injury done him. Evidently there was an actual case at the business meeting of the Eastern Division of the American Philosophical Association in 1970. I am told that a women's group introduced some resolutions about policies regarding women, which were immediately passed, and passed unanimously. The women concerned were furious; they had wanted to hold a discussion of the resolutions, and to be listened to.[31]

NOTES AND REFERENCES

Primitive ideas for this paper were tried out on a visit to Joanne Arnaud's class in political theory during the spring quarter of 1971 at the University of Minnesota; and early versions were read to the members of Pi Sigma Alpha, the honorary political science fraternity at Macalester College, after their annual banquet in May 1971, and to the Halifax Philosophy Circle in October. I am grateful both to those who listened patiently on these occasions and to those (patient listeners or not) who talked back, especially to William R. Mathie of the Dalhousie political science department, who acted as commentator at the Circle meeting and made a number of penetrating points, which I have tried to accommodate in the present version. I have also made visible use of points and examples offered by Bernard Davis, Rolf Gruner, and Alexander Rosenberg, in their contributions to the same meeting. Finally, I have had, and in large part have exploited the advantage of having, helpful detailed comments by J. Roland Pennock. During the meetings on participation in New York, the point was raised that the vogue for "participation" as a vehicle for popular slogans and current demands may already have passed, faster than the program committee allowed for. That may be. The issues surrounding the concept remain important ones, politically as well as philosophically, and so little explored by political philosophers that the subject still requires a preliminary survey, late though the survey may be, perhaps too late for fashion.

1. For evidence that my illustration keeps reasonably close to the historical facts that inspired it, see Alison Burford, "The Builders of the Parthenon," in G. T. W. Hooker, ed., *Parthenos and Parthenon* (Supplement to Vol. X, 1963, *Greece and Rome*) (Oxford: The Clarendon Press, 1963), pp. 23-34; also, Robert Scranton, "Greek Building," in Carl Roebuck, ed., *The Muses at Work* (Cambridge, Mass.: MIT Press, 1969), pp. 2-34, especially pp. 3-5. I am indebted to Alice Braybrooke for these references.
2. Joanne Arnaud called my attention to "partake."
3. I shall not make any serious attempt to relate "participation" in the senses I am treating to "participation" as a technical philosophical term used in translating Plato. There is a passage in Simmel that indicates, however, that such a relation might be found, and not appear too contrived. Simmel says, "The larger the number of groups to which an individual belongs, the more improbable is it that other persons will exhibit the same combination of group-affiliations. . . . Concrete objects lose their individual characteristics as we subsume them under a general concept in accordance with one of their attributes. And concrete objects regain their individual characteristics as other concepts are emphasized under which their several attributes may be subsumed. To speak Platonically, each thing has a part in as many ideas as it has manifold

attributes, and it achieves thereby its individual determination. There is an analogous relationship between the individual and the groups with which he is affiliated. . . . As the person becomes affiliated with a social group, he surrenders himself to it. . . . But he also regains his individuality, because his pattern of participation is unique." Georg Simmel, "The Web of Group-Affiliations," trans. Reinhard Bendix, in Simmel, *Conflict* (and) *The Web of Group-Affiliations* (Glencoe, Ill.: The Free Press, 1955), pp. 140-141. If for "groups" we substitute "characteristic activities of the groups," the passage applies directly to "participation" in the senses I am treating.

4. *Cf.* the discussion by Carole Pateman, in her *Participation and Democratic Theory* (Cambridge: Cambridge University Press, 1970), chap. ii, of Rousseau, John Stuart Mill, and G. D. H. Cole.

5. These points about discovering interests were inspired by hearing Professor Bachrach's paper (in this volume, pp. 39-55); there advances in defining and articulating interests not previously known to the participants are particularly stressed. I shall leave the points for Bachrach to elaborate, but since they have now helped determine my conception of the educative aspects of participation, I have to mention them here in the course of explaining how the educative aspects can be brought to view within my general scheme for explicating demands to participate. The scheme was originally set up without asking whether would-be participants might still have to learn what their own interests are.

6. I owe this objection to William R. Mathie, whose illustration was exclusion on racial grounds from college fraternities. It has been suggested to me that my own example of a beauty pageant, which follows, is rather "dated": I am inclined to admit that it is, in most parts of the U-.ited States and Canada, say, even outside self-consciously liberal circles. It may not be dated everywhere: Are there not still news stories about black coeds becoming homecoming queens where only white girls were chosen before? And in South Africa the example, far from being dated, would surely appear bizarrely premature. At any rate, I have not been able to think of a better example: Mathie's example involves joining a group, rather than (directly) a joint activity; an orgy, which would be a more topical example, and certainly qualifies as a joint activity, has the drawback that I myself am not sure an orgy is to be disapproved (given various conditions), whereas I do consider beauty pageants degrading. So the present example accords with my own feelings, as well as being correct in structure.

7. Cf. Bernard R. Berelson, Paul F. Lazarsfeld, and William N. McPhee, *Voting* (Chicago: The University of Chicago Press, 1954), especially as cited (along with Schumpeter and Dahl) by Carole Pateman, *Participation,* p. 5ff.

8. *Apology* 31-33; *Republic* 496 and 520b.

9. *Politics* 1325b.

10. Anthony Downs, *An Economic Theory of Democracy* (New York: Harper, 1957).

11. Mancur Olson, Jr., *The Logic of Collective Action* (Cambridge, Mass.: Harvard University Press, 1965).

12. Downs, *Economic Theory,* p. 267ff.

13. Thucydides, II, 40 (trans. R. W. Livingstone [London: Oxford University Press, 1943]). Commenting on the phrase, οὐκ ἀπράγμονα ἀλλ' ἀχρεῖον, which Livingstone translates "not as 'quiet' but as useless," A. W. Gomme (*A Historical Commentary on Thucydides* [Oxford: The Clar-

endon Press, 1956], pp. 121-122), says that ἀπράγμων was a compli-
mentary term in Athens as elsewhere; in that case "detached" might be
a better translation than "quiet." See also the interesting rendition of
the passage offered in the comments on it by Thomas Arnold, in his
edition of Thucydides (Oxford: Parker, 8th ed., 1882), who considers
the passage to express an emphatic opposition to dividing civil society
into "two distinct castes; the one wholly devoted to the care of the
state (like the φύλακες of Plato's Utopia) and maintained by the labour
of a vassal people, like the Spartans with their Helots; the other degraded to the exclusive pursuit of trade or labour, and held unfit to concern
themselves with any higher objects." "With us," Pericles, in Arnold's
rendition, continues, "the statesman does not lay aside his humbler
duties and employments; nor is the mechanic thought incapable of form-
ing a judgment on public affairs. We consider no man to be so incapable;
nay, we do not allow that or any other plea to be urged as an excuse for
a member of civil society taking no part in that society's concerns" (pp.
236-237).

14. I give a slight technical twist to the word "outcome" by supposing that
these outcomes are not necessarily mutually exclusive.

15. Or, some people who deserve to be better off will be better off and no
one who does not deserve to be worse off will be worse off. N's demand
may be motivated by disinterested moral considerations, though it will
not necessarily be accepted as nonintrusive just because it is. A religious
fanatic who means only to save the souls of the present members of the
group by stopping them from drinking, dancing, and making love will
nonetheless be treated, if he demands to participate, as making an intrusive demand. There is much to say, which I shall not try to say here,
about how groups are to distinguish between intrusive enthusiasts, whose
demands may be rejected, and genuine reforming prophets, who ought
to be given at least a cautious welcome. My phrases, e.g., "better off"
and "deserve to be better off," are perhaps general enough, however,
especially if we assume that G and A are not illicit, to accommodate
under the second exception all the disinterested demands to participate
that are likely to be accepted by reasonable people as nonintrusive.

16. L. S. Shapley and Martin Shubik, "A Method for Evaluating the Distribution of Power in a Committee System," *American Political Science
Review,* 48 (1954), 787-792; reprinted in Martin Shubik, ed., *Game
Theory and Related Approaches to Social Behavior* (New York: Wiley,
1964), pp. 141-150.

17. Simmel, *Web,* p. 193.

18. *Ibid.,* p. 195.

19. *Cf.* James M. Buchanan and Gordon Tullock, *The Calculus of Consent*
(Ann Arbor: University of Michigan Press, 1962), on the "decision-mak-
ing-costs function," which rises dramatically as the requirement of
unanimity is approached, for in that region the costs of bargaining for
the consent of any one voter are likely to be very high. "If we include
(as we should) the opportunity costs of bargains that are never made, it
seems likely that the bargaining costs might approach infinity in groups
of substantial size" (p. 69).

20. See Pateman, *Participation,* pp. 61-62. "Gang" is the British term.

21. *Cf.* Paul Ziff, *Semantic Analysis* (Ithaca, N.Y.: Cornell University Press,
1960), sections 165, 193, 195, 198.

22. *Cf.* Robert A. Dahl and Charles E. Lindblom, *Politics, Economics,* and
Welfare (New York: Harper, 1953), which gives the price system,

88   DAVID BRAYBROOKE

polyarchy, and bargaining as three alternative sociopolitical processes
available for combining with hierarchy in various mixed techniques for
calculation and control.

23. A complaint well expressed, probably in a representative way, by John
Platt, in *Perception and Change* (Ann Arbor: University of Michigan
Press, 1970), pp. 116-117: "The new idea of participatory democracy
does not simply concern election of officials; it concerns the administrative decisions of those public officials between elections, to make sure
they are not simply pushing people about for their own class purposes
or administrative convenience. It is no longer enough for us to go to the
polls and cast our ballots. We also want to be consulted. We do not
want to be treated any longer as objects. . . . We want to be treated as
co-subjects . . . not manipulated by an elite, but instead shared with as a
group, a group which is collectively determining its own decision."

24. *Cf.* William P. Alston, "Vagueness," in *The Encyclopedia of Philosophy,*
ed. Paul Edwards (New York: Macmillan & The Free Press, 1967), vol.
VIII, pp. 218-221. Alston's term for "multiple-criteria vagueness" is
"combinatory vagueness."

25. See above, p. 66.

26. Such provisions might include increased use of polyarchy or of bargaining or of the price system. *Cf.* Dahl and Lindblom, *Politics.*

27. *Cf.* André Gorz, *A Strategy for Labor,* trans. Martin A. Nicolaus and
Victoria Ortiz (Boston: Beacon Press, 1967), pp. 43-44; also pp. 58-59.

28. James Boswell, *The Life of Samuel Johnson,* ed. Rodney Shewan (London: The Folio Society, 1968), vol. II, p. 160 (the anecdote dates from
1777 and Johnson's 68th year).

29. Theodore Roszak, *The Making of a Counter Culture* (New York: Anchor Books, 1969), pp. 148-149.

30. *Ibid.,* p. 150.

31. I have to thank William R. Mathie for his insistence on the point that
even when outcomes are important, outcomes do not matter alone; and
Alexander Rosenberg, for recalling the incident at the Eastern Division.

4

COMMENTS ON DAVID BRAYBROOKE'S "THE MEANING OF PARTICIPATION AND OF DEMANDS FOR IT"

GEORGE KATEB

I do not think that we would have held a philosophical conference on participation were it not for the fact that almost ten years ago the SDS began to speak about "participatory democracy." They made participation into an *issue*. Unless we in our discussion, and others in discussions like it, remember the genesis in recent events of concern for participation, conceptual analysis of it will come out sounding artificial. It will sound as if it were analysis of some traditional thorny cluster of problems; of some nice, hard subject with a settled demarcation. I am not certain participation is, or is yet, a subject. There may be less intellectual substance than meets the eye: a *fashion* pretending to intellectual substance. Reality may take its revenge on such moral forwardness. Or, to the contrary, we may be seeing the beginning of a tendency that will grow larger and more urgent, and therefore call for a lot of good thought: conceptual as well as historical analysis.

Of course there is no absolute novelty: the thought of Aristotle, Machiavelli, Rousseau, Sorel, and Dewey—especially Rousseau and Dewey—covers some of the ground that is now again being looked at, surveyed, occasionally explored. Then too, as Hannah Arendt says,

> ... no tradition, either revolutionary or pre-revolutionary, can be called to account for the regular emergence and re-emergence of the council system ever since the French Revolution. . . . It was nothing more or less than this hope for a transformation of the state, for a new form of government that would permit every member of the modern egalitarian society to become a "participator" in public affairs, that was buried in the disasters of twentieth-century revolutions.[1]

But there has been an altered emphasis in idealist expression and writing. Professor Braybrooke alludes to that point. The call for participation has in it as much intellectual novelty as one can expect from a doctrine meant to inspire action. Yet this novelty seems also to revive memories, to speak to something old but ignored in American life. The call has had an effect: in the mid-to-late sixties the moral complexion of American life changed, and one of the most noticeable changes was the widespread demand for participation, or for more participation. What that all means, how deep the change went, what its present status is, what really was achieved, what the shape of the demand in the near future will be—whether it has been *only* a fashion, though a fascinating one—I cannot say. In any case, if we are going to talk about participation, let us say that a recent political tendency has *pushed* the matter before us, and then pay some heed to the ill-defined, new, and tentative qualities of that tendency. I say this not to disparage our effort, but to show its essential difference from other efforts undertaken by this Society in the past. A conference on participation cannot yet be like a conference on liberty, equality, authority, or sovereignty. It cannot presuppose the same richness of background, the same need for strict sorting out and making of distinctions, and the same appetite for coaxing out a new perception or connection from a familiar but inexhaustible literature.

I shall approach Braybrooke's paper indirectly, by indicating a few of the elements that figure when people talk and write about participation. One had only to listen half-attentively to college students to have picked up most of the content of the idea of participation. What they said, what some of them may still be saying, is first said in the "Port Huron Statement," apparently prepared mostly by Tom Hayden for the SDS in 1962. There is a lucid and complex codification in Staughton Lynd's essay, "The New Radicals and 'Participatory Democracy,'" which an unsympathetic but generous Irving Howe published in *Dissent* in 1965. Some of the manifestos and occasional statements of student movements in America, Germany, and France, particularly the words that burst on Paris and the world in May and June 1968, give hints and clues of further development from Hayden and Lynd. The student of participation must start, then, with the so-called Movement; else he will, when he talks about participation, not be talking about participation.

I think a serviceable summary of this new idealism is as follows: the aim is to rehabilitate the idea of citizenship and to extend the practice of citizenship into as many areas of life as possible; from the original locus of citizenship, i.e., public affairs, to private institutions and associations and activities of almost every sort. What is in play is a positive concept of politics, and a corresponding desire to make as many kinds of human relations as possible into political relations. Put negatively, there is a disdain for passivity. There is a repugnance toward being administered, commanded, or manipulated; and not only that, but a repugnance toward being governed; and beyond that, a repugnance toward being represented. The perversions of "usual politics" are not the only object of attack: usual politics itself stands under indictment. The spokesmen for participation want, insist on, politics; want it for themselves and for others; seek to extend it as far as it can be extended, until tiredness sets in. But it is politics without hierarchy, procedures, delimited purposes, legalism, practiced compromise, and permanent roles, as well as politics without frozen postures, fakery, cheating, arrogance, self-imposition, and rivalry. It is politics as conversation, not speeches; transaction, not battle. Politics at its best defines experience at its best, whether the form of experience be political (strictly speaking) or not.

Just two brief illustrations get at what I have been trying to suggest. In the Port Huron Statement, we read: "channels should be commonly available to relate men to knowledge and to power so that private problems—from bad recreation facilities to personal alienation—are formulated as general issues." [2] In "The Appeal from the Sorbonne: The Open Assembly of June 13-14, 1968," the seventeenth thesis is: "It is necessary that everyone have rights, not 'roles.' Let us be other than characters in a tragi-comedy which is no longer even comical." [3]

We then must ask what passions supply the force behind the demand for participation. Originally, it was not so much the immemorial grievances: abuse of power, corruption, privilege, and so on, though these had a place, especially in the form of feeling for the grievances of *others,* like the blacks. The primary considerations were less tangible, more refined: as the opening words of the Port Huron Statement indicate, the petitioners are middle-class people rather well provided for. Only, there was some awful lack nevertheless, some alienation or malaise not explicable just by reference to the Bomb and the persistence of the cold war. There was a wish to live more fully, shake off apathy, cease leading a purely private life, stop the role playing forced on people by a meritocratic and materialist ethos. There was a desire for movement: the Movement is movement. A desire for movement is a desire for action, for free, spontaneous, "unstructured" action; as well as for symbolic action, for the self-expressive gesture, the extravagant deed; as well as for commotion, the *mélée,* roughhouse. This desire was satisfied characteristically by participation in confrontations, demonstrations, and ad hoc groups. If politics as the search for power is the politics of the uncertain, the impotent, and the old, then the alternative politics, the parallel politics of the SDS and other student groups in the early days, is the politics of the boyish, the innocent, the unformed, the energetic, and the conscience-ridden, politics with a blush on its face.

After the primal impulse to move, to do, to act in public, there follows the wish for self-mastery in organizational and institutional life, the wish to participate with others in determining the common fate, the wish to be the source of benefits and not merely the passive recipients of them. This wish, the Rousseauist wish, is, I suppose, that aspect of the new idealism which was most publicly salient. It was ideologically the easiest for the outsider to understand, so in the American grain was it, and did it appear to be; yet it was in practice the hardest to accommodate.

Balanced with this wish for self-mastery was the thirst for community: some dialectic for participation was wanted, for gaining and losing yourself time and again, for dancing with but not holding your partner. The aim was to convert organizations and institutions into communities of deliberation and affection, to have the discipline of informal democracy replace the discipline of straight rules. One wanted an audience for what one did; one also wanted to be part of an audience, but the audience was to be made up only of players. And more than one game or play should go on at the same time. Included in the concern for community was the wish to improvise communities, to create them out of an aggregation, to abolish the concept of stranger. These communities were short-lived or even evanescent, as at Columbia or Paris or Woodstock, but not liked the less for that. The congregational principle found there its latest church. The social contract found there its major metaphorical existence (leaving aside the numerous new communes).

In short, citizenship should embrace movement, self-mastery, and community; and the occasions for citizenship can be nearly extensive with life itself. That is the heart of the matter of participation. As the Port Huron Statement says "politics [ought to] be seen positively, as the art of collectively creating an acceptable pattern of social relations. . . . " [4]

Thus, the recent doctrine of participation is an account of the psychological gratifications and moral worth of political action— inside and outside organizational and institutional life—before it is anything else, like, say, a plan for reform or revolution. At the same time its scope is large enough to permit us to say that it intends to be taken as a prescription for an entire way of life, or "life-style," to use the newly coined and rather weightless term. To put it schematically: the human relations that political activists have with each other anticipate the human relations that would characterize the better society which the activists may be working for; [5] the human relations in one successfully politicized institution or organization are a contagious example for all others. One could call these relations "purified politics." This students' doctrine does have some resemblances to that of workers' controls; it also eases the way for notions of community action and community control in the cities. Let us, however, recall what it was in its origins. Whatever it was, it was not (a) a justification for the pursuit of self-interest, by conventional definition; (b) a general theory of membership, its rights and duties, and the qualifications for joining; or (c) a general theory of organization, of the roles and procedures necessary to get a job done or a purpose achieved, and of the methods for insuring that the led keep the leadership decent and rational. As Staughton Lynd put it, "The spirit of a community, as opposed to an organization, is not, We are together to accomplish this or that end, but, We are together to face together whatever life brings." [6]

I propose that the student of participation would then have many questions once the present-day context of participation has been established. Among these questions are:

1. What relation does the new delight in political action have to older or other recent theories? For example, action as the expression of practical wisdom, action as the doing of great deeds and saying of great words, action as equivalent to manhood, action as the expression of a good will, action as self-discovery, action as therapy, action as serious play, action as theater, action as cure for self-contempt—all theories that espouse political action for nonpractical, noninstrumental reasons.

2. Are there no limits to the desirability of extending the idea of citizenship? Does participation choke individuality and kill the taste for solitude? Is impulse sanctified, while morally valuable procedures are dismissed as petty or heartless legalisms? Surely there are *some* human relations which are corrupted by politics, by the best politics, but which are not to be condemned for being unamenable to politicization?

3. How does one reintroduce the question of practicality, instrumentality, especially after the failures of political action? Are success and participatory democracy in a political movement incompatible? Has Michels' Iron Law been discredited? How seriously, given our condition, can we take the view that *all* that matters is the quality of the participation, and not anything outside itself? Is the *sense* of community really enough? Is it enough to appease pangs of conscience, or make a beautiful or shocking gesture, or engage in meaningful personal relations, or have a moment in the limelight, or enjoy the pleasure of self-expression, or have fun while coming alive or shaking things up? Can these things be enough—great as they are—if the structure of privilege and the system of cruelty remain intact?

4. In organizational and institutional life, what is the relation between increased participation and the power of the established leadership or authority? How much real power is usually given? May participation, under many circumstances, provide the best cover for manipulation by authority, in the style recommended by Elton Mayo? Is there such a thing, then, as "repressive participation"? In nominally leaderless groups, does power fall to those who, having greater psychological skill, know how to wield power invisibly and therefore undemocratically? Or can full participation end the need for any authority whatever? Is harmonious anarchism the *telos* of participation?

5. What is the relation between the demand for participation and the institutions of representative government? Peter Bachrach[7] and Robert Dahl[8] have recently struggled with this question. Yet we must ask them, and others more radical,[9] whether more areas of policy can be made subject to participatory democracy, with less reliance on representative government, *even as representative government suffers constant attenuation as a result of presidential and bureaucratic assertion.* If the most important questions, the mortal questions, life and death in the nuclear age, are settled more or less at the unaccountable pleasure of the presidency, how much does it matter that a few other questions get resolved more and more democratically? If big power is arbitrary, is it not trivial and misleading to democratize lesser power? How much plausibility does an idea like the one sketched by Michael Rossman have? He says, "High computer/communication technology makes possible the abolition of representative government and the institution of simple, direct popular-democratic government." [10] Does one participate by sitting at a console?

There are of course many other points (practical and theoretical) to be raised in connection with the subject of participation. Friends and critics of the tendency have raised them. Professor Braybrooke has contributed greatly to the elucidation of some of them. My opinion is, however, that his paper is really two papers, and that only the second one is directly on the subject as I think it ought now to be conceived; though I see that parts of the first also fit. I hope that what I have already said about participation indicates with sufficient emphasis my misgivings about some of Braybrooke's effort. These misgivings end at the moment he asks whether there may be a psychological point in using the word "participation" even if it should turn out—as rightly it does not turn out—that all the new demands for participation add up only to demands for traditional values like liberty, equality, fraternity, and justice. Braybrooke's rejection of the charge of redundancy is excellent, and his four reasons for rejection, added to the psychological consideration, are in my opinion true to the sources of the movement for participation which we have been witnessing. Afterward, his stress on the inescapable but not discreditable vagueness of the demand, on the wish of people to have more say and to have more to do, and his acknowledgment of the fact that the more specific the role a person asks for the less likely he is to use the word "participate"—all this is cogent, and faithful to the events. Then, his development of the idea that the demand is not always related to wanting to protect one's stake or to have a chance to use one's skills, but rather is intimately joined to the large concern to be treated as a person and to have certain experiences not otherwise attainable, is quite skillful.

My only point about his paper is that this part of it deals with the essential matters, but the first part does not. It does not because it provides the outlines for a general combined theory of membership and organization along lines that obscure the politically radical and radically political nature of the demands that have been made for participation. Braybrooke wants "general principles for matching people with appropriate activities." I quarrel with this conception because it places the emphasis on the demand for inclusion, on letting new members in who have been left out arbitrarily and to the disadvantage of their interests. But the movement has often taken inclusion for granted. Indeed, some fled inclusion to found "parallel structures." Its doctrine deals primarily with what to do to transform any organization or institution people already happen to be in. Braybrooke seems to assume that once membership has been enlarged, the demand for participation would be satisfied. The organizations and institutions could go about their business in the old way, though with increased numbers. But when membership has been expanded, and the structure has remained otherwise unaffected, participation languishes. Doing business in the old way is the very enemy. The doctrine of participation is at war with traditional structures and routines, carefully drawn jurisdictional lines, neatly defined roles, and sharp boundaries that are meant to keep the rest of the world out. And where there has been a demand for participation in the sense of inclusion, as in the insistence on community action and community control in the cities, new structures and routines that are more open and popular, more populist, have been called for to replace the existing ones.

The movement for participation thus is the movement for participatory *democracy*. The motto is not "Join everything you can, it hurts to be left out." No, the motto is "Democratize everything you find yourself in, citizenship can exist everywhere." We see new exemplifications in army and prison, as well as in church, school, firm, and so on. The first part of Braybrooke's paper, compelling as it is on its own terms, leads us away from the moral meaning and practical perplexities of the drama we have been watching, and perhaps participating in.

NOTES AND REFERENCES

1. Hannah Arendt, *On Revolution* (New York: Viking, 1963), pp. 265, 268.
2. Reprinted in Paul Jacobs and Saul Landau, eds., *The New Radicals* (New York: Vintage, 1966), p. 156.
3. Reprinted in Carl Oglesby, ed., *The New Left Reader* (New York: Grove, 1969), p. 270.
4. Jacobs and Landau, *New Radicals,* p. 156.
5. Murray Bookchin graphically speaks of "the living nuclei of utopia in the decomposing body of bourgeois society," in *Post-Scarcity Anarchism* (Berkeley, Calif.: Ramparts, 1971), p. 168.
6. Staughton Lynd, "The New Radicals and 'Participatory Democracy,' " *Dissent,* XII:3 (Summer 1965), 333.
7. Peter Bachrach, *The Theory of Democratic Elitism* (Boston: Little, Brown, 1967).
8. Robert A. Dahl, *After the Revolution?* (New Haven, Conn.: Yale, 1970).
9. See C. George Benello and Dimitrios Roussopoulos, eds., *The Case for Participatory Democracy* (New York: Viking Compass, 1972).
10. Michael Rossman, *On Learning and Social Change* (New York: Vintage, 1972), pp. 257-258.

5

THE ETHICS OF PARTICIPATION

JOHN LADD

The purpose of this essay is to explore the ethical basis of the demand for participation. There are, of course, many different senses of "participation" as well as many different contexts in which the concept is used. (Mr. Braybrooke has given us a careful analysis and classification of many of these uses.) I shall concentrate on the notion of participation in decision making invoked in political, social, and institutional contexts, as embodied, for example, in the notion of "participatory democracy." Participation, in this sense, has a much more extended area of relevance than just the "confrontations, demonstrations, and ad hoc" groups of the sixties, as exemplified, say, in the Port Huron statement. The theme of participation, once the hallmark of youth in the university, is now an important factor in city planning, school decentralization, control of the police, intelligence operations, international relations, and so on. Of particular interest today is the use of participation in the medical context, where the old-fashioned paternalistic attitude of the medical practitioner is coming under increasingly critical scrutiny. It seems to me that, as viewed in these manifold contexts, the concept of participation has some interesting ethical features that cannot be accounted for in utilitarian terms or by means of other categories of traditional liberalism. Instead, I shall try to link the concept of participation to the idea of the moral autonomy of individuals. The approach that I outline here might therefore be appropriately called "the ethics of participation."

At the very outset, I should warm the reader that my principal aim in this essay is theoretical and philosophical, rather than practical and polemical. I do not claim to establish the case for participation in any specific context, e.g. that students should participate in the selection of deans at institutions of higher learning! Nor do I consider whether or not new structures ought to be established or old ones reshaped in order to accommodate the requirements of participation. These specific questions depend on additional considerations involving particulars that are not the concern of this essay.

The ethics of participation that I outline here is intended, therefore, only as a logical framework for certain kinds of arguments supporting claims to participation. My hope is that it will help us better to understand and evaluate the specific arguments that have been or that might be given in debates over participation. Accordingly, the examples that I use are introduced only for purposes of illustration; if the reader objects to any of them, he is invited to think of other examples on his own and to test my analysis against them.

There is an additional philosophical reason for not being too finicky about the examples in a discussion of this sort. Examples relating to participation are obviously by their very nature controversial. The debatable character of the examples in this area, as in most of ethics and political philosophy, makes it impossible to use them either to substantiate or, as counterexamples, to refute, a philosophical analysis of the concepts involving them. As I have argued elsewhere, the familiar counterexample technique, one of the tools in trade of the analytical philosopher in other areas, is a specious mode of argument in ethics and political philosophy.[1]

The kind of argument covered by what I call the ethics of participation departs radically from the usual pragmatic justifications of participation. In order to see the difference, I shall briefly review some of these pragmatic arguments, that is, arguments based on the claim that participatory structures of some kind or other are an effective means to socially desirable ends of some kind or other.

The pragmatist often argues, for instance, that participation is productive because it provides a means of communication between different elements in a social system, say, within an organization between administrators and those affected by their decisions, the recipients.[2] Participation leads to "better service" by providing "input" and "feedback" from the recipients, e.g., clients or employees. (In this regard, students are, of course, clients, and professors employees!) In addition to providing a good way of gathering information, participation is often advocated as a means of adapting general policies to local conditions; thus, insofar as participation involves decentralization, a local group of recipients may be in a better position than a central authority to formulate and implement decisions. Needless to say, pragmatic arguments of this sort resemble in their logic arguments for installing local thermostatic controls in a heating system to replace or supplement a central control: the local thermostat is more likely to "know" the specific heating needs in a particular area and so is able to operate the switches more efficiently. But this sort of pragmatic argument can also be used for social organizations that have immoral purposes: the hard drug trade, for example, might operate more efficiently, at least as far as sales are concerned, through decentralization and participation on the part of its clients.

The justification of participation need not be merely technological, however. A more human justification for it is expressed in the saying that he who wears the shoe knows best where it pinches. A local group of recipients knows better than a federal bureau what their needs are, e.g., for housing or transportation. Another important and worthy purpose served by participation is educational. Rousseau, Mill, and John Dewey all have important and noteworthy things to say in this regard.[3]

Obviously one could go on and on with a list like this. Some of these pragmatic considerations are worthy, some are contemptible, and some are plainly indifferent. I certainly do not wish to downgrade the worthy reasons for participation.[4] However, in my opinion, they clearly belong to *social engineering,* as Mr. Braybrooke aptly calls it, rather than to what I regard as *ethics.*

OBJECTIVE AND SUBJECTIVE APPROACHES TO THE QUESTION OF PARTICIPATION

There are two entirely different points of view from which participation in general and participation in particular cases can be analyzed and evaluated. I shall call them the objective and the subjective points of view. The *objective point of view* approaches participation from the point of view of the group (the organization, the community, or the society). It takes what Baier calls the God's eye point of view and considers participation as it affects society in terms of public utility, and so on.[5] Participation is viewed by it as a social mechanism for promoting social goals. The *subjective point of view,* on the other hand, starts from the individual as an autonomous moral being and considers participation in terms of its meaning for the individual person. This approach tries to show how participation is connected with the individual's own special moral concerns and interests and his social relations with his family, neighbors, associates, and fellow citizens. Key concepts in the subjective approach are conscience, freedom, and responsibility. (There are, of course, other meanings associated with the terms "objective-subjective" that are not intended here. I do not wish to imply that the subjective approach, as I have called it, is subjective in the sense of being idiosyncratic, fanciful, sentimental, emotional, prejudiced, ill-founded, lacking in reality and substance, etc. The subjective approach, in my sense, is none of these; indeed, it is more likely to be realistic and intersubjectively valid than what I have called the "objective approach," which is often patently speculative.)

In contrast to social engineering, which takes the objective approach, the ethics of participation that I present in this essay approaches participation from the subjective point of view. It asks: What does participation mean to the individual? Why, from his point of view, is participation desirable or necessary? How does it relate to his conscience, his freedom and his responsibilities? These are what I should call moral questions, rather than questions of social engineering.[6]

Taking the subjective approach, it is easy to see why participation has suddenly become an acute social and political issue. Participation provides one obvious way of coping with bigness: big government, big industry, big universities, big medical organizations, and big organizations of all sorts. In one way or another, the individual nowadays feels that his moral autonomy is threatened by these structures, which systematically exclude him from decision and plan making in areas of his own immediate moral concerns. When viewed subjectively, the demands for participation represented in movements for community control of schools and of the police, e.g., by blacks, or for participation in university governance by students and faculty, for workers' councils for participation in welfare programs, etc., simply reflect this sense of alienation, an alienation that has a moral as well as a psychological and social basis. For such people participation provides a constructive method of disalienation, one that is consistent with their moral principles and their sense of moral responsibility.

Why, one might ask, has protest against government and other authoritative organizations suddenly taken on the new form of demands for participation? After all, it might be argued, since time immemorial the ordinary man has been on the receiving end of things; he has been the victim of institutions (e.g., slavery) and the unwilling subject of social and political processes. The meliorist might add: and we should be satisfied that we live in a society that is more enlightened, more rational, and more socially oriented than any previous ones. In contrast to former times and to other societies, we now have bureaucratic organizations like school departments, federal agencies, and university administrations, whose explicit official function is to promote socially worthwhile ends. Furthermore, for the most part, the officials in these organizations are sincere and dedicated public servants selected on the basis of their professional expertise.

Why, asks the objectivist, should we give up all these solid gains for a will-o'-the-wisp, which is all that these demands by "ignoramuses" amount to? Participation by such people would never ever be able to provide us with as effective a means to our acknowledged goals as those that are already provided by our formal organizations of expert administrators.

In asking this sort of question, the objectivist quite misses the point, which is not what is the most effective form of governance to promote worthwhile goals. The real question from the subjective point of view is: *who is to decide?* For, in contrast to earlier times, when social processes and outcomes were perceived as the inevitable result of forces beyond the control of individual men, these same social processes and outcomes are now perceived to be the result of someone's decision, the decision of an identifiable individual, e.g., the president, the director, or some official. What is new is the picture (often on the tube) of individuals who are far away (socially, psychologically, and economically, if not geographically) making crucial decisions affecting our everyday lives and our most deeply felt moral concerns: [7] we see an old man deciding that young people should kill innocent people in a war; we see a rich man deciding what kind of welfare the poor should receive; we see a white man deciding who should police the streets in a black neighborhood, and so on. Moreover, the individuals we see making these decisions are obviously fallible human beings like the rest of us, and frequently misinformed and stupid to boot. What is most important is that they lack the kind of involvement in the outcome that is forced on the recipients of the decision. It does not seem entirely absurd to think that a decision maker ought to have some kind of personal moral interest in what is decided. Q.E.D. The recipients ought to be decision makers, or at least have some part in the decision-making process.

The key concept, from the subjective point of view, is moral responsibility. Participation, as I shall argue, cannot be understood apart from various conceptions of moral responsibility. The central role that responsibility plays in discussions of participation is quite obvious. In one or another of its different meanings the constant reference to responsibility is a recurrent feature of all debates about participation, general and specific.

Participation arises out of and leads to responsibility. To participate itself means to become responsible for something or other. In demanding participation, the individual claims that he needs or ought to have responsibility. As a participant or a decision maker, he is expected to take responsibility, to be responsible for seeing that various things are done, to act responsibly, to be responsible for the results of his decisions, and so on. And in the refusal of participation the notion of responsibility is also invoked: it is averred that the claimants are irresponsible or are, e.g., too young and inexperienced to be responsible, that responsibility cannot be shared, that if everyone is responsible no one is responsible, and so on. The refusers say among themselves that it would be the height of irresponsibility to give responsibility to the irresponsible!

It is unnecessary to belabor the point that a good deal of name-calling is involved in the rhetoric of responsibility; each side attacks the other for being irresponsible. The older generation holds that the younger generation is irresponsible and hence has no right to participate in important decisions; the younger generation, on the other hand, holds that the older generation has been irresponsible and therefore the least it can do is to share its powers with the younger generation, which has a greater sense of responsibility. It is easy to see from the way "responsibility" is used in such debates that the parties to the dispute are arguing past each other, not because they have different conceptions of the material facts, but because they have mutually inconsistent conceptions (or misconceptions) of responsibility. It is quite obvious, therefore, that one of our first tasks will be to unravel the notion of responsibility and to show how, in its various senses, it is related to participation.

As we study the ethics of participation from the subjective point of view, it soon becomes clear that we need to revamp many of the basic ethical categories taken for granted in most discussions of participation. The reason for this is that the prevailing categories are designed to analyze action, participation, and responsibility from the objective point of view. Specifically, they are for the most part causal categories, and, as I shall try to show, a causal analysis of our key ethical concepts results in a completely distorted version of the ethics of participation.

To begin with, I shall argue that we cannot apply a causal theory of action to participation in any meaningful sense, so we need to find some other theory that will help us understand what is at issue in discussions of participation.

Second, we confront a somewhat similar difficulty in the notion of responsibility. Here too the objectivist tends to favor a causal approach, which, as we shall see, wreaks havoc with the concept of participation. Indeed, the application of a causal theory of responsibility to participation may make the latter entirely senseless from an ethical point of view. Hence, an extended discussion of responsibility is necessary for an ethics of participation. It is evi-

dent that there are a number of different meanings of "responsibility," and so our first task will be to define and differentiate
them.[8] After that it will be possible to show how responsibility, in
each of its different meanings, has a bearing on participation.

Finally, having restructured these various categories, I shall try
to show how in their modified form they can be used to support
claims for participation. I shall also point out what follows with
regard to the relationship between participation and competence
and power.

FOUR WAYS OF LINKING AN INDIVIDUAL
TO A SOCIAL PROCESS ETHICALLY

Participation, in the sense that interests us here, is a
way of engaging in a social process. By *social process* I simply
mean a process in which a group of individuals is involved, acting
or interacting together, that has a significant outcome of some sort
or other. It is sometimes said that by participating an individual
has an "impact" on the social process and a "significant relation"
to the outcome. These terms appear to me unclear and ambiguous,
for there are obviously many different ways in which the actions
and activities of an individual can be related to a social process
and a social outcome. Unless we distinguish between various types
of linkage connecting the individual to these processes and outcomes, the ethical issues surrounding participation will be utterly
confused. In particular, I want to stress that from the subjective
point of view, that is, from the point of view of the individual involved in social processes, these linkages are quite distinct and
different, although the word "participation" has been used for all
of them.

For our purposes, the main question we need to ask about each
of these different kinds of linkage is what follows from it concerning the individual's responsibility for the outcome to which
he is linked. Is he responsible for it at all and, if so, in what sense
of "responsibility" is he responsible? It will become clear as we
proceed that only one of these linkages provides us with the kind
of responsibility that is relevant to the conception of participation that is at issue in the social and political contexts mentioned
earlier.

To begin with, there is a trivial, and for our purposes unimportant, sense of "participation" in which an individual's action directly determines the outcome of a social process. There are obviously many situations in which the action of each and every individual has a direct impact, i.e., his action is necessary and (partly) sufficient to make a difference to the outcome. For example, in the case of two people getting married, either of the individuals is able to determine whether or not the marriage will take place. This kind of *direct determination,* in which the outcome is a direct product of the combined activities of the individuals involved, is not an issue, as far as we are concerned, in the discussion of participation.

More interesting from our point of view are those cases in which the relationship of any particular individual to the outcome is equivocal. For the most ticklish questions concerning the individual's responsibility arise when an aggregate of individuals is involved in a social process and it is impossible to determine unequivocally that the efforts of any particular individual, as distinct from the efforts of the set of individuals, effectively determine the outcome. The actions of these individuals are like the strands in a rope; no single one of them is necessary or sufficient to make a rope, yet a number of them are when put together. Similarly, any particular individual's action can be added or taken away without significantly changing the outcome of a social process. It only determines the outcome statistically, so to speak.

Given this sort of indeterminate relation between the outcome and the actions of any particular individual, we seem faced with a paradox: we can say that the individual himself has no good reason for participating, and yet there is a reason for his doing so. For example, people often say: "I have no reason to vote in this election since my vote won't make any difference to the outcome." Yet, if people do not vote, there will be a difference in the outcome. So there is a reason for voting.

From the objective point of view, the answer is easy, since apart from direct determination cases, the individual simply counts as a statistic. From the subjective point of view, however, that is, from the point of view of the individual who does not take the God's eye view, there are genuine and understandable doubts about the *meaning* of his own actions and, in particular, his own responsibility for the outcome. The resolution of this paradox, if it is possible, requires an examination of various ways of viewing the relationship of the individual's action to a social process. There are at least four such "linkages" worth examining. (There may, of course, be others as well.)

First, there are a number of social processes in which the outcome is exactly the opposite of what is desired or intended by the individual involved in them. There are many examples of this kind of *reverse effect:* individuals may enter the market to buy a certain commodity and thereby force the price up by raising the demand. Or people may take to the road on a holiday for a pleasant ride in the country, thereby causing a traffic jam, etc. The word "participate" is occasionally used for acting with this kind of effect, but this kind of linkage does not seen to be relevant to the central issue.

Second, there are social processes in which the outcome is intended by the individuals involved in them. Such individuals may be said to *contribute* to the outcome—statistically, of course. Examples of contribution in this sense would be individuals engaged in a joint project such as the making of an automobile, writing letters to congressmen, or fighting in a war. Under this category I want to include acts that contribute to an outcome and that are intended to do so by the actor, but where the outcome is not in his own personal interest or where it is not approved by him personally. Paying taxes might be an example: in paying one's taxes one contributes (intentionally) to the total amount received in taxes, yet one may disapprove of the money being used to fight a war.

Interesting questions concerning responsibility and "complicity" arise in connection with contributory action. If one pays his taxes or buys Saran Wrap, is he an accomplice in the war? Is he thereby responsible for the use of napalm bombs? In a causal sense, perhaps he is. But surely there is something paradoxical in this sense of responsibility. For if responsibility is a function of causal efficacy and the efficacy of any one individual's contribution is merely statistical, then the responsibility would attach to the individual only as a statistic, as a member of a class of people no single one of which is responsible. Furthermore, in this sense of responsibility, the more people who are involved in an undertaking, the more who contribute, the less each individual is responsible. Numbers diminish responsibility! From an ethical point of view, such consequences do not make any sense, for we think of responsibility as attached to specific individuals considered separately and not as unidentifiable members of a group.

A third kind of link between the individual's action and a social process and its outcome is like the one just mentioned, except that in addition to contributing to the outcome, the individual also approves of it or endorses it. In order to distinguish this linkage from contribution, I shall call it *supporting* an outcome. A man who donates money or time to a cause of which he approves (e.g., a political party or hospital) may be said to support it, in my sense. Likewise, someone who supplies information or advice to a group working for an end which he endorses also may be said to support it; he supports it by providing "input"—to use the jargon expression.

At first, support might appear to provide a firmer basis for ascriptions of responsibility than contribution, for we are more likely to condemn a person for aiding a bad cause if he also approves and endorses it. On reflection, however, it turns out that logically there is no important distinction between contribution and support, for we may find a person condemnable for his attitudes or for his contribution, but combining them does not make him any more condemnable.[9]

Despite the fact that the word "participation" is used for all of these three linkages, it seems clear that none of them really captures the meaning of "participation" in the sense that interests us here. These three linkages reduce participation to causal influences of some kind or other, but causal influence seems to be neither sufficient nor perhaps even necessary to constitute participation. The causal relationship, especially where direct determination is not involved, seems far too casual. To participate means to act *in* the process rather than *on* the process. For example, when the process includes decision making, the demand for participation is a demand to be a decision maker rather than simply to have the opportunity of exerting an influence on the decision maker. Indeed, influence in the form, e.g., of pressure, may be very powerful, but that still does not make it participation.

What is missing is the reference to responsibility that is present in the notion of participation but not in the notion of influence. As I have already pointed out, to participate entails having responsibility, taking responsibility, being responsible for the results of what one does, and so on. The principal kind of responsibility involved here is what I call *accountability*, that is, the kind of accountability that attaches to actions as such. For participation is a kind of action as distinct from an influence on action. In this regard, the only difference between participation and other ordinary kinds of action is that participation is an action that is performed in association with others. It is, in other words, a *joint action*.

In order to understand the ethically relevant aspects of participation, we must now examine the concepts of action, accountability, and joint action in more detail.

ACTION, ACCOUNTABILITY, AND JOINT ACTION

The concept of action is often linked up with the concept of responsibility: it is sometimes said, for example, that a free human agent is responsible for his voluntary actions. The thesis I want to defend here is that if a person participates in a social process, then he is responsible for what he does as he participates, in this general sense of "responsibility."

I prefer not to use the word "responsibility" in this context, however, for I shall argue later and have argued elsewhere that it is linguistically odd to say that a person is responsible for his actions, e.g., that he is responsible for going for a walk, for hitting someone, or for eating supper.[10] It is sounder, both linguistically and philosophically, to say that he is responsible for states of affairs rather than for actions, admitting, of course, that he is responsible for those states of affairs that are consequences of his actions.

Instead of using the word "responsibility," I prefer to use the word "accountability" when speaking of actions as distinguished from the consequences they bring about. "Accountability" here means "capable of being accounted for" or "of having an account given of it." Actions are typically the kinds of things for which reasons can be given, that can be justified and explained by reasons, that is, that one can account for. As I use it here, I assume that a person who performs an action (as contrasted, say, with a bodily movement) is able to give an account of it, i.e., say *what* he is doing and *why* he is doing it. *Mutatis mutandis* he can give an account of past and future actions (intentions). Without going into a full-scale exposition of a *reasons theory of action,* a few points are worth noting with regard to it.[11]

Accountability is not an extra moral requirement of some sort, but part of the very meaning of the concept of action. An action is by definition the kind of thing for which it makes sense to ask a reason, and it is this aspect of action that differentiates an action from a mere bodily movement. Accountability, I should contend, is in certain respects ethically neutral in that the reasons given in reply to our questions need not be moral reasons; they might be prudential or emotional. "Because I enjoy doing X" is a reason for doing X in the sense intended here. One might also, as Anscombe points out, reply "for no reason," and that would be a reply just as "none" is a reply to the question how much money I have in my pocket. In addition, there are excuses, and so on. It is impossible to enter into an extended discussion of various ways of answering the question: why did you do that? I merely want to give a rough indication here of what I mean by "accountability."

Returning to participation, we can now see that it can be subsumed under actions for which we are accountable. As such, participation belongs in the category of *joint actions,* that is, actions that we perform together with other people.

Many of the actions that one performs every day are joint actions in this sense, that is, actions that one cannot perform except together with other people. One cannot shake hands, play tennis, or dance a waltz all by oneself; one needs others, as it were, to complete the action. Nevertheless, these actions are no less actions of individual persons than other kinds of actions that they can perform alone. Joint actions are actions in the full sense of the term.

A person is accountable for his joint actions as he is for his individual actions. The fact that others are involved in the action in no way diminishes his accountability. In this sense, it can be said that joint actions are actions for which a number of people are jointly and separately accountable. (As far as "jointness" is concerned, joint accountability is like having a joint bank account —each owner is a complete owner and can draw the total amount from the account; or it is like partners in committing a crime— they are jointly and separately punishable to the full extent for their crime.) The complete accountability of each participant in a joint action is obviously what distinguishes participation from influence of any of the three types mentioned in the last section. A person who influences a social process is not accountable for it, whereas a person who participates in it is.

It might be objected that the part played by a particular individual participant may not be the decisive factor in determining what actually takes place. After all, without the help of others, the action would not transpire; hence, since his role is not sufficient to produce the action (or outcome), he is not accountable. For instance, if eight men join in moving a car, while only six are necessary to do it, we can say that the efforts of two men are superfluous and do not contribute, therefore, to the car's being moved. If their efforts are neither necessary nor sufficient to move the car, how could they be held accountable for moving it?

This kind of objection is based on the assumption of a causal theory of action; if actions were definable as the effects of causes of some kind or other (e.g., the agent or his volitions), then the objection would be well taken. However, I deny that a person (or something in him) is in any meaningful sense the *cause* of his actions.[12] Accountability, which I offer instead as a distinctive feature of action, is not necessarily a function of causal efficacy and is therefore not affected by the fact that actions by others are required to complete the action.

In this connection, it should be observed that accountability attaches not only to actions whose completion depends on others but also to incomplete actions of one's own, e.g., tryings. It is interesting to note that when we are asked why we tried to do X, our answer, more often than not, is the same as it would have been had we done X. For example, in reply to the question: why did you *try* to buy that house? one might say: "because it was conveniently located, well-built, the price was right, etc." And these answers give the same kind of reasons one would give if one had succeeded in buying the house. The crucial difference between an action and trying (and not succeeding) to perform the same action is that there has been an intervention of external circumstances to prevent completion of the action. The accountability for the completed action and for the attempt to complete it is basically the same, in some cases at least, quite independently of the fact that a completed action A and an incompleted action A′ might have entirely different causal consequences.

If we press this point further it becomes clear that perhaps everything we do is dependent for its completion on external circumstances of some sort or other. If there is no reason on this account to deny the accountability of actions and tryings that are so dependent, then there seems no good reason to deny it in the case of joint actions. Indeed, if we attribute accountability to joint actions, we are on our way to a better understanding of the meaning of "participation."[13]

RESPONSIBILITY: DESCRIPTIVE AND NORMATIVE

Having distinguished accountability from responsibility, it is now possible to proceed on the assumption that, properly speaking, responsibility attaches to persons in their relation to states of affairs rather than in relation to their actions as such. We are, of course, particularly interested in states of affairs that are the consequence or outcome of actions, either in the past or in the future. Inasmuch as joint actions are actions with outcomes, we can say that joint actors, i.e., participants in a joint action, are responsible for a state of affairs brought about by their action or, *mutatis mutandis,* ought to be responsible for a state of affairs that could be brought about by their action. In all these cases, responsibility is to be construed as a relationship between an actor (or group of actors) and a state of affairs, actual or possible, and past, present, or future.

The common element in almost all, if not all, of the morally relevant senses of "responsibility" is the stress on the "forethought, care, intelligence, and initiative" demanded of the actor who is the subject of the responsibility.[14] This is, of course, the connotation of "responsible" as an adjective: "Jones is a responsible person" means that he has forethought, etc. The opposite of responsibility, its absence where it is expected, is neglect, negligence, remissness, disregard, etc.

Having noted these two general characteristics of responsibility in general, we must now observe that there is a basic ambiguity in the term "responsibility" itself, namely, that it may be used descriptively or normatively. That is, "responsibility" may refer to an actual relationship between an actor and a state of affairs (usually past) or to a relationship that ought to exist between them (usually future). Thus, I can say, for example, that Ann is (descriptively) responsible for the mess, i.e., she made it, or that she is (normatively) responsible for cleaning up the mess, i.e., she ought to clean it up.

Accordingly, we have basically two different kinds of responsibility: descriptive responsibility and normative responsibility. The only way to avoid utter confusion when talking about responsibility, especially in connection with participation, is to bear this distinction constantly in mind.

Most ascriptions of responsibility in the descriptive sense are causal, that is, the responsibility is held to rest on a causal relationship between an actor's action and the results of his action. Jones is responsible for the accident because he was driving too fast, etc., and his driving too fast caused the accident. Sometimes, indeed, we use "responsibility" in a purely causal sense, applying it, e.g., to nonhuman agents as well as persons. For example, we say that the storm is responsible for the broken window, meaning that the storm caused the window to break.

In this connection, a great deal has been made of the distinction between event-responsibility (or event-causation) and thing-responsibility (or thing-causation). The most interesting case of the latter is, of course, person-responsibility (or agent-causation). The fact that we can use these two different kinds of subject for an imputation of responsibility (a causal attribution) has been used to justify a metaphysical distinction between events and persons (agents). I am not sure that I understand the rationale for using this distinction for metaphysical purposes. It seems to me that the distinction between these two kinds of descriptive responsibility (or causation) is purely pragmatic: the choice of locution depends on what we intend to use the imputation for. When I say, for example, that the dirty spark plugs are responsible for the engine's loss of power, I mean to direct attention to the spark plugs as a continuing thing, with a view to implying that they ought to be fixed; whereas when I say that the storm (an event) is responsible for the broken window, I am implying that the cause no longer exists and, for that reason as a one-time happening, cannot be changed. When we use thing-responsibility to apply to persons, our reason is probably similar to the case of the spark plugs, namely, we want to identify a continuing thing, with a view to doing something like repairing the thing, e.g., punishing or blaming the person who is responsible.

From the moral point of view, normative responsibility may be more important, especially if, as a moralist, one focuses on future conduct rather than past misconduct. Sometimes, of course, normative responsibility, i.e., an ought, arises out of descriptive responsibility, i.e., something that one has caused. Ann is responsible for the mess, therefore she is responsible for cleaning it up.

However, most individuals have moral responsibilities over and above those that arise out of their past actions and omissions, i.e., their descriptive responsibilities. Incidentally, I might point out that the concept of normative (or moral) responsibility is an important one for a nonutilitarian ethics, for it allows the introduction of consequentialist considerations into the determination of a person's duties without reducing the latter to a means-end relationship.

We must now note some important logical differences between descriptive and normative responsibility. First, descriptive responsibility is almost always used in relation to undesirable states of affairs, e.g., injuries, deprivations, or destructions; whereas normative responsibility is almost always used in relation to desirable states of affairs, e.g., health, safety, welfare, and education. Second, the states of affairs referred to in ascriptions of descriptive responsibility (e.g., causes) are usually specific and determinate (e.g., the accident at such and such a place); whereas the states of affairs connected with normative responsibilities are general and diffuse, e.g., the health and education of one's children.

Because of our special interest in participation, perhaps the most significant logical difference between the two kinds of responsibility is that descriptive responsibility is closed and exclusionary, whereas normative responsibility is open and inclusionary. By "exclusionary" I mean that descriptive responsibility is fixed on one party (object, person, or group) to the *exclusion* of others: Jones, not Smith, is responsible for the accident; the Electric Company, not the Gas Company, is responsible for the rise in pollution; the spark plugs, not the carburetor, are responsible for the loss of power. Descriptive responsibility, in other words, is imputed to one party and by implication *not* to others. (A clear instance of this kind of responsibility is legal liability, which would be a worthless concept in law if it did not imply the distinction between parties that are liable in a particular case and that are not.) The same kind of exclusive responsibility is presupposed in the attribution of criminal responsibility to a person, for in this context it is important to distinguish between those who are and those who are not responsible.

Normative responsibility, on the other hand, is not exclusionary in this sense. Sharp lines between who is and who is not responsible cannot be drawn. From the fact that one person (party) is responsible, it does not follow that no one else is. For example, one person's moral responsibility for the health and welfare of his children does not bar the moral responsibility of others, e.g., grandparents, aunts and uncles, neighbors, doctors, or government officials. A particular responsibility may devolve on one individual or group, that is, it may rest more heavily on them; but that fact does not cancel out the responsibility of others. To a moralist it is evident, for example, that *all* of us are in some sense responsible for the safety, health, and welfare of others, our neighbors and our fellow men in general. We cannot plead, as Cain did, that we are not our brother's keeper—that our moral responsibilities are limited to certain people and not to others. Nor can we excuse ourselves, like those who watched Kitty Genovese being beaten to death, by saying that someone else is responsible. Someone else's being responsible does not necessarily imply that you are not responsible.

Thus there is a fundamental logical difference between the two kinds of responsibility. Negation (or denial) of responsibility is possible with regard to descriptive responsibility; in fact, the possibility or implication of excluding some parties as not responsible is an essential logical feature of descriptive responsibility.

On the other hand, disclaiming normative moral responsibility for, say, the safety and welfare of others, is simply a sign of moral callousness or blindness. That is not to deny, of course, that moral responsibilities may vary in exigency and that some people are more responsible than others for certain persons, say, their children. Perhaps this kind of responsibility might be said to vary in exigency inversely with the distance between persons, actors and recipients. I am more responsible for my children and friends than for the children and friends of a Chinese peasant. But that does not mean that I have no responsibility at all for the latter.

In sum, the difference between the two basic kinds of responsibility is that descriptive responsibility permits a negative posture toward one's own or another person's responsibilities whereas normative responsibility does not. Normative responsibility is positive in a sense in which descriptive responsibility is not.

The immediate application of these two different logics of responsibility to controversies surrounding participation is obvious: the demanders of participation take a positive, nonexclusionary approach, whereas the refusers of participation take a negative, exclusionary one. Exactly how this is possible leads us to another crucial distinction, namely, the distinction between official and moral responsibility.

OFFICIAL RESPONSIBILITY AND MORAL RESPONSIBILITY [15]

It might be objected at this point that the remarks made in the previous section concerning the two types of responsibility are simply beside the point, because neither type represents the only kind of responsibility that is relevant to controversies about participation, namely, the kind of responsibility that goes with a job, e.g., the job of being a policeman or an administrator of some kind. This new kind of responsibility, which is typically attached to jobs, offices, and roles, I shall call *official responsibility*. It is sometimes called "task responsibility."

Official responsibility resembles descriptive responsibility in being exclusionary and normative responsibility in being normative, i.e., in generating prescriptions for conduct. Where, then, does official responsibility fit into our scheme? Is it descriptive or is it normative? Or is it a hybrid? Or is it a third kind of responsibility?

Let us begin by examining the exclusionary aspect of official responsibility. It is obvious that the kind of responsibility that is attached to offices is exclusionary—A's job is not B's job—for the bureaucratic approach to organization requires drawing hard and fast lines between spheres of responsibility. Responsibility goes with one office and not another, and certainly not to outsiders (= meddlers). For if everything were everyone's responsibility, i.e., if responsibility were nonexclusionary, then we would have anarchy and nothing would ever get done. Pragmatically speaking, we must divide up our labor and responsibilities in order to be more efficient and "rational." [16]

We must now look more closely at responsibility as it occurs in this context. Clearly official responsibility receives its basic rationale from the fact that bureaucratic organizations are structured along lines of authority: authority is delegated by superiors to subordinates, who, in turn, are responsible to their superiors (and no one else!). Responsibility in this sense may be called *answerability:* the subordinate is answerable to his superior; his superior in turn is answerable to another superior, and so up the line. Lines of authority are drawn in terms of answerability relations.

It is easy to see why answerability has to be exclusionary. For it is associated with the kind of authority and tasks that are delegated to a subordinate by a superior. The exact nature of the relationship between these two persons is immaterial for present purposes, but it might be pointed out that in regard to answerability the superior is related to a subordinate somewhat as a principal is related to his agent, and this relationship is, of necessity, exclusionary; for we must know who is and who is not someone's agent. In logical form, then, the answerability relation is exclusionary in precisely the same way as the contractual relationship, that is, it is tied to particular people and is personal in this sense. However, like things contracted for, the rights and duties associated with offices are alienable. In particular, official responsibility is a kind of responsibility that can be delegated, transferred, created, and extinguished.

Now we see why official responsibility (= answerability) differs from both kinds of responsibility mentioned in the previous section. Unlike official responsibility, neither descriptive nor normative responsibility, at least in the moral sense, can be alienated. Having admitted the (descriptive) responsibility for a person's death, for example, one cannot transfer or delegate it to someone else. Nor can anyone transfer or delegate his moral responsibility for the safety and welfare of others to someone else; for example, none of the spectators could transfer his own responsibility to Kitty Genovese to the other spectators. Nor, indeed, can anyone take away either kind of responsibility from the person to whom it belongs and give it to someone else, as a superior can with regard to answerability. Only an official can bestow, remove, or transfer responsibility (= answerability); a moralist cannot do this with moral responsibility.

It should be clear now that the key issue separating the two sides of the controversy over participation is the question of the alienability of responsibility and its correlate, negateability. An official who refuses participation is thinking in terms of official responsibility and accordingly, from that point of view, he can say that the responsibility is his and *not* someone else's, and since it was given to him by a superior, it is not his to share or give away, etc. He can then add that the participation seeker has no authority (e.g., no office) and hence is answerable to no one. Not being answerable, he has no responsibility, etc., etc.

The participation seeker, on the other hand, is thinking in terms of moral responsibility, a kind of responsibility that is inalienable and cannot be taken away from him by any kind of executive fiat. The official, he contends, has only official responsibility, which, being nonmoral, has only a casual relationship to morality and cannot, of course, override or cancel a person's moral (normative) responsibilities, etc., etc.

CONSEQUENCES AND CONDITIONS OF
MORAL RESPONSIBILITY

So far I have argued that from the ethical point of view, the rationale for participation rests on the notion of moral responsibility. To be morally responsible for a state of affairs X means that, other things being equal, one ought to do everything in one's power to bring about X, e.g., the welfare of one's children. To participate in a joint action is a means of promoting social outcomes of one sort or another, in particular, the safety, health, welfare, and education of particular people for whom one is responsible. Hence, other things being equal, one ought to participate in such joint actions.

Although moral responsibilities in general create oughts, we cannot neglect the all-important qualifying phrase, "other things being equal." Every individual has numerous duties, obligations, and responsibilities that vary in stringency and compatibility with each other. Thus, a particular person's responsibility with regard to a particular outcome may be minimal and that responsibility may have to give way to other more pressing responsibilities. Again, if a responsibility requires wrongful acts, e.g., deception or the use of violence, the oughts it generates may be cancelled. Hence, the decision whether or not to act on one's responsibility may turn out to be a complex one, depending not only on the nature of the responsibility itself but also on one's other commitments. For the same reason, decisions about whether or not to participate, or to allow others to participate, may be complex and not susceptible to simple answers.

The conditions that give rise to moral responsibilities in the first instance and the criteria that determine how much one particular responsibility should count compared with other moral requirements are characteristically fuzzy and vague. To some extent one's responsibilities depend upon one's social relations, e.g., relations to family, to friends, to associates, or to other members of the community. Another factor that creates moral responsibilities is proximity or affinity: psychological, sociological, or physical. Students naturally have a responsibility for other students (including future generations of students), blacks naturally have a responsibility for other blacks, neighbors are responsible for each other, and so on. This brief list is by no means exhaustive, but it suffices for the present.

Two other facets of the relation of a moral responsibility to action should be mentioned here. First, whether as a result of having a moral responsibility one ought to do something or not often depends on what other people have done or will do, or, on the other hand, have failed to do or will not do. For example, if another person or group that is responsible acts first and entirely effectively, then it may not be necessary for us to do anything at all. If several people had come to the rescue of Kitty Genovese, it would have been unnecessary for others to do so, even though they had a moral responsibility for her safety. Similarly, if others default on their moral responsibility to bring about X, then we are required to act to bring it about. If parents neglect their children, then someone else, the grandparents, aunts, or uncles, must jump into the breach and take care of them.

A second facet of the relation between a person's moral responsibilities and possible action is their connection with his power and competence. To begin with, power and competence by themselves generally create moral responsibilities; a person who acquires the power or competence to bring about an outcome X automatically acquires a moral responsibility with regard to it. An expert swimmer, for instance, by virtue of his expertness has a special responsibility to rescue a person from drowning. Perhaps a person (or country) with special resources has a greater responsibility to help others than a poor person (or country). Inasmuch as power and competence tend to create moral responsibilities, it is plausible to regard them as sufficient conditions of moral responsibility.

However, it is frequently contended that power and competence are not only sufficient conditions but also necessary conditions of moral responsibility. The lack of power or competence, in other words, is held to wipe out moral responsibility. This contention provides the premise for another argument against participation, one based on powerlessness and incompetence. It is averred that since students or the poor have neither power nor competence, they have no moral responsibility and therefore their claim to participate has no merit. Since the issue is crucial in debates concerning participation, we must examine this contention more closely. It will be the subject of the final section of this essay, to which we now turn.

OUGHT IMPLIES CAN

There is a well-known maxim, usually attributed to Kant, that "ought implies can."[17] This maxim is often employed by philosophers to show that a certain supposed ought must be cancelled if it can be shown that it is impossible to perform the action that it requires. For example, if Jones promises to do A and it turns out that, for reasons beyond his control, he cannot do A, then the "ought to do A" is cancelled. For the same kind of reason, the argument goes, if a person is responsible for X and he cannot do anything to produce X, then his moral responsibility with regard to X is *eo ipso* obliterated. In other words, moral responsibility is eliminated when one lacks the ability to perform because, say, he lacks the requisite power, competence, or opportunity.

This negative use of the maxim is familiar to all of us. It is also obvious that it can be misused, as when someone uses it as an excuse for his failure to do what he ought to do or to avoid his moral responsibilities. "I could do nothing about it" is an all-too-common subterfuge. In the context of debates over participation, the same maxim is invoked to deny the responsibilities of others: we say that it is outside Jones' power or competence to decide X, therefore he has no responsibility with regard to X. (The growing frequency of denials of this sort explains the prevalence of moral apathy among those not allowed to participate, for moral apathy is the natural effect of being told or of feeling that one's actions are worthless and that one cannot do what he feels he ought to do.)

Although the maxim "ought implies can" has sometimes been incorporated as a theorem in systems of deontic logic, I have argued elsewhere that logically it functions as a presupposition of certain kinds of ethical discourse rather than as a component proposition in the discourse itself.[18] I also believe that "ought implies can" is not as self-evidently true as it is usually thought to be.

In any case, the maxim can obviously be applied in two different ways: in *modo ponendo* and in *modo tollendo,* i.e., by affirming a can or by denying an ought. It is instructive in this regard to observe that Kant himself, the supposed inventor of the maxim, employed it positively rather than negatively. For example, he argued that perpetual peace is possible because all men have a duty to strive for it: i.e., because one ought to strive for it, one can achieve it. Taking our cue from Kant, let us see what follows if we use the maxim positively rather than negatively. Granted that moral responsibility implies power and competence, we can infer therefrom not that a person who has no power or competence has no responsibility, but that because he has moral responsibility (an ought) he can (and should) have the requisite power and competence.[19]

This conclusion is hardly farfetched, for we usually do assume that a person who has a responsibility and no power or competence ought to do everything that he can to remedy the deficiency. A parent's responsibility for the health or welfare of his child implies, for example, that if he does not have the power (e.g., the money) or the competence (e.g., the knowledge) to take care of his child, he should forthwith try to get them. There is no reason to think that the same logic does not apply to participants in a social process: if they do not have the power or competence to fulfill their responsibilities, they should take all the necessary steps to obtain them. In general, if a person is, say, incompetent, then it seems more reasonable to say that he ought to make himself competent than to deny that he has the moral responsibility.

A more interesting, though much neglected, facet of this maxim is its bearing on other parties. There is no reason to deny that the same logic that applies to the individual actor himself applies to others as well, namely, that if an individual has responsibilities, oughts, but lacks the power or competence that they imply, then others who do have the power or competence have a duty to help him obtain the power and competence necessary to fulfill his responsibilities. In other words, instead of justifying the contention that a participation seeker does not have the moral responsibility on which his demand for participation rests, the fact of his non-competence or powerlessness creates a special onus on the person who has these prerequisites, e.g., the official to whom the demands are addressed, to do everything he can to help the participant acquire competence and power.

Thus, if the maxim "ought implies can" is correctly interpreted, precisely the opposite of the conclusion mentioned at the end of the preceding section follows. Incompetence or lack of power neither excuses the individual himself from his moral responsibilities nor excuses others from the duty of facilitating his fulfilling his responsibility. Instead, it creates an obligation on the part of both the individual and others to remove his incompetence and lack of power. That is the morality of it. The politics, of course, will be different.

Underlying the whole concept of the ethics of participation, therefore, is the\ moral principle that as moral beings we ought to refrain from hindering others in fulfilling their moral responsibilities, and their duties in general. We ought instead to give them every assistance possible in carrying out these responsibilities and duties. This principle is simply another way of saying that we ought to respect our fellow men as autonomous moral beings.

In closing, I want to remind the reader that what I have given here are only the "prolegomena," so to speak, to a theory of participation. What I have tried to do is to call attention to certain logical and moral principles that seem to me highly relevant and cogent to disputes in general about participation. These principles emerge clearly when one approaches the issue from what I have called the subjective point of view; they are easily overlooked if one takes the objective point of view. The fact that those engaged in arguing about participation can proceed from such entirely different bases explains why communication breaks down so easily between two parties, each of which sincerely thinks that it is right and that the other one is irrational.[20]

NOTES AND REFERENCES

1. I have argued this point in more detail in "The Interdependence of Ethical Analysis and Ethics," ETYKA (Warsaw, Poland), 11, 1973.
2. In discussions of action it is often necessary to distinguish between the person performing the action and the person acted on. The former is generally called the "agent" by philosophers and the "actor" by sociologists; there is no good name for the latter. "Patient," which would be etymologically correct, suggests suffering, whereas I want to convey the idea that the person concerned may be a beneficiary. In order to preserve the neutral connotation and to avoid ambiguities, I shall speak of the two as *actor* and *recipient*.
3. A good discussion of this kind of argument, with historical references, is to be found in Carole Pateman, *Participation and Democratic Theory* (Cambridge: Cambridge University Press, 1970), chap. 2. John Dewey's classical discussion is to be found in his *The Public and Its Problems* (Chicago: Gateway Books, 1946), chap. 6.
4. A good summary of the arguments for participatory democracy may be found in Terrence E. Cook and Patrick M. Morgan, *Participatory Democracy* (San Francisco: Canfield Press, 1971). It is clear that, in addition to the sort of argument mentioned here or in this book, there are some very persuasive arguments based on political expediency: participation is granted as a way of "defusing" a crisis, and so on.
5. Kurt Baier, *The Moral Point of View* (New York: Random House, 1965), p. 107.
6. Even those who emphasize the moral aspects of evaluation tend to couch them in objectivist terms. For example, they dwell on the psychological consequences of dividing "men from a sense of moral responsibility for the ultimate consequences of their actions, etc." Cook and Morgan, *Participatory Democracy,* p. 15.
7. It is important in discussions of participation to distinguish between a person's interests and his concerns. Interests tend to be material and, as such, are not the chief foundation of demands for participation. Concerns, on the other hand, include moral concerns, e.g., matters of conscience and principle. Thus, it may be in a man's interest to accept the draft but his conscience may tell him to do otherwise. Unfortunately, the Establishment tends to recognize only interests as legitimate grounds for participation. My argument here is that moral concerns, rather than interests, are the foundation of a right to participate. For some interesting remarks on the concept of interest, see Brian Barry, *Political Argument* (London: Routledge and Kegan Paul, 1965), pp. 174-186.
8. In the following pages, distinctions will be made between: accountability, descriptive and causal responsibility (liability), normative responsibility, moral responsibility, and official responsibility (answerability). These are only a few of the many meanings of this ambiguous term.
9. Although voting, e.g., in a national presidential election, is often regarded as a form of participation, it probably belongs under what is here called "support." The actual participation in ongoing political processes by the electorate is minimal. As Schumpeter says, "once they (i.e., the voters) have elected an individual, political action is his business and not theirs" (Joseph A. Schumpeter, *Capitalism, Socialism and Democracy* [New York: Harper and Row, 1962], p. 295). For an interesting discussion of Schumpeter's theory in historical perspective, see Pateman, *Participation,* chap. 1.

10. See my "The Ethical Dimensions of the Concept of Action," *Journal of Philosophy*, LXII: 21 (November 4, 1965). See also Glenn Langford, *Human Action* (Garden City, N.Y.: Doubleday, 1971), p. 51.

11. The general approach adopted here is like that found in G. E. M. Anscombe, *Intention* (Ithaca, N.Y.: Cornell University Press, 1957), especially pp. 24-28. It is also to be found in somewhat different versions in Alan Gewirth, "The Normative Structure of Action," *Review of Metaphysics*, XXV: 2 (December 1971) and Irving Thalberg, *Enigmas of Agency* (New York: Humanities Press, 1972), especially pp. 73-86. In detail, of course, there are significant differences between the theories presented in these writings, among themselves, and with my own. There is no room for the elaboration and justification of a "reasons" theory of action in the present essay.

12. See Thalberg, *Enigmas*, pp. 35-47, and Alvin I. Goldman, *A Theory of Action* (Englewood Cliffs, N.J.: Prentice-Hall, 1970), pp. 23-25. For a contrary view, see Roderick M. Chisholm, "Freedom and Action," in Keith Lehrer, ed., *Freedom and Determinism* (New York: Random House, 1966).

13. Here it might be mentioned that there is an enormous variety of joint actions that can be represented as participation. The theory offered here is not restricted to formal participation in decision making of, say, organizations. There are unorganized as well as organized activities, e.g., people working together to put out a fire and people deciding together what to do to help a neighbor in distress. Joint actions need not be composed of simultaneous actions of individuals, but they may be related sequentially, as in a relay race. They may involve utilizing existing structures or creating new ones. There is, furthermore, no restriction as to areas of concern. For example, one area that needs to be explored from the point of view adopted here is the area of health care, decisions about life and death, operations, transplants, and doctor-patient-nurse relationships. Unfortunately, there is a growing tendency to ignore the recipient's role in these matters.

14. The list is taken from Kurt Baier, "Responsibility and Action," reprinted in Myles Brand, ed., *The Nature of Human Action* (Glenview, Ill.: Scott, Foresman, 1970), p. 104. My analysis departs radically from Baier's, however.

15. Strictly speaking, some forms of moral responsibility can be subsumed under descriptive as well as normative responsibility. In this section, however, I shall generally assume that moral responsibility is a species of normative responsibility.

16. See my "Morality and the Ideal of Rationality in Formal Organizations," *Monist*, 54: 4 (October 1970), where I argue that for logical reasons there is often a head-on collision between bureaucratic rationality and morality.

17. See David Baumgardt, "Legendary Quotations and Lack of References," *Journal of the History of Ideas*, VII: 1 (January 1946). Also Lewis W. Beck, *A Commentary on Kant's Critique of Practical Reason* (Chicago: University of Chicago Press, 1960), pp. 189, 200n.

18. See my "Remarks on the Conflict of Obligations," *Journal of Philosophy*, IV: 19 (September 11, 1958).

19. Kant's argument for the possibility of perpetual peace is to be found in his *Metaphysical Elements of Justice*, trans. John Ladd (Indianapolis: Bobbs-Merrill, 1965), pp. 127-129. The key question in the negative application of "ought implies can" is whether or not the absence of com-

petence or power is corrigible. I am indebted to Philip Quinn for pointing this out to me.

20. I wish to thank my colleagues in the Brown Philosophy Department for their helpful comments and criticisms when I read this essay to them at a colloquium. Some of the ideas presented here have been elaborated in relation to issues of medical decision-making in a forthcoming essay entitled: "Freedom and Responsibility in Medicine."

6

THE VALUE OF PARTICIPATION

M. B. E. SMITH

It is by now a commonplace that in this and in the other Western democracies citizen participation in the process of government is not large. (In common with most political theorists I do not count mere voting as participating in government.) The average citizen has virtually no influence in national affairs, and little more in setting the policies of subordinate governments to which he is subject. Even when he has an opportunity of influencing government, most often at the local level, he rarely seizes it. Thus, in the small town of Ashfield, Massachusetts, where I live, perhaps half of those eligible to participate ever bother to attend the town meeting. Of those who do attend, only few rise to speak. The town meeting serves chiefly to ratify the plans of the selectmen; when, some years ago, an article in the town warrant was defeated, no one could remember a previous meeting in which such a thing occurred. At the heart of traditional democratic theory is the vision of the average citizen participating actively in government, at least in the process of setting its policies, but this vision is nowhere fulfilled in any of the Western democracies.

Rather than finding this cause for concern, some political theorists have applauded it. They have held that widespread participation would have several untoward consequences: decision making would be unwieldy and inefficient because of the number to be heeded and persuaded; since most citizens lack the specialized knowledge needed to govern competently, the decisions reached would frequently be defective; political passions would run high, thus hampering government and perhaps rendering it unstable; and, finally, much time would be lost in political activity that could better be spent in other ways. It is important, such theorists hold, that the ordinary citizen have an opportunity of participating in political activity and that occasionally he do so, in order to maintain a reserve of influence with government so that it will be responsive to his desires. Nevertheless, so they hold, it is in general a good thing that the business of government be left to a small portion of the populace. Such theorists have been said to hold a "realistic" democratic theory, and I shall adopt this label here.[1]

In recent years, the realists' celebration of citizen apathy has drawn considerable fire.[2] First, they are often accused of a conservative bias, on the ground that their view of participation serves to justify and to safeguard present political arrangements. This, so it has been claimed, tends to discourage speculation as to whether widespread participation might better serve the general good than does citizen apathy, e.g., by bringing unarticulated and unfulfilled desires or interests into the light, so that they may be dealt with. Second, their critics complain that in assessing the merits of political arrangements the realists limit their concern to efficiency and stability, ignoring such considerations as justice and human development. Considerable emphasis is placed upon this last. Moral development, so it is argued, requires that a man look beyond his private interests and have some vision of the common good; and it is held that participation in some level of government is indispensable to this process. Moreover, by participating in government the citizen will gain a sense of self-esteem, will better learn to safeguard his interests, and may even discover interests of which he was previously unaware. Traditional democratic theory, the critics point out, held widespread participation in government desirable, not so much as an efficient and stable method of conducting the public business, but rather as a prerequisite for the improvement of mankind. They castigate the realists for abandoning this faith.

It is, I shall argue, fair to say that in the present state of the controversy the realists' position has emerged relatively unscathed. It must, I think, be kept in mind that the realists have pointed to certain prima facie desirable features of government which, virtually all hands concede, have been brought about by voter apathy, viz., stability and efficiency. Their critics have rightly pointed out that there are other desirable features of government, among which are social justice and improvement of the citizenry, and they are perhaps right in holding that the realists have not been sufficiently concerned with these features. Nevertheless, they surely have not shown that these will be secured by widespread participation in government. To begin, there is surely no evidence now to make it even probable that widespread participation would better promote the general good than does widespread apathy. As Dahl has recently argued, a group of active participants must be relatively small if it is to be efficient in making decisions, and yet the problems faced by large industrial societies require for their solution governments with authority over large numbers of persons.[3] It therefore seems reasonable to suppose that widespread participation in government would result either in policy setting and administrative bodies that are too large to move effectively against the problems which beset society, or else would result in a large number of small bodies that are efficient in making decisions but lack power to attack significant problems. In either case, although the benefits of government would perhaps be distributed more equally, it seems reasonable to suppose that no one could be significantly better off than he now is under a relatively stable and efficient government in which citizen participation is not great. And, although a state of affairs in which benefits are distributed more equally may in some circumstances be preferable to one in which a larger number of benefits is distributed, this is surely so only when the level of benefits enjoyed by the least favored members under the first distribution is significantly higher than that enjoyed by the least favored members under the second. Hence, even if it be granted that participation will allow unexpressed and unfulfilled desires to come to light, that the average citizen can acquire the knowledge sufficient to deal with the multifarious problems we face, and that most persons can transcend their personal, group, and class prejudices in order to work selflessly for the common good, there is reason to suppose that widespread participation would not better secure the public good, i.e., an acceptable amount of individual goods distributed in a reasonably just way.

One last point: in his paper in this volume, Braybrooke suggests that our culture condemns aloofness from the political process, its main reason being that "everyone stands to lose if the outcome is diminished by the failure of even one of the people eligible to participate to make his contribution, indeed the best contribution that he is capable of (taking into account his other responsibilities)." [4] There is reason to suppose that most persons in our culture make no such condemnation.[5] Nevertheless, even if Braybrooke is right in supposing that they do and even if he has correctly identified the ground of their condemnation, it is clear that the proposition advanced as ground is absurd. Political activity is an extraordinarily time-consuming activity, and there are, after all, other activities equally valuable. What is more, many persons are by temperament or native ability not particularly well suited to politics and government. I count myself as one such. For the most part I remain aloof from politics, but there is no reason at all to think that everyone in the United States, or even in the small town in which I live, has lost anything remotely worth having.

What, then, about human development? Here the realists' critics appear to be on even weaker ground. To begin, a moment's reflection discloses that participation in government is neither necessary nor sufficient for "full moral development." It is not necessary, for it is perfectly possible that a man have a vision of the common good and yet not take part in government or politics. Indeed, this often occurs when men believe that government is in tolerably good hands and that the common good will not better be served by their participation. Nor is it sufficient, for many who participate are not conspicuously better developed morally than those of us who do not. Nor is participation necessary for development of one's sense of self-esteem, for many persons who do not participate are not racked by doubts about their worth and doubtless many who do participate are prey to such doubts. Nor is participation necessary for identifying one's interests. In the case of the educated and articulate this is doubtless obvious enough; but, perhaps somewhat surprisingly, it seems also to be true of the uneducated and poverty-stricken.[6] In his paper included in this volume, Bachrach claims that the poor have interests which no one, not even themselves, can now identify; and he suggests that they may discover these interests through participation.[7] Bachrach's claim seems to me incredible, a perverse inversion of Scott Fitzgerald's famous remark that "The very rich are different from you and me." Surely, the problem is not that the interests of the poor are mysterious and opaque—being human, their important interests may be expected to be identical to those of any other economic class. Rather, the problem is that the structure of our economic and social arrangements is either such that their interests cannot be satisfied or else those who hold power are unwilling to allow them to be satisfied. Lastly, participation in government is neither necessary nor sufficient for being able to secure one's interests, although it is often a useful tool for so doing. However, it is doubtful whether it would continue to be a useful tool were everyone to use it: for, as was suggested in the paragraph above, were everyone to participate there is reason to think a state might result in which no one's interests are adequately met.

A caveat is in order here: I am suggesting only that actual participation in government is not reasonably supposed to be a prerequisite for full human development, not that this is true of the opportunity of participating. Perhaps it is true that, if a man has no opportunity of participating, if he could not participate even if he strongly desired to do so and bent all of his energies toward this end, his self-esteem, vision of the common good, and ability to safeguard his interests might suffer. But, since the realists in general think it important that citizens have the opportunity of participating, this is in no way inconsistent with their position.

Again, it perhaps may be objected that I have been unfair to the realists' critics, that what they maintain is not that participation in government inevitably makes one a better person, but rather that the level of human development would be higher in a society in which participation in government is widespread. Doubtless, this is at least part of what they are contending for; but, that it is true remains to be proven. Until this is done, their contention is the mere expression of a hope.

In sum, the realists have pointed to certain dangers which it may reasonably be supposed would result from widespread participation in government, viz., that it would be rendered so inefficient, powerless, or unstable that it could not carry out its ordinary and necessary functions, or could not carry them out well. Their critics have countered, not by providing evidence that widespread participation would have beneficial results, but rather by saying in effect that the realists have not shown that these benefits would not obtain. The critics are therefore perhaps justified in asserting that the realists' assessment of participation has not been proven to a certainty. Nevertheless, until they produce evidence which makes it reasonable to suppose that widespread participation would have the beneficial results they claim for it, it is surely more reasonable to adopt the realist position. As Hume once remarked, "A wise man . . . proportions his belief to the evidence," and in the present state of the controversy the evidence is on the side of the realists.

It is interesting to note, however, that both the realists and their critics agree that widespread participation in government is to be valued instrumentally, i.e., on the basis of whether it would have good or bad consequences. One critic, Lane Davis, suggested that classical democratic theory regards the "method of political democracy" (by which he means in part widespread participation in government) as being "valuable in itself regardless of the results which it produces," although he immediately robbed his suggestion of interest by assuring us that it is but a convenient, elliptical way of saying that the method results in a better citizenry.[8] Nevertheless, the suggestion is worth taking seriously in a nonelliptical way: for, if it is correct, a substantial amount of inefficiency and instability which might be caused by widespread participation might be overshadowed by its intrinsic goodness; and so it may be that we ought to adopt it as a social goal even though we do not expect it to have more good results than bad. In what follows I shall attempt to foreclose this line of attack against the realists.

The notion of intrinsic goodness is notoriously difficult—so much so that many philosophers profess not to understand it. However, since I shall not attempt to show that anything is intrinsically good, but rather to show that something is not, I shall bypass the difficulties of explicating the notion in favor of framing a necessary condition for something's being intrinsically good. Intrinsically good things are said to be good in themselves, independently of all other things (including their consequences), and it is held that their goodness is apparent to us upon reflection. Seizing upon this last supposed feature of intrinsically good things, we might be inclined to think that a thing can be intrinsically good only if under any circumstances whatever it cannot reasonably be denied to be good: that is, if someone denies under any circumstances that such a thing is good, he must either not have sufficiently reflected upon its value, or else his reasons for his denial must either themselves lack rational support or must obviously fail to support his contention.

However, this condition is too strong. If we are to take the notion of intrinsic goodness seriously, we ought obviously not adopt a necessary condition which eliminates all possible candidates. And, it is plausible to suppose that adopting this condition would have this effect. It is often held that pleasure and acting on moral principle are intrinsically good, and I shall take them to be among the most obvious candidates for this title. There are, however, circumstances in which these things may reasonably be denied to be good. Thus, it is sometimes held that sadistic pleasure is positively bad— not merely that the activity which produces the pleasure is bad, but that the pleasure itself is bad and makes a state of affairs in which pain is inflicted worse than it otherwise would have been. And, it is sometimes held that there is no value in conscientious action when, because a person has mistaken moral principles or is ignorant of a situation, his action has disastrous results. Now, these latter contentions may be mistaken. According to Moore's principle of organic wholes,[9] the intrinsic value of a state of affairs is not determined by the intrinsic values of its parts; and so perhaps the correct thing to say of sadistic pleasure and unfortunate conscientious action is that they are goods which at times can contribute to bad states of affairs. Nevertheless, it is surely not *unreasonable* to deny that pleasure and conscientious action are in such circumstances good: we may not accept this contention, but we can feel its tug and understand why someone might hold it. Hence, if we adopt this first condition for intrinsic goodness, we must rule out pleasure and conscientious action and, I believe, all other candidates as well.

Nevertheless, we can frame a weaker condition that yet does justice to the supposed fact that the goodness of intrinsically good things is supposed to be apparent to all reasonable men. We might say that things of a certain kind X can be intrinsically good only if it is unreasonable for anyone to deny that a particular x is good, provided that he admits that x is not the result of a bad state of affairs and has no bad consequences. I believe that virtually all things that are commonly supposed to be intrinsically good will meet this condition. Let us revert to the example of pleasure. Were someone to admit that a person's pleasure was not brought about by a bad state of affairs and had no bad consequences, and were he yet to deny that the pleasure was good, I think we should consider him unreasonable. At the very least we should demand of him a reason for denying it to be good: were he to say "I don't know why I refuse to count it good, but I just do," we should not adopt this as a reasonable stance, conflicting as it does with the reflective judgment of virtually all moralists and moral philosophers, who are nearly unanimous in considering innocent pleasure to be a good worth promoting.[10] And, it is difficult to think of a reason he might offer that we would accept. Were he to say, e.g., that God does not favor happiness, the theists among us might accept this as a relevant consideration; but surely no one would admit that there is evidence as to make it reasonable to believe that God holds such an attitude. Or, were he to say that his father did not favor pleasure and that that is sufficient reason for him, we should deny that this bears at all upon the question of whether pleasure is a good. A similar argument is easily devised to show that acting on moral principle passes the weaker condition for intrinsic goodness.

Since, therefore, the weaker condition allows intrinsic goodness to those things commonly considered to have it and since it does justice to the belief that the goodness of intrinsically good things is revealed upon reflection to reasonable men, we are then justified in using it as a negative test for intrinsic goodness. And it is, I think, plain that participation in government fails this test. It is surely not unreasonable to hold that participation has no value except when it has good results, and so not unreasonable to deny that someone's participating is good while admitting that it has no bad consequences and was not brought about by an untoward state of affairs. Indeed, it is surely because most persons hold this position that the controversy between the realists and their critics has been confined to the results of participation. Participation is therefore not intrinsically good, and so there is no intrinsic value in widespread participation in government which could balance off any instability or inefficiency which might result from it.

This has two immediate consequences. First, it implies that the battle between the realists and their critics has been joined on the right ground. Widespread participation in government, and so democracy according to the classical model, has no value in itself: if it is valuable at all, it is so because of its consequences. Second, it implies that, since the value of widespread participation is determined by its consequences and since this is an empirical matter, whether it is valuable is primarily a question for political science and not one for political philosophy. The only useful role for the philosopher in the controversy between the realists and their critics is to set out clearly and concisely the opposing positions and, on the basis of the evidence offered in support of each, to assess their cogency. In the earlier portions of this paper I have attempted to do this.

NOTES AND REFERENCES

1. Many of the most noted contemporary political theorists count as realists, and so it would be both tedious and unnecessary to provide a bibliography of realist theorists. However, were one to pick out a single work as representative of the realist view on citizen participation, perhaps the best choice would be G. Almond and S. Verba, *The Civic Culture* (Princeton, 1963), chap. viii. I have taken the term "realist" from L. Davis, "The Cost of Realism: Contemporary Restatements of Democracy," reprinted in C. A. McCoy and J. Playford, *Apolitical Politicals* (New York, 1967).
2. The most important papers critical of the realist celebration of citizen apathy are collected in McCoy and Playford, *Apolitical Politicals*. These include: C. Bay, "Politics and Pseudopolitics: A Critical Evaluation of Some Behavioral Literature"; G. Duncan and S. Lukes, "The New Democracy"; L. Davis, "The Cost of Realism"; and J. L. Walker, "A Critique of the Elitist Theory of Democracy." P. Bachrach's *The Theory of Democratic Elites* (Boston, 1967) is an important criticism of the realists, as is his paper in this volume.
3. R. A. Dahl, *After the Revolution?* (New Haven, 1970), especially pp. 64-77.
4. This volume, chapter 3.
5. Cf. Almond and Verba, *The Civic Culture,* chap. v.
6. Cf. L. Lipsitz, "On Political Belief: The Grievances of the Poor," in P. Green and S. Levinson, eds., *Power and Community* (New York, 1969).
7. This volume, chapter 2.
8. Davis, "Cost of Realism," p. 190.
9. G. E. Moore, *Principia Ethica* (Cambridge, 1903), p. 27f.

10. It may be objected that the mere fact that reflective men are nearly unanimous in thinking innocent pleasure a good in no way shows that it is unreasonable to deny it to be good without having a reason, particularly in view of the fact that there is no accepted explanation of why innocent pleasure is a good. This objection touches upon fundamental issues in moral philosophy, whether moral judgments are true or false, whether moral positions can be reasonable or unreasonable, etc. I cannot deal with these questions here. Nevertheless, it is worth noting that there are many propositions which are reasonable to believe without reason, but unreasonable to deny without reason, e.g., the principle of contradiction, the principle of sufficient reason, that there are other minds, etc. I believe that a good many ethical propositions fall in this category and that, if virtually all reflective men agree upon a particular moral judgment without having a reason for believing it, there is good reason to place it in this category.

PART II

7

PARTICIPATION IN GOVERNMENTAL PROCESSES: A SKETCH OF THE EXPANDING LAW

SAMUEL MERMIN

In thinking of what constitutes public participation in government processes,[1] one tends to seek examples first of *direct* participation. There are of course town meetings and initiative and referendum procedures. But the most frequent example is voting for representatives (turning into *indirect* participation in government through representatives).

VOTING

The field of voting, indeed, now involves a much broader participation than it once did. Recent Supreme Court decisions have applied federal statutes and the Constitution so as to overcome certain barriers to voting: racial discrimination; poll taxes; English literacy requirements; restrictive state requirements on residency and absentee voting; disqualification of voters aged 18 to 20; and provisions requiring that voters in school board elections be parents or property owners, that voters on certain bond issues be property taxpayers, and that military residents be excluded from voting.[2] Other Supreme Court decisions have attempted to insure a roughly egalitarian participation through the one-man one-vote rule.[3] The attempt to invalidate a state law denying ex-felons the right to vote failed in 1974, but largely because of the language of Sec. 2 of the 14th Amendment itself, which seemed to assume the validity of such disfranchisement.[4] As for participation by would-be candidates, the Supreme Court has blocked some state statutory restraints on ballot access by candidates who are impecunious, represent minority parties, or are running independently,[5] though some restraints deemed reasonable have been upheld.[6]

ADMINISTRATION

Further, one thinks of the citizen's participation in government administration. This field deserves a more extended mention, because it is not as well known or perhaps not as readily remembered. One is aware, of course, of indirect public participation through representatives—members of executive or administrative agencies—who have been either popularly elected or, more usually, appointed by the elected executive. One may be further aware of public participation in "advisory committees" of various government bodies—perhaps because of recent Congressional hearings, and the resulting statute which may broaden the representation and improve the system of advisory committees throughout the Government.[7]

But the term "participation" seems more appropriately applied when the participation through representatives is not in far-off Washington or state capitols but in the "grass roots." Examples would be the role of citizen groups and local governments in administration of the TVA program; of local farmer committees in administering the loan program of the New Deal's Farm Security Administration (to be distinguished from the *direct* participation represented by currently familiar farmers' *referenda,* in which a specified percentage of farmer votes is needed before a marketing program affecting them becomes legally valid); of the thousands of local price and rationing boards of World War II, composed of unpaid volunteers appointed by OPA district directors from those nominated by the community; of the use of citizen advisory committees by OPA and other agencies; of the thousands of local draft boards, whose unpaid members were appointed by the president from the governor's nominees.[8]

Of special contemporary import is the legislation of the 1960s in the antipoverty, housing, health, and education fields. The Economic Opportunity Act of 1964 as amended [42 U.S.C. 2791 (f)] authorized the setting up of "community action" boards with at least one-third of the members chosen democratically so as to assure representation of the poor in the area served. The law emphasized that the poor and the area residents were to be able to influence the character of programs affecting their interests and regularly participate in planning and implementation. "Maximum feasible participation" of this kind was called for.[9] Under the "model cities" legislation of 1966, a city demonstration program is eligible for assistance under the Act only if it is of sufficient magnitude to provide, among other things, "widespread citizen participation in the program" [42 U.S.C. 3303(a)(2)]; and a 1968 amendment to the Housing Act of 1937 [42 U.S.C. 1415(10)], in the provision for financing of service programs for tenants in low-rent public housing, gives "preference to programs providing for the maximum feasible participation of the tenants" in formulating and operating the program.

A number of federal provisions in the field of health "provide for some form of citizen participation in the planning and delivery of health services."[10] Congress in 1970 authorized the Commissioner of Education to encourage "parental participation" in educational programs at the State or local level [20 U.S.C. 1231(d)]; and there have been administrative regulations along this line dating from even before the statutory authorization.[11] New York school legislation illustrated the desire for more public participation by its provision for locally elected community school boards for New York City, which were to exercise some of the power previously concentrated in an appointed central board.[12]

OPPORTUNITY TO BE HEARD ADMINISTRATIVELY

Another expanding type of participation is in the opportunity to be heard administratively before adverse government action is taken, as distinguished from taking part in administration of government action.

a. Consider first the situations of individuals or groups against whom the government action is being directly taken. Courts have come to recognize the constitutional right of public housing tenants to be fully heard administratively before eviction or refusal to renew leases.[13] A hearing, not on the full trial-type model but including some opportunity to present the tenant's views, on proposed rent increases, has been accorded to public housing tenants[14] and sometimes to tenants in government subsidized private housing.[15] A similar right of the locally affected public to be heard administratively in connection with urban renewal has been statutorily recognized.[16] Courts are now acknowledging that public university students have a constitutional right to an almost full administrative hearing (i.e., almost the trial-type model) before suspension or expulsion, and that even public school students in this situation are entitled to certain minimal procedural safeguards.[17] The Supreme Court has substantially liberalized previous procedures by recognizing the right of welfare recipients to an almost full administrative hearing before termination of benefits,[18] a rather similar hearing right of parolees and probationers before parole or probation revocation,[19] and a lesser administrative hearing right before imposition of discipline on prisoners for alleged misconduct within the prison.[20]

Also more fully recognized in recent years are the hearing rights of those doing business with, or employed by, the Government. In spite of an earlier view that the Government need not extend due process in dealing with its contractors, courts now would doubtless follow a leading 1964 Court of Appeals decision[21] to the effect that a Government contractor cannot be administratively "debarred" or suspended from dealing with the Government without having had a full opportunity to be heard at an administrative hearing. As for public employees, the Supreme Court has held: (1) A professor or teacher who is discharged while holding a tenured job, or before expiration of the period for which he has an express or implied employment contract, has a constitutional due process right to a full predischarge hearing. (2) Even the public employee with a limited-term contract, and neither an express nor implied assurance of renewal, is entitled to a full hearing before nonrenewal *if* the reason for nonrenewal is constitutionally impermissible, e.g., employer opposition to the employee's exercise of free speech rights.[22] The Court has found it constitutional, however, for the federal Government to allow less than a full administrative hearing (a written response) prior to discharge of a civil service employee, where a full hearing would be allowed upon an appeal within the administrative structure, and with the right to back-pay benefits if the employee won on appeal.[23]

Licensees or would-be licensees within a profession or business, or other activity subject to licensing, are not in all circumstances or in every jurisdiction entitled to an administrative hearing before the license can be withheld or revoked. Though there are some well-known cases in which the constitutional right of an opportunity to be heard was recognized,[24] a number of jurisdictions are still under the spell of the thought that a license is a mere privilege which the grantor can grant, withhold, or revoke under whatever conditions the grantor sees fit to recognize—especially in the case of less "respectable" businesses such as taverns and pool halls. As one case put it, "due process . . . does not apply to matters concerning liquor licenses."[25] But even as to liquor, a much-cited federal case on local liquor licensing has pointed the other way.[26] And so, as to licensing generally, has an influential Supreme Court case of 1971 dealing with suspension of auto drivers licenses: ". . . it is fundamental that except in emergency situations . . . due process requires that when a State seeks to terminate an interest such as that here involved, it must afford 'notice and opportunity for hearing appropriate to the nature of the case' *before* the termination becomes effective . . ."[27] As a leading commentator stated in 1972: "Many licenses that were once regarded as privileges have become rights. The movement is strong and clear, although some traces of the privilege doctrine remain in the state courts."[28]

Indeed, in most of the types of cases above considered (the public employee, the welfare recipient, etc.) we are witnessing a massive erosion of the traditional legal view that recipients of Government benefits or largesse have mere "privileges" rather than constitutional rights to fair procedure.[29]

b. Consider now the situation where the individuals or groups involved are not the specific object of adverse government action but wish to participate in an agency proceeding which they think may adversely affect their interest. Of course, the Administrative Procedure Act has long provided that an "interested person may appear" in federal agency proceedings "so far as the orderly conduct of public business permits" [5 U.S. Code 555 (b)] and has long required the giving of notice of rule-making hearings, and giving "interested persons an opportunity to participate in the rule-making through submission of written data, views, or arguments with or without opportunity for oral presentation" [5 U.S. Code 553 (c)]. Some statutes applying to particular agencies have analogous provisions. In 1966, representatives of the listening public were held to have standing to intervene as statutory "parties in interest" under the Federal Communications Act, to contest in FCC hearings the renewal of a TV station license. Chief Justice Burger (then D.C. Court of Appeals judge) argued that "experience demonstrates consumers are generally among the best vindicators of the public interest. In order to safeguard the public interest in broadcasting, therefore, we hold that some 'audience participation' must be allowed in license renewal proceedings." [30] In 1970, welfare organizations and individual welfare recipients were held to have standing (though the Social Security Act had no language construable as conferring standing) to intervene and fully participate in HEW "conformity hearings" to determine whether certain state welfare laws were in conformity with the federal Act's standards.[31]

To be noted also is the fact that the influence of a participating citizens' organization may extend beyond its formal participation in the hearing. A book from Ralph Nader's Center for Study of Responsive Law points to "negotiated settlements between intervenors and licensees" as a technique successfully used in some proceedings before the AEC and FCC. The settlement creates a "contract between a licensee and a citizens' group which has intervened in opposition to the granting of a license by the agency in question. In exchange for withdrawal of opposition by the citizen group, the licensee promises to provide environmental safeguards or to eliminate discrimination in employment." [32]

There are limits, however, to the possibility of intervention. While it seems presently to be true that, with some exceptions, "intervention has assumed the proportions of a right, even where the applicable statute or rules are phrased permissively," [33] still a proposed intervention can be blocked by a restrictive interpretation of the above-quoted Administrative Procedure Act provisions on "orderly conduct of public business" and on the permission to "appear" (as distinct from having full rights of participation).[34] Another limitation resides in the fact that the above-stated participation opportunities embodied in the Administrative Procedure Act's rule-making provisions are inapplicable to, among other things, proceedings relating to "public property, loans, grants, benefits or contracts."[35] In 1969 the Administrative Conference of the U.S. recommended eliminating this exception.[36] So did the 1970 Report of the Public Land Law Review Commission, as far as public lands are concerned.[37]

A variety of other factors may limit intervention. To name a few: Agencies may be less willing to allow intervention in an adjudicative proceeding (as distinguished from rule-making), or to listen to a public intervenor's contentions in such proceeding when the contentions are tangential to the main issue, or are more appropriately raised in a rule-making proceeding which is then pending or which the intervenor can petition for. Agencies may be less willing to allow intervention where the prospective intervenor's interest is not direct, substantial, and unrepresented by existing parties, or the proceeding is focused on past misconduct in order to determine whether an individual cease and desist order should be issued or an individual broker's license revoked; or less willing where a consent order is being negotiated, prior to agency filling of the complaint on which an adjudicatory hearing would be based.[38]

Realization in the latter 1960s and early 1970s that public participation in agency proceedings had been rather restricted in scope and effectiveness stimulated a number of scholarly studies[39] and a push for reforms. Consumer and public interest organizations circulated among the agencies in 1970 a set of model rules for broadened citizen participation.[40] The Administrative Conference of the U.S. in 1971 made recommendations along similar lines.[41] It asked that public participation be freely allowed in ordinary rule-making ("notice and comment rule-making")—with the agency, to the extent feasible, making available the documents, etc., on which the proposed rule was based. Public participation was also to be freely allowed in trial-type proceedings ("adjudicatory" hearings and "on-the-record rule-making") where agency action was likely to affect the interests asserted.[42] But here the

Conference laid down some limits in the case of enforcement and license revocation proceedings[43]; listed some factors for balancing in the process of "selection of intervenors" [44]; set some bounds on the "scope" of participation[45]; and pointed to ways of reducing the financial burden on intervenors, including making less expensive transcripts available, and furnishing information, staff assistance, and access to experts.[46] Agencies were also asked to give better public notice of their proceedings.[47]

An earlier recommendation of the Administrative Conference had been for representation of the interests of the poor by a People's Counsel (which, it was suggested, might take the form of a public corporation like the Corporation for Public Broadcasting) in federal agency rule-making proceedings substantially affecting the poor, as well as in judicial review.[48] Senator Edward Kennedy subsequently sponsored a bill for representation of the public interest before several major administrative agencies by a public counsel corporation funded by government and directed by a board of Presidential appointees [S.3434, 91 Cong. 2 Sess. (1970)].[49] In the last few years, a sharply contested bill for representation of consumer interests before federal administrative agencies and courts by a Consumer Counsel or Agency for Consumer Advocacy has been close to passage.[50] Expanded public participation in antitrust proceedings has been proposed, before the FTC and Department of Justice as well as in court; and the Administrative Conference of the United States, as well as others, has urged broader participation by the ultimate beneficiaries of federal grant-in-aid programs, in enforcement of the federal standards for such programs.[51]

Finally, three attenuated forms of participation or opportunity to be heard administratively should be mentioned: (1) The first is represented by the institution of the "ombudsman," an official receiver of public complaints about the action or inaction of government officials. Citizen participation may be discerned not only in the filing of complaints. Through the ombudsman's power to investigate, recommend, criticize, and publicize, members of the public may be said to be vicariously taking part or being heard in the process of rectifying government deficiencies, and more effectively than they could on their own. Long used in some European countries, the device is making some, though very slow, headway in American federal, state, and local governments. (2) The second is the "freedom of information" type of statute, already enacted in a few states, and enacted by Congress in 1966 and strengthened in 1974. Though excluding some categories of information from coverage, these laws make large amounts of agency information available to requesting citizens. In addition to the fact that the request for and receipt of such information might itself be viewed as a kind of participation, it seems clear that the process makes citizen participation in subsequent government proceedings more effective because it is more knowledgeable. (3) The third is a form of administrative participation which may not deserve to be called "participation" at all because of its silent and passive character. I refer to what is aimed at by the recent movement for legislation throwing open to the public the meetings of public bodies. A large number of states have enacted these "sunshine" or "open meeting" laws, though not many are adequately enforced or have sufficient breadth to cover most state and local bodies.[52]

OPPORTUNITY TO BE HEARD IN COURT

The necessary "standing" to represent a consumer or public interest before a *court* is not governed by exactly the same considerations as those governing participation in the agency proceeding.[53] For example, some restraint on standing that is not expressly applicable to agency proceedings comes from a constitutional requirement (the "case or controversy" clause) applicable to standing in a federal court, and from a substantially similar restraint recognized in state courts. However, this generation, and especially in recent years, has witnessed an expanding interpretation of "standing" in court, not only for consumers of goods and services[54] but also for users and appreciators of the environment[55] —indeed, as the Supreme Court said in 1970, for anyone whose interests are in fact injured and who comes within a "zone of interest" protected by the statutory or constitutional provision involved.[56] This latter approach brought a certain amount of clarity and liberalization to the confusing mass of case-law on standing, once described by Justice Frankfurter as a "complicated specialty of federal jurisdiction." But the meaning of the new test is not altogether clear. And it has been forcibly argued that the "zone of interest" portion adds an ambiguous and restrictive element to a test which would better read in terms of "injury in fact" alone (in the absence of affirmative indication of a legislative intent to restrict).[57] At any rate, it has been possible, under its current approach, for the Supreme Court to say that the necessary legal interest to support standing need not be economic—it may be aesthetic, conservational, recreational, or spiritual.[58]

An indication of how accommodating this attitude can be for the standing of citizens' environmental groups in court was given in a 1973 case, in which SCRAP, a Washington, D.C. environmental group was suing to restrain enforcement of an ICC order which had allowed a′ 2½% emergency surcharge on railroad freight rates to go into effect.[59] The Supreme Court had no trouble with the "zone of interest" requirement,[60] or in finding that the necessary "injury" existed. The chief injury claimed was that the freight rate increases caused "increased use of nonrecyclable commodities as compared to recyclable goods, thus resulting in the need to use more natural resources to produce such goods, some of which resources might be taken from the Washington area, and resulting in more refuse that might be discarded in national parks in the Washington area." [61] The Court made clear that standing was not to be denied because the plaintiffs would be suffering the injury together with large numbers of others who were not suing,[62] or because the alleged injury was small.[63] The alleged injury was "direct" and "perceptible," plaintiffs having alleged actual use of the Washington metropolitan area resources in question (for camping, hiking, fishing, and sightseeing) rather than a mere "interest" in environmentalism. True, the chain of causation assumed in the allegation may have been dubious, but the case, the Court emphasized, was at the pleading stage, and since it was conceivable that the plaintiffs could prove their assumptions, the allegations were sufficient to withstand a pretrial motion to dismiss.[64] The attitude here shown toward the "injury in fact" test is a liberal one—though other recent cases suggest that the Court may on occasion take a tougher view of what constitutes the necessary "direct," "concrete," or "specific" injury.[65]

Liberalization has also occurred in the area of taxpayer standing in court. Overruling in 1968 a traditional view that the economic interest of a federal taxpayer was too remote to give standing for an attack on expenditures of general Treasury funds, the Court recognized a federal taxpayer's standing to attack certain expenditures of educational funds as violating the church-state separation clause of the First Amendment.[66] Standing as a federal taxpayer was to be recognized only where the attack was on constitutionality of exercises of Congressional power under the taxing and spending clause, and when the constitutional clause allegedly violated was a "specific" restriction on federal expenditure. The Court has already applied these limitations to bar some taxpayer suits.[67]

Significance of the trend toward liberalized standing is of course increased by the contemporary ascendancy of two techniques for maximizing the public's access to courts: (1) the "class action," which makes economically feasible the bringing of lawsuits by consumers, welfare recipients, etc., who could not afford to bring individual lawsuits[68]; (2) availability of "public interest" law centers and law firms to bring the lawsuits—whether class actions or otherwise.[69]

Standing is not the only area in which the court participation right has been enhanced. Supreme Court cases have been recognizing a right to be heard in court at an *earlier* stage of certain legal processes than has traditionally been permitted: the right of a wage earner to be heard in court before part of his wages is "frozen" through garnishment by his creditor, rather than merely in the later court hearing on the alleged debt[70]; the right of an unwed father, who had been living with the children and their mother, to a court hearing after the mother's death on the question of his fitness, before the children could be taken away from him.[71] It was thought in 1972 that the Supreme Court had also recognized the right of a buyer of goods on a conditional sales contract to a court hearing before rather than after the goods are seized for alleged nonpayment—but now this right is only somewhat more available than it was prior to 1972.[72]

These decisions are in addition to those specifically focused on enlarging participation of the *poor* in court processes—by invalidating a state's refusal to permit a divorce action by an indigent unable to pay certain court fees,[73] by invalidating a state's refusal to permit a criminal appeal by an indigent unable to pay the cost of the transcript necessary for the appeal,[74] and by ruling that no criminal defendant who has not waived his right to counsel can be sentenced to any jail term without having been represented by counsel of his own or by free counsel if he can't afford his own.[75]

In addition to the poor, certain other classes of litigants have been accorded greater participation rights than previously enjoyed. The traditional paternalistic attitude toward juveniles has given way to granting them almost as full an opportunity to be heard on the delinquency adjudication as an adult would have on criminal charges.[76] The sex deviate who has, after a criminal court hearing, been convicted of a sex crime, and instead of being sentenced could under the statutes be institutionally examined and recommended for a treatment commitment, can now insist upon a full court hearing before such commitment.[77] In the case of the criminal defendant who has been found not guilty by reason of insanity at the time of the alleged offense, some courts are finding that an *automatic* commitment thereafter for institutional examination, and, if necessary, treatment (as opposed to an immediate hearing in court on whether the acquitted defendant's present mental state requires institutional commitment) is invalid.[78] In civil commitments for mental illness, some courts are beginning to recognize that fuller hearing rights than have traditionally been granted are constitutionally required.[79]

A final aspect worth noting about court participation is that, as far as court review of federal agencies is concerned, the Supreme Court has come to recognize a *presumption* that Congress intended the administrative action to be reviewable in court.[80] At the same time, the Court has not yet determined that Congress cannot preclude judicial review of allegedly arbitrary administrative decisions; i.e., has not determined that there is a *constitutional right* to judicial review of the substance of administrative decisions—including those arrived at by fair procedure.[81]

MISCELLANEOUS

I have been discussing participation in the adjudicative process. One might argue further that the very nature of our *adversary system* of adjudication underscores the participative aspect of the role of the litigant's counsel: the opportunity for full presentation of his own arguments and version of the facts, in a system permitting full cross-examination and rebuttal of the opposing side. In a nonadversary system, the participation of the litigants' counsel is less and that of the judge greater.

My reference to "counsel" stems of course from the fact that the typical participation in adjudication is not direct; it is through lawyers. But some are now urging more direct participation, at least in some kinds of cases (e.g., welfare, criminal) via either self-representation or the use of lawyers in an advisory rather than a controlling role.[82] Even today in a criminal case the defendant has the ultimate authority, after consulting counsel, on the decisions whether to plead guilty, whether to waive jury trial, and whether to testify on his own behalf.[83] In civil cases it has generally been held that without the client's authority the attorney cannot compromise or settle the case, or ask on behalf of the plaintiff for dismissal on the merits. But all this still leaves the main burden of preparing and conducting criminal and civil cases on the attorney. Should the client have much greater participation?

A blunderbuss attack in terms of "everyman his own lawyer," is almost as senseless as an "everyman his own doctor" prescription. But in medicine we are witnessing a movement supporting a broader meaning and more vigorous application of the notion of "informed consent." Similarly, it has seemed desirable to some observers to allow greater participation by the client in his legal case, not in the sense of performance at the trial but at least in receiving full information and explanation from his lawyer on each aspect and stage of the case, discussing the problems with his lawyer, and retaining ultimate authority to make the major decisions. Something like this has been called, in a recent study, a "participatory model" for lawyer-client relations as distinct from the "traditional model" in which the lawyer is in complete charge, keeping the client in relative ignorance.[84] The "traditional model" was found to prevail in practice, though the theoretical foundations of the other model were laid down in 1969 by the American Bar Association's new Code of Professional Responsibility.[85] What makes particular sense about more participation by the client is that, in general, the client bears the burden of the mistakes of his agent, the lawyer[86]—with only an uncertain right of recovery against the lawyer for negligence.[87]

In the court process there is another form of lay participation, the *jury*—which gained greater breadth by Supreme Court decisions invalidating systematic exclusions of racial minorities and, more recently, of women, from jury service in criminal cases.[88] Jury service of course is lay participation on less broad a scale than that found in the "comrades courts" in Marxist countries. There one can find a public participation even in the police function, through the volunteer·people's police.[89] In this country, too, there are calls for community control, and neighborhood control, of the police.[90]

But at present, public participation in *enforcement* activity is perhaps best illustrated by lawsuits or interventions or "amicus curiae" participation by environmentalist and public interest law groups because of alleged law violations. Some statutes specifically authorize citizen enforcement suits against law violators.[91] These are of course supplemented by informal enforcement through infrequent vigilante groups or posses, as well as by "whistle blowing" on offenders through co-employees' or citizens' complaints to Ralph Nader or to the relevant government agency.

What I have sketched is, in large part, formalistic, superficial, and incomplete. It is concerned mainly with rights of participation laid down by legislatures or courts, and to some extent with participation practices. But I have not attempted to explore the degree to which the rights on the books have become rights in action, or the scope, nature, and diffusion of the participative practices. Empirical studies are necessary to flesh out my skeletal outline. For instance, the University of Chicago Jury Project has helped correct our theoretical views of how the jury participates in our system. Some studies of the operation of the statutory "maximum feasible participation" standard suggest that it has generated, in Moynihan's phrase, "maximum feasible misunderstanding." [92] Administration of voting laws deviates from the court decisions. And so on. Neither have I systematically confronted the normative issues: optimum solutions to the problems arising from existing public participation, or the issue of to what extent an increasing public participation, in the various areas considered, is "a good thing."

NOTES AND REFERENCES

1. As originally presented orally, this paper concerned itself with two additional aspects of the meaning of participation to one trained in law and jurisprudence. Those additional aspects were excised because they were deemed incongruent with the focus of the rest of the volume. An excised

portion dealing with the problem of defining "participation," viewed as analogous to the problem of defining "law," appears in slightly revised form in Samuel Mermin, "On Defining 'Law'—A Dissent from Fuller's Approach," 6 *Indiana L. Rev.* 683 (1973). The present paper is confined to outlining the ways in which the legal system has recently been expanding its allowance of public participation in government processes. Restricting myself in this way, I am not concerned with participation in such nongovernment activity as community economic enterprise, which some members of Congress have urged for ghetto residents. See S.33, 91 Cong., 1 sess. (1969); S.3875, 90 Cong., 2 sess. (1968); John A. C. Hetherington, "Community Participation: A Critical View," 36 *Law and Contemp. Prob.* 13, 16 (1971). Nor have I concerned myself with the indirect participation which is represented by political campaign contributions or by pressure upon, or lobbying, a government agency.

2. South Carolina v. Katzenbach, 383 U.S. 301 (1966); Harper v. Va. State Bd. of Elections, 383 U.S. 663 (1966); Katzenbach v. Morgan, 384 U.S. 641 (1966); Dunn v. Blumstein, 405 U.S. 330 (1972); Oregon v. Mitchell, 400 U.S. 112 (1970); Kramer v. Union Free School District, 395 U.S. 621 (1969); Cipriano v. City of Houma, 395 U.S. 701 (1969); City of Phoenix v. Kolodziejski, 399 U.S. 204 (1970); Carrington v. Rash, 380 U.S. 89 (1965).

3. E.g., Reynolds v. Sims, 377 U.S. 533 (1964); Wesberry v. Sanders, 376 U.S. 1 (1964); Avery v. Midland County, 390 U.S. 474 (1968); Hadley v. Junior College District of Metrop. Kansas City, 397 U.S. 50 (1970); Mahan v. Howell, 410 U.S. 315 (1973); Gaffney v. Cummings, 412 U.S. 735 (1973); White v. Regester, 412 U.S. 755 (1973).

4. Richardson v. Ramirez, 418 U.S. 24 (1974).

5. Williams v. Rhodes, 393 U.S. 23 (1968); Bullock v. Carter, 405 U.S. 134 (1972).

6. See discussion in "The Supreme Court, 1973 Term," 88 *Harv. L. Rev.* 91-101 (1974).

7. See Public Law 92-463, 86 Statutes at Large 770 (1972), and the legislative history summarized in 2 U.S. Code and Congressional Service, 92nd Cong., 2d Sess. (1972), pp. 3491-3512; Markham, "The Federal Advisory Committee Act," 35 *U. of Pitt. L. Rev.* 557 (1974).

8. Comment, "The Role of Citizen Advisory Boards in Administration of Natural Resources," 50 *Oregon L. Rev.* 153 (1971); Barlow Burke, Jr., "The Threat to Citizen Participation in Model Cities," 56 *Cornell L. Rev.* 751 at 751-5 (1971); Joseph P. Witherspoon, "The Bureaucracy as Representatives," in J. Roland Pennock and John W. Chapman, eds., *Representation:* Nomos X (New York: Atherton Press, 1968), pp. 245-253; Philip Selznick, *TVA and the Grass Roots* (Berkeley: University of California Press, 1949); Sidney Baldwin, *Poverty and Politics: Rise and Decline of the Farm Security Administration* (Chapel Hill: University of North Carolina Press, 1968); Imogene H. Putnam, *Volunteers in OPA* (Washington: Government Printing Office, 1947); Harvey C. Mansfield, Jr., *A Short History of OPA* (Washington: Government Printing Office, 1947), pp. 241-252; James W. Davis and Kenneth M. Dolbeare, *Little Groups of Neighbors: The Selective Service System* (Chicago: Markham, 1968).

9. See Note, "Participation of the Poor: Section 202(a)(3) Organizations under the Economic Opportunity Act of 1964," 75 *Yale L.J.* 599 (1966); Daniel Moynihan, *Maximum Feasible Misunderstanding: Community Action in the War on Poverty* (New York: Free Press, 1969).

10. See Barry A. Herzog, "Participation by the Poor in Federal Health Programs," 1970 *Wis. L. Rev.* 682.
11. See Note, 1972 *Wis. L. Rev.* 583.
12. N.Y. Education Law, Art. 52-A (McKinney Supp. 1971). See discussion in Howard I. Kalodner, "The Right to Participate," in Norman Dorsen, ed., *The Rights of Americans* 203-5 (1970).
13. Thorpe v. Housing Authority of City of Durham, 393 U.S. 268 (1969); Glover v. Housing Authority of City of Bessemer, Ala., 444 F.2d 158 (5 Cir., 1971); Caulder v. Durham Housing Authority, 433 F.2d 998 (4 Cir., 1970) cert. den. 401 U.S. 1003 (1971); Escalera v. N.Y. City Housing Authority, 425 F.2d 852 (2 Cir., 1970). The first two cases enforced the right under agency regulations. The latter two went further, to recognize a due process constitutional right to a full hearing—though they recognized the possibility that in some circumstances there might be a compelling Government interest in a more summary form of adjudication. These two cases have also been distinguished on the ground that under the relevant state eviction statutes, the eviction proceeding in state court did not afford a full hearing on the facts allegedly justifying eviction, hence the full administrative hearing was necessary. Johnson v. Tamsberg, 430 F.2d 1125 (4 Cir. 1970).
14. Burr v. New Rochelle Municipal Housing Authority, 479 F.2d 1165 (2 Cir., 1973) (due process grounds); Thompson v. Washington, 497 F.2d 626 (D.C. Cir., 1974) (statutory grounds).
15. Geneva Towers Tenants Organiz. v. Fed. Mtge. Investors, 504 F.2d 483 (9 Cir., 1974). This involved privately built housing for low and moderate income tenants, under Sec. 221(d) (3) of the Housing Act of 1961, subsidized by low-interest Government loans and certain tax advantages. Contrary to the *Geneva Towers* decision are Hahn v. Gottlieb, 430 F.2d 1243 (1 Cir. 1970); Langevin v. Chenango Court, 447 F.2d 296 (2 Cir. 1971). Agreeing with the *Geneva Towers* result on statutory grounds is Marshall v. Lynn, 497 F.2d 643 (D.C. Cir. 1973). The latter court arrived at a contrary result when it dealt with housing constructed under Sec. 220 of the Housing Act as part of area redevelopment plans, with Government loan guarantees—there being no Congressional intent apparent to benefit any particular class of tenants. Tenants' Council of T. I.–C. Sq. v. Lynn, 497 F. 2d 648 (D.C. Cir. 1974). For a general discussion, see Note, "Procedural Due Process in Government-Subsidized Housing," 86 *Harv. L. Rev.* 880 (1973).
16. See, e.g., Powellton Civic Home Owners' Assoc. v. H.U.D., 284 F.Supp. 809 (E.D. Pa. 1968), enforcing a statutory right to present written evidence. Standing of such plaintiffs to be heard in *court* is now well recognized, though previously dubious. See Shannon v. U.S. Dept. of H.U.D., 436 F.2d 809 (3 Cir., 1970); Norwalk CORE v. Norwalk Redevel. Agency, 395 F.2d 920 (2 Cir. 1968).
17. On university students, see Note, "Judicial Review of the University-Student Relationship: Expulsion and Governance," 26 *Stanf. L. Rev.* 95 (1973); Note, "Students' Constitutional Rights on Public Campuses," 58 *Virginia L. Rev.* 552 (1972); Symposium, "Procedural Due Process and Campus Disorder," 1970 *Duke L.J.* 763; Charles A. Wright, "The Constitution On the Campus," 22 *Vanderbilt L. Rev.* 1027 (1969). As to public school students, the Supreme Court ruled on the issue in 1975, in Goss v. Lopez, 95 S. Ct. 729 (1975). An Ohio statute which allowed a high school principal to suspend a pupil for up to 10 days (notifying the parents within 24 hours and giving reasons for the suspension) was

held unconstitutional, in that it failed to require "oral or written notice of the charges against him, and if he denies them, an explanation of the evidence the authorities have and an opportunity to present his side of the story." This rudimentary hearing, the Court thought, could be informal, and in emergency situations the notice and hearing could follow the suspension, as soon thereafter as practicable.

18. Goldberg v. Kelly, 397 U.S. 254 (1970).
19. Morrissey v. Brewer, 408 U.S. 471 (1972); Gagnon v. Scarpelli, 411 U.S. 778 (1973).
20. Wolff v. McDonnell, 418 U.S. 539 (1974). Due process was held to require that the inmate receive written notice of the charges, and a written statement by the fact-finders as to evidence relied on and reasons for any disciplinary action, but did not require confrontation and cross-examination of witnesses against the prisoner. The prisoner's right to call witnesses and present evidence would be recognized only if this would not be unduly hazardous to institutional safety or correctional goals. There was no right to counsel, but if the prisoner were illiterate or the case complex, the prisoner "should be free to seek the aid of a fellow inmate, or if that is forbidden, to have adequate substitute aid in the form of help from the staff or from a sufficiently competent inmate designated by the staff" (p. 570). The same case recognized the validity of another form of prisoner participation (inmate preparation of petitions to court for habeas corpus relief) by reiterating a somewhat earlier holding: "unless and until the State provides some reasonable alternative to assist inmates in the preparation of petitions for postconviction relief, inmates could not be barred from furnishing assistance to each other" (pp. 578-580).
21. Gonzalez v. Freeman, 334 F.2d 570 (D.C. Cir. 1964). Though basing the right on its interpretation of the statute, the Court stressed that a contrary interpretation would raise a serious constitutional issue.
22. Board of Regents v. Roth, 408 U.S. 564 (1972); Perry v. Sindermann, 408 U.S. 593 (1972).
23. Arnett v. Kennedy, 416 U.S. 134 (1974). The case dealt with the federal statute and regulations authorizing discharge of federal civil service employees without pay, for such cause as would promote the efficiency of the service, after notice of charges and opportunity to file a written response, the decision being by the official who brought the charges (who in this case had been publicly accused by the employee of bribery). Some agencies allowed a full hearing at this first stage, rather than the mere written response guaranteed by statute, but the agency in this case did not. The administrative *appeal* was to be before an impartial decision-maker. The Court held that procedural due process had not been violated.
24. Willner v. Committee on Character and Fitness, 373 U.S. 96 (1963) (attorney); Goldsmith v. U.S. Board of Tax Appeals, 270 U.S. 117 (1926) (accountant); Milligan v. Bd. of Registration, 348 Mass. 491, 204 N.E. 2d 504 (1965) (retail drug store); Koster v. Holz, 3 N.Y. 2d 639, 148 N.E. 2d 287 (1958) (insurance broker); House of Tobacco, Inc. v. Calvert, 394 S.W. 2d 654 (Tex., 1965) (cigarette seller).
25. Lewis v. City of Grand Rapids, 356 F.2d 276, 286 (6 Cir.), cert den. 385 U.S. 838 (1966).
26. Hornsby v. Allen, 326 F.2d 605 (5 Cir. 1964). See also Manos v. City of Green Bay, 372 F. Supp. 40 (E.D. Wis. 1974) (three-judge court).
27. Bell v. Burson, 402 U.S. 535, 542 (1971). A Georgia statute providing

for administrative suspension of an uninsured motorist's license in the event of failure to post security for the amount of damages claimed by injured parties in their reports of an accident, was held to violate due process in this respect: it did not require that there be, *prior* to any suspension, (1) a determination by administrative hearing or court hearing, of whether there was a reasonable possibility of a judgment being rendered against him; or (2) a court adjudication of the action for damages.

28. Kenneth C. Davis, *Administrative Law Text* 184 (St. Paul: West, 3rd ed. 1972). Be it noted, however, that in the matter of licensing by federal agencies the federal Administrative Procedure Act of 1946 does not guarantee full administrative hearings in all cases of license issuance or suspension or revocation [5 U.S. Code, Sec. 558(c)]. Statutes dealing with particular subject matter however, on both the federal and state level, are likely to contain a hearing requirement.

29. See the language in Goldberg v. Kelly, 397 U.S. 254 (1970) at p. 262, and Board of Regents v. Roth, 408 U.S. 564 (1972) at p. 571 and note 9; Davis, *Administrative Law Text,* 175-193 (1972).

30. Office of Communication of United Church of Christ v. FCC, 359 F. 2d 994, 1005 (D.C. Cir. 1966).

31. National Welfare Rights Organization v. Finch, 429 F.2d 725 (D.C. Cir. 1970).

32. James R. Michael with Ruth C. Fort, eds., *Working On the System* (New York: Basic Books, 1974), pp. 20-21.

33. Albert K. Butzel, "Intervention and Class Actions Before the Agencies and the Courts," 25 *Admin L. Rev.* 135, 136 (1973).

34. See David L. Shapiro, "Some Thoughts On Intervention Before Courts, Agencies and Arbitrators," 81 *Harv. L. Rev.* 721, 766 (1968).

35. For critical comment see Arthur E. Bonfield, "Public Participation in Federal Rulemaking Relating to Public Property, Loans, Grants, Benefits or Contracts," 118 *U. of Pa. L. Rev.* 540 (1970).

36. 1969 Annual Report, Administrative Conference of the United States (Washington: Government Printing Office, 1970), pp. 45-46.

37. "One Third of the Nation's Land," *Report of Public Land Law Review Commission* (Washington: Government Printing Office, 1970). The Report not only supported the already existing use of citizen advisory boards in administering natural resource legislation but also asked that agencies be required "to give meaningful public notice of all proposed public land transactions to the maximum extent feasible, and to provide for the intervention and participation by, among others, members of the public." See Comment, "The Role of Citizen Advisory Boards in Administration of Natural Resources," 50 *Oregon L. Rev.* 153, 163-8 (1971). An example on the state level of the public's opportunity to be heard in the area of public property, loans, etc., is the federal requirement that a *state highway department* seeking federal aid for a highway project must hold a public hearing to get community views on the design, route, and effects of the proposed highway. 23 U.S. Code, Sec. 128.

38. In the latter situation, a case finding neither a statutory nor a constitutional right of a consumer protection group to intervene before the Federal Trade Commission is Action on Safety and Health v. FTC, 498 F.2d 754 (D.C. Cir. 1974). The agency denial of intervention was also held to be the kind of discretionary determination that was judicially unreviewable. Discussion of the other kinds of agency unwillingness mentioned in the text paragraph above will be found in Ernest A. E. Gell-

horn, "Public Participation in Administration Proceedings," 81 *Yale L. J.* 359, 368, 378-382 (1972).

39. Roger C. Cramton, "The Why, Where and How of Broadened Public Participation in the Administrative Process," 60 *Georgetown L. J.* 525 (1972); Ernest A. E. Gellhorn, "Public Participation in Administrative Proceedings," 81 *Yale L. J.* 359 (1972); Comment, "Public Participation in Federal Administrative Proceedings," 120 *U. of Pa. L. Rev.* 702 (1972); Simon Lazarus and Joseph Onek, "The Regulators and the People," 57 *Va. L. Rev.* 1069, 1094-1108 (1971); Roger Noll, "The Economics and Politics of Regulation," 57 *Va. L. Rev.* 1016, 1031-2 (1971). For a critical view, especially as to how a broadened participation might affect the FTC, see A. Everett McIntyre and Joachim J. Volhard, "Intervention in Agency Adjudications," 58 *Va. L. Rev.* 230 (1972).

40. See 116 *Cong. Rec.* S18939-18943 (daily ed., Nov. 25, 1970).

41. Conference Recommendation 28, in *1971-72 Report, Administrative Conference of the United States* (Washington: Government Printing Office, 1972), pp. 59-66.

42. And agencies were to be "cautious in advance of actual experience in anticipating that intervention will cause undue delays" (p. 61).

43. Public participation "in enforcement or license revocation proceedings should be permitted when a significant objective of the adjudication is to develop and test a new policy or remedy in a precise factual setting or when the prospective intervenor is the de facto charging party. Public participation in enforcement proceedings, license revocations or other adjudications where the issue is whether the charged respondent has violated a settled law or policy should be permitted only after close scrutiny of the effect of intervention or other participation on existing parties" (pp. 60-61).

44. These were: (a) nature of contested issues; (b) prospective intervenor's precise interest in subject matter or possible outcome; (c) adequacy of representation of its interest and views by existing parties; (d) availability of other means (e.g., "amicus curiae" status) to protect its interest; (e) its ability to present relevant evidence and argument; (f) effect of its intervention on agency implementation of its statutory mandate (p. 61).

45. "A public intervenor generally should be allowed all the rights of any other party including the right to be represented by counsel, participate in prehearing conferences, obtain discovery, stipulate facts, present and cross-examine witnesses, make oral and written argument and participate in settlement negotiations." However, the "nature of the issues, the intervenor's interests, its ability to present relevant evidence and argument, and the number, interests and capacities of the other parties should determine the dimensions" of the participation. Further, the public intervenor is not to render the hearing "unmanageable," should "not be allowed to determine the broad outline of the proceeding, such as the scope or compass of the issues," and if the intervenor "focuses on only one aspect of the proceeding or doesn't seek to controvert adjudicative facts, consideration should be given to limiting its participation to particular issues, written evidence, argument or the like" (p. 61).

46. Existing agency requirements as to filing and distribution of documents by a hearing participant were to be reexamined, to make the costs less burdensome. Transcripts of proceedings were to be furnished "at a minimum charge reflecting only the cost of reproducing copies of the agency's transcript," and were to be "available without charge to indigent participants to the extent necessary for the effective representation of

their interests." Also, an "agency should provide assistance to participants in proceedings before it or another agency, provided that the agency's resources will not be seriously burdened or its operations impaired. Assistance should include advice and help in obtaining information from the agency's files. Each agency should experiment with allowing access to agency experts and making available experts whose testimony would be helpful in another agency's proceeding" (p. 62). The Conference decided to make no recommendation regarding the subsidizing or other meeting of the highest costs of all, i.e., attorneys' fees. See discussion of the problem in Gellhorn, supra note 39 at 394-398, and Cramton, *id.,* at 541-546.

47. Where public participation in agency proceedings would be appropriate, agencies were to give public notice of them in addition to the official public notice given in the Federal Register. "Among the techniques which should be considered" were: press releases in lay language, television and radio announcements, mailings and advertisements where the affected public was located, invitations to groups able to represent otherwise unrepresented interests and views. "The initial notice should be as far in advance of hearing as possible in order to allow affected groups an opportunity to prepare." Finally, agencies "should consider publication of a monthly bulletin" identifying and summarizing the purposes of the proceedings "in which public intervention may be appropriate," and giving the date, name and place of hearing, as well as the agency and official to be contacted (pp. 62-63).

48. 1969 Annual Report, Administrative Conference of the United States (Washington: Government Printing Office, 1970), 31-34. See also Arthur E. Bonfield, "Representation of the Poor in Federal Rule-marking," 67 *Mich. L. Rev.* 511 (1969) (Appendix reproduces the Conference recommendation); Allan Ashman, "Representation for the Poor in State Rulemaking," 24 *Vanderbilt L. Rev.* 1 (1970).

49. See Comment in *Oregon Law Rev.,* supra note 8, at 174-76 for discussion of the Kennedy bill. The bill was introduced in 1970 as S.3434 and in 1971 as S.1423. See Hearings before Subcommittee on Administrative Practice and Procedures of Senate Committee on Judiciary on S.3434, 91 Cong. 2 sess. (1970), and on S.1423, 92 Cong. 1 sess. (1971).

50. See House Report No. 91-1361, to accompany H.R. 18214, 91 Cong., 2 sess. (1970); House Report No. 92-542, to accompany H.R. 10835, 92 Cong., 1 sess. (1971); House Report 93-962 to accompany H.R. 13163, 93 Cong., 2 sess. (1974); Senate Reports 91-1331 and 91-1365, to accompany S.4459, 91 Cong., 2 sess. (1970); Senate Report 92-1100 to accompany S.3970, 92 Cong., 2 sess. (1972); Senate Reports 93-792 and 93-883, to accompany S.707, 93 Cong., 1 sess (1973). Among the relevant hearings are these: Hearings before Subcommittee on House Committee on Government Operations, on H.R. 16 and Related Bills, H.R. 3809 and Related Bills, H.R. 254 and H.R. 1015, 92 Cong., 1 sess. (1971), and on H.R. 6037 and Related Bills, 91 Cong. 1 sess. (1969) and 91 Cong., 2 sess. (1970); Hearings before Subcommittee on Intergovernmental Relations of Senate Committee on Government Operations, on S.607, 92 Cong., 1 sess. (1971); Hearings before Subcommittee on Executive Reorganization and Government Research of Senate Committee on Government Operations, on S.2045, S.3097, S.3165, and S.3240, 91 Cong., 2 sess. (1970) and on S.1177, 92 Cong., 1 sess. (1971); Hearings before Consumer Subcommittee of Senate Committee on Commerce, on S.2959, 91 Cong., 1 sess. (1969) and 91 Cong., 2 sess. (1970);

Joint Hearings before Subcommittees of Senate Committee on Commerce, on S.707 and S.1160, 93 Cong., 1 sess. (1973); Hearings before Subcommittee on Legislation and Military Operations of House Committee on Government Operations, on H.R. 14, 21, 564, 93 Cong., 1 sess. (1973).

51. On anti-trust proceedings, see Richard M. Buxbaum, "Public Participation in the Enforcement of the Anti-trust Laws," 59 *Calif. L. Rev.* 1113 (1971). On the other point, see *1971-72 Report, Administrative Conference of United States* (Washington: Government Printing Office, 1972), pp. 73-76; Edward A. Tomlinson and Jerry L. Mashaw, "The Enforcement of Federal Standards in Grant-in-Aid Programs: Suggestions for Beneficiary Involvement," 58 *Va. L. Rev.* 600 (1972).

52. On the ombudsman device, see Walter Gellhorn, *Ombudsmen and Others* (Cambridge: Harvard, 1966), and *When Americans Complain* (Cambridge: Harvard, 1966); Roger Cramton, "A Federal Ombudsman," 1972 *Duke L. J.* 1.

On the open hearing laws, see Walter Gellhorn and Clark Byse, *Administrative Law,* Cases and Comments, 6th ed. (Mineola, N.Y.: Foundation, 1974), pp. 573-574; Notes, 49 *Tex L. Rev.* 764 (1971) and 75 *Harv. L. Rev.* 1199 (1962).

On freedom of information, see 80 *U.S. Statutes At Large* 250 (1966) codified in 5 U.S. Code, Sec. 552, amended by Public Law No. 93-502 (1974) (legislative history of 1974 amendments being shown in *U.S. Code Congressional and Administrative News,* Dec. 15, 1974, pp. 6203-6229); Kenneth C. Davis, *Administrative Law Text,* 3rd ed., Sec. 3A.3; 3A.20 (St. Paul: West, 1972); Gellhorn and Byse, *supra* note 52 at pp. 565-573.

53. Kenneth C. Davis, *Administrative Law Text,* 3rd ed., Sec. 8.09 (St. Paul: West, 1972); David L. Shapiro, "Some Thoughts on Intervention Before Courts, Agencies and Arbitrators," 81 *Harv. L. Rev.* 721 (1968); Louis L. Jaffe, *Judicial Control of Administration Action* (Boston: Little, Brown, 1965), pp. 524-525; Comment, "Public Participation in Federal Administrative Proceedings," 120 *U. of Pa. L. Rev.* 702, 718-722 (1972).

54. Office of Communication of United Church of Christ v. F.C.C., 359 F.2d 994 (D.C. Cir. 1966); Associated Industries v. Ickes, 134 F.2d 694 (2 Cir. 1943); Reade v. Ewing, 205 F.2d 630 (2 Cir. 1953); City of Pittsburgh v. F.P.C., 237 F.2d 741 (D.C. Cir., 1956).

55. United States v. Students Challenging Regulatory Agency Procedures (SCRAP), 412 U.S. 669 (1973); Citizens to Preserve Overton Park v. Volpe, 401 U.S. 402 (1971) (standing assumed without discussion); Scenic Hudson Preservation Conference v. F.P.C., 354 F.2d 608 (2 Cir. 1965), cert. den. 384 U.S. 941 (1966); Citizens for Alleghany County, Inc. v. FPC, 414 F.2d 1125 (D.C. Cir. 1969); Citizens Committee for Hudson Valley, etc., v. Volpe, 425 F.2d 97 (2 Cir. 1970); Coalition for the Environment v. Volpe, 504 F.2d 156 (8 Cir. 1974).

56. This was the new test announced in Assoc. of Data Processing Service Org. v. Camp, 397 U.S. 150 (1970).

57. Kenneth C. Davis, *Administrative Law Text,* Secs. 22.07-22-08, 3rd ed. (St. Paul: West, 1972). Davis' substitute test reads: "A person whose legitimate interest is injured in fact or imminently threatened with injury by governmental action should have standing to challenge that action in absence of legislative intent that the interest is not to be protected."

58. Assoc. of Data Processing Service Org. v. Camp, 397 U.S. 150, 154 (1970); Sierra Club v. Morton, 405 U.S. 727, 734 (1972).
59. United States v. Students Challenging Regulatory Agency Procedures (SCRAP), 412 U.S. 669 (1973).
60. The group had alleged the ICC's failure to comply with the National Environmental Policy Act's requirement for the filing of an environmental impact statement. The Supreme Court said it was "unnecessary to reach any question concerning the scope of the 'zone of interests' test or its application to this case. It is undisputed that the 'environmental interest' that the appellees seek to protect is within the interests to be protected by NEPA . . ." (p. 686, n. 13). The Court's opinion, taken together with those in earlier cases, suggests that Sec. 10 of the Administrative Procedure Act which gives standing to those who are "suffering legal wrong because of agency action," or are "adversely affected or aggrieved within the meaning of a relevant statute," is to be interpreted in the light of the Court's present test for standing, i.e., (1) injury in fact, (2) being within the necessary "zone of interests." That is, the statutory adverse effect or aggrievement represents the "injury in fact"; the statutory "within the meaning of a relevant statute" represents the "zone of interests." Thus in this case, NEPA was the "relevant statute" that created a zone of interests protecting the plaintiffs.
61. 412 U.S. at 688.
62. *Id.,* at 686-688.
63. *Id.,* at 688, n. 14: " 'Injury in fact' reflects the statutory requirement that a person be 'adversely affected' or 'aggrieved,' and it serves to distinguish a person with a direct stake in the outcome of a litigation— even though small—from a person with a mere interest in the problem."
64. *Id.,* at 684-685, 687, 688-689.
65. An example is Schlesinger v. Reservists Committee to Stop the War, 418 U.S. 208(1974). Anti-war activists claiming that the Constitution's compatibility clause (Art. 1, sec. 6, clause 2: ". . . no person holding any office under the United States shall be a member of either House during continuance in office") was violated by the Pentagon policy allowing members of Congress to retain their status in the Armed Forces Reserves, were held not to have standing as citizens or taxpayers. As to citizen standing, the Court thought the alleged impairment of a citizen's right to independent representation in Congress, free from executive undue influence, was speculative; and, besides, injury to a general interest in "constitutional governance" was not concrete enough. Another example is Laird v. Tatum, 408 U.S. 1 (1972) involving the Army Intelligence surveillance reports on citizens' political activities that had a potential for domestic disorder. Though most of the plaintiff individuals or their organizations had been the subject of the reports, they were held to have no standing to complain of the chilling effect of the surveillance system on their First Amendment rights of speech and association—in the absence of more specific present harm or threat of specific future harm.
66. Flast v. Cohen, 392 U.S. 83 (1968).
67. One instance was United States v. Richardson, 418 U.S. 166 (1974) where a taxpayer who claimed that the Executive Branch's failure to reveal CIA expenditures violated the statement and account clause of the Constitution (Art. I, sec. 9, clause 7: ". . . and a regular statement and account of the receipts and expenditures of all public money shall be published from time to time") was held not to have standing as a tax-

payer to enforce the clause. In this case as well as in the Schlesinger case discussed in note 65 above (where the plaintiffs sued also as taxpayers) the Court declared that the double test announced in Flast v. Cohen had not been met: the challenge was not to an exercise of the taxing and spending power; and the constitutional provision allegedly violated was not a specific restriction on taxing and spending.

68. See Senate Committee on Commerce, 93rd Congress, 2d session, *Class Action Study* (1974); Symposium, "Class Actions," 12 *San Diego Rev.* 1-243 (1974); Note, "Managing the Large Class Action," 87 *Harv. L. Rev.* 425 (1973); Eisen v. Carlisle and Jacquelin, 417 U.S. 156 (1974).

69. F. Raymond Marks, et al., *The Lawyer, the Public and Professional Responsibility* (Chicago: American Bar Foundation, 1972); Symposium on public interest law practice, 79 *Yale L. J.* 1005-1152 (1970); The Ford Foundation report, *The Public Interest Law Firm: New Voices For New Constituencies* (New York: Ford Foundation, 1973).

70. Sniadich v. Family Finance Corp. of Bayview, 395 U.S. 337 (1969). And in 1975 the principle was extended to garnishment of a corporate bank account. North Georgia Finishing, Inc. v. Di-Chem, Inc., 95 S. Ct. 719 (1975).

71. Stanley v. Illinois, 405 U.S. 645 (7972).

72. Apparently there is no such right today if certain procedural safeguards exist in the jurisdiction, e.g., if the creditor must (instead of activating a sheriff's seizure by simply filling out a form available at request from a court clerk) file a verified affidavit stating the specific facts before a judge, who alone can issue the seizure writ; if the creditor must post a bond; and if the debtor is entitled to an immediate post-seizure hearing. If the debtor had "waived" the right, this in itself may be fatal, though such factors as inequality of bargaining power, or lack of clarity in or communication of a fine-print waiver clause, may be a pertinent counterfactor. See generally Fuentes v. Shevin, 407 U.S. 67 (1972); D. H. Overmeyer Co. v. Frick, 405 U.S. 174 (1972); Swarb v. Lennox, 405 U.S. 191 (1972); Mitchell v. W. T. Grant Co., 416 U.S. 600 (1974).

73. Boddie v. Connecticut, 401 U.S. 371 (1971). The Court refused, however, to extend the principle to bankruptcy filing fees, United States v. Kras, 409 U.S. 434 (1973), or to a $25 filing fee applicable to appeals from welfare agency decisions (made after hearing) reducing old-age assistance and welfare payments, Ortwein v. Schwab, 410 U.S. 656 (1973).

74. Griffin v. Illinois, 351 U.S. 12 (1956).

75. Argersinger v. Hamlin, 407 U.S. 25 (1972).

76. In re Gault, 387 U.S. 1 (1967). See also Matter of Winship, 397 U.S. 358 (1970); McKeiver v. Penn., 403 U.S. 528 (1971).

77. Specht v. Patterson, 386 U.S. 605 (1967); Huebner v. State, 147 N.W. 2d 646 (Wis. 1967). See also Humphrey v. Cady, 405 U.S. 504 (1972).

78. See, e.g., Schubert v. Kovach, 219 N.W. 2d 341 (Wis., 1974), cert. den. 95 S.Ct. 816 (1975); Bolton v. Harris, 395 F.2d 642 (D.C. Cir. 1968). *Cf.* the Court's due process limitations on duration of institutional commitment of a criminal defendant adjudged mentally incompetent to stand trial, in Jackson v. Indiana, 406 U.S. 715 (1972).

79. See, e.g., Lessard v. Schmidt, 349 F. Supp. 1078 (E.D. Wis. 1972) (three judge court), vacated and remanded on procedural grounds, 414 U.S. 473 (1974); Bell v. Wayne County General Hospital, 384 F.Supp. 1085 (E.D. Mich. 1974) (three judge court).

80. Abbott Laboratories v. Gardner, 387 U.S. 136 (1967).

81. It has sometimes been said that "due process is not necessarily judicial process" (Reetz v. Michigan, 188 U.S. 505, 507 (1903), and there is support for this view in the reasoning of Ortwein v. Schwab, 410 U.S. 656 (1973) cited above in note 73. But there are lines of Supreme Court cases that seem to assume otherwise, and the recent case of Johnson v. Robison, 415 U.S. 361 (1974), on judicial review of veterans' benefit decisions, recognizes that the constitutional issue remains open. In posing the constitutional issue, I am assuming that a statutory preclusion of judicial review is being applied to a plaintiff who (1) has hurdled the barriers in the various doctrines permitting a court to legitimately decline or postpone review: the plaintiff has "standing," has "exhausted" any administrative remedies that he may properly be required to exhaust, the particular court has "jurisdiction," the issue is "ripe" for review, is not "moot," is "justiciable" (i.e., not a "political question" to be resolved by the legislature or executive), and is not for the "primary jurisdiction" of the agency; (2) has not been precluded from testing in court the constitutional fairness of the administrative *procedure* used to make the administrative decision.

82. Stephen Wexler, "Practicing Law for Poor People," *79 Yale L. J.* 1049, 1057-8, 1063-6 (1970); Comment, "Self-Representation in Criminal Trials: The Dilemma of the *Pro Se* Defendant," 59 *California L. Rev.* 1479 (1971). The California Supreme Court has held that an indigent defendant in a criminal case does not have the constitutional right to reject an appointed attorney in order to be his own lawyer. People v. Sharp, 499 Pac. 2d 489 (Cal. 1972), cert. den. 410 U.S. 944 (1973). As this goes to press in 1975, the U.S. Supreme Court has the same issue under advisement, in Faretta v. California, Docket No. 73-5772.

83. See A.B.A. Project on Standards for Criminal Justice, *The Prosecution Function and the Defense Function* (Chicago: A.B.A., 1970), especially pp. 237-241.

84. Douglas E. Rosenthal, *Lawyer and Client: Who's in Charge?* (New York: Russell Sage Foundation, 1974).

85. These foundations are to be found not in the "disciplinary rules" but in the more abstract "ethical considerations" of the Code (p. 25): *Ethical Consideration 7-7.* In certain areas of legal representation not affecting the merits of the case or substantially prejudicing the rights of a client, a lawyer is entitled to make decisions on his own. But otherwise, the authority to make decisions is exclusively that of the client, and if made within the framework of the law, such decisions are binding on his lawyer. As typical examples in civil cases, it is for the client to decide whether he will accept a settlement offer, or whether he will waive his right to plead an affirmative defense.

    Ethical Consideration 7-8. A lawyer should exert his best efforts to insure that decisions of his client are made only after the client has been informed of relevant considerations. A lawyer ought to initiate this decision-making process if the client does not do so. Advice of a lawyer to his client need not be confined to purely legal considerations. A lawyer should advise his client of the possible effect of each legal alternative. A lawyer should bring to bear upon this decision-making process the fullness of his experience as well as his objective viewpoint. In assisting his client to reach a proper decision, it is often desirable for a lawyer to point out those factors which may lead to a decision that is morally just as well as legally permissible. He may emphasize the possibility of harsh consequences that might result from the assertion of

legally permissible positions. In the final analysis, however, the lawyer
should always remember that the decision whether to forego legally
available objectives or methods because of nonlegal factors is ultimately
for the client and not for himself. In the event that the client in a non-
adjudicatory matter insists upon a course of conduct that is contrary to
the judgment and advice of the lawyer but not prohibited by the Disciplinary Rules, the lawyer may withdraw from the employment.
86. See Link V. Wabash R. Co., 370 U.S. 626, 633 (1962); Lester Mazor,
"Power and Responsibility in the Attorney-Client Relation," 20 *Stanf. L.
Rev.* 118 (1966). Rosenthal, *supra* note 84 at pp. 120-123.
87. Rosenthal, *supra* note 84 at pp. 123-127.
88. Smith v. Texas, 311 U.S. 128 (1940); Taylor v. Louisiana, 95 S.Ct. 692
(1975).
89. For information on both the comrades courts and the volunteer police
in the Soviet Union, see Leon Lipson, "Law: The Function of Extra-
Judicial Mechanisms in the USSR," in Terrence E. Cook and Patrick M.
Morgan, *Participatory Democracy* (San Francisco: Canfield, 1971), pp.
441, 442-454. See also John Dawson, *A History of Lay Judges* (1960);
Harold J. Berman and James W. Spindler, "Soviet Comrades' Courts,"
38 *Wash. L. Rev.* 842 (1963); W. E. Butler, "Comradely Justice in
Eastern Europe," 25 *Current Legal Problems,* 200 (1972); Gerhard
Casper and Hans Zeisel, "Lay Judges in the German Criminal Courts,"
1 *J. of Legal Studies* 135 (1972); Gordon Smith, "Popular Participation
in the Administration of Justice in the Soviet Union: Comrades' Courts
and the Brezhnev Regime, 49 *Indiana L. Review* 238 (1974); Robert
Cantor, "Law Without Lawyers: Popular Tribunals in Cuba," *Juris
Doctor,* Feb. 1974, p. 24; Jesse Berman, "The Cuban Popular Tribunals,"
69 Colum. L. Rev. 1317 (1969).
90. See "Black Panther Petition for Neighborhood Control of the Police,"
and Arthur I Waskow, "Community Control of the Police," in Cook
and Morgan, *Participatory Democracy,* pp. 428-431 and 432-440.
91. These include statutes authorizing a victim of law violation to obtain
multiple damage recovery (e.g., the employee's double-damage remedy
for violation of the Fair Labor Standards Act, 29 U.S. Code, Sec. 216);
the Clean Air Act authorization of citizen suits to enforce air emission
standards, limits, and orders, or to require the Administrator to perform
any nondiscretionary duty (42 U.S. Code, Sec. 1857 h-2); Statutes giving an "informer" the right to share a monetary penalty after the government's successful prosecution (e.g., what is known as the "Refuse
Act," 33 U.S. Code 407, 411, which is part of the Rivers and Harbors
Act); and the neglected "qui tam" statutes, authorizing a citizen to sue
on behalf of the government for a civil penalty and to share recovery
with the government (e.g., under the Federal False Claims Act, 31 U.S.
Code, Sec. 231-235). For discussion of the latter, see Comment, "Qui
Tam Actions: The Role of the Private Citizen in Law Enforcement,"
20 *U.C.L.A. L. Rev.* 778 (1973).
92. See *supra* note 9. For a later, more favorable assessment of community
participation, see J. David Greenstone and Paul E. Peterson, *Race and
Authority in Urban Politics: Community Participation and the War on
Poverty* (New York: Russell Sage Foundation, 1973).

8

CITIZEN PARTICIPATION IN EMERGING SOCIAL INSTITUTIONS

HOWARD I. KALODNER

"Citizen participation"—the very words are designed to evoke an affirmative response. Do we not, after all, live in a nation devoted to democratic principles, a nation based on the concept that only that government governs justly which does so with the consent of the majority, consent expressed or denied by exercise of the now universal franchise? And if this is so, then why some special speech, or essay, or book, on citizen participation in the 1970s, almost two hundred years after these democratic ideals were codified in the United States Constitution?

I take it that the subject is selected because the issue seems unsettled—somehow unresolved. One can or should be troubled by the limitations of the topic—citizen participation in emerging social institutions. Logically, if there has been some failing of citizen participation in existing institutions, only if emerging institutions were to replace or at least become dominant over existing institutions would the most extreme citizen participation in new institutions be significant. With the usual apology to the conference planners, then, I will state my topic somewhat more broadly than the title suggests.

But I am content to begin with citizen participation in the "emerging institutions" of the title. I will include among them community action programs under the Economic Opportunity Act of 1964, workable program certification requirements, urban renewal, model cities, and federal aid to elementary and secondary schools. The list is not exhaustive, but a further proliferation would be unproductive. Even as I begin with these, let me say that they are not at the heart of the matter; citizen participation in these comparatively newly arrived government benefit programs is secondary in importance to three more basic issues: first, an alteration in the character of the operation of more traditional governmental regulatory and service functions; second, the equalization of political power, or rather the neutralization of establishment power whenever it negates political power expressed in the democratic ideal; and third, the radical alteration of the political, social, and economic structure to allow equal participation in the economic growth of the United States.

COMMUNITY ACTION PROGRAMS UNDER
THE ECONOMIC OPPORTUNITY ACT OF 1964

After a study of twelve community action programs in 1968, the black psychologist Kenneth Clark concluded: "As we have seen, the record of the community action programs is, even at best, a qualified success. Even the most effective show only tentative signs of observable social change. At their worst, they are a charade and elaborate exploitation of the poor."[1]

The explanation of the word "charade" requires an excursion into Congressional and administrative action in the enactment and implementation of the Economic Opportunity Act of 1964, the legislative embodiment of President Lyndon Johnson's "War against Poverty." Among other things, that Act called for community action programs which were to be "developed, conducted, and administered with the maximum feasible participation of residents of the areas and members of the groups served."

This statutory mandate, however uncertain its origin, purpose, or meaning,[2] necessitated an inquiry into both the word "participation" and the standard by which one measures "maximum feasibility." Various efforts have contributed toward the elaboration of a typology of citizen participation in governmental planning decisions, defining a continuum from the threshold point of provision of information to citizens regarding decisions to be made, through consultation, negotiation, shared policy and decision making, joint planning, delegation of planning responsibility, and neighborhood control.[3]

Early administrative interpretation did little to clarify which of the manifold meanings the Office of Economic Opportunity, created by the Economic Opportunity Act, intended to adopt. In a memorandum dated August 21, 1964, the President's Task Force on the War against Poverty, in discussing the Community Action Program, described mainly service programs and specified that these should "involve the poor themselves in developing and operating the antipoverty programs." This same memorandum did clearly embrace the idea that residents of the poverty areas could be used as "workers in projects," listing specifically the roles of "aides to professionals," "recreational and day care assistants," "helpers in homemaker and health services," "community research aides," and so forth. Thus, maximum feasible participation at least included employment of some residents and, additionally, involvement of residents in some kind of planning ("developing") capacity. This emphasis on a planning role as a significant component of citizen participation reappears again and again in the developments of the last six years.

The history of community action programs is not consistent throughout the United States. In common with the other provisions for participation by the poor in new, predominantly service-oriented programs, too little time has passed and still too few empirical studies are available to reach final conclusions about the effectiveness of citizen participation in the community action program. However, certain generalizations will probably survive later evaluation. The first is that where the community action agency threatened to become an effective device for mobilizing the residents of a poverty area toward political action, the existing political institutions reacted by terminating or rendering ineffective the community group, through reorganization or withdrawal of funds. One such experience, in Syracuse, New York, was reported by Kenneth Clark and Jeanette Hopkins in their study of community action programs entitled, "A Relevant War against Poverty."[4] A community organization called Community Action Training Center (CATC) was established with the help of Syracuse University. It was funded as a demonstration program by OEO. As quoted by Dr. Clark from CATC's statements, CATC's philosophy was that: "the central problem of the poor is their dependency, their powerlessness, the fact that their lives are controlled by persons and forces outside themselves, that there are no socially provided structures through which they can exercise control over their lives." In line with this power analysis, CATC acted politically, though without political partisanship. CATC began a voter registration drive. Since most of the poor registered Democratic, this effort was viewed by the Republican mayor as a direct threat to him. He in turn engaged in a public attack against other programs of CATC and a pattern of harassment of CATC followed. After the mayor's reelection, OEO refused further direct funding to CATC, instead suggesting that CATC apply for funds through Crusade for Opportunity, a city-wide umbrella organization. CATC refused. When Crusade held an election for its own neighborhood boards, Dr. Clark reports, only about 1,500 persons voted. Crusade for Opportunity was the conventional community action structure—one-third of its board was composed of the poor and elected by the local elected neighborhood boards. The balance of the board represented existing institutions (described by Dr. Clark as the "majority culture")—social agencies, political groups, and the like. Crusade for Opportunity was service-oriented and not, as was CATC, oriented toward political goals. Nevertheless, Dr. Clark reports, Crusade itself lost financial support from OEO when the majority of the board fell to representatives of the poor. Dr. Clark summarizes his view of the CATC and similar experiences as follows: "But as soon as such programs came in conflict with local political and civic leadership, the local and federal governments began to show strong signs of a strategic retreat and began to mollify local establishment leadership while nevertheless pushing verbally 'participation of the poor.'"[5] Nor is Dr. Clark alone in his observation of this phenomenon. In his book on the community action programs, Dr. Moynihan has drawn the following conclusions with respect to their effectiveness:

> Seemingly it comes to this. Over and over again, the attempt by official and quasi-official agencies . . . to organize poor communities led first to the radicalization of the middle-class persons who began the effort; next to a certain amount of stirring among the poor, but accompanied by heightened racial antagonism *on the part of the poor* if they happened to be black; next to retaliation from the larger white community; whereupon it would emerge that the community action agency, which had talked so much, been so much in the headlines, promised so much in the way of changes in the fundamentals of things, was powerless. A creature of a Washington bureaucracy, subject to discontinuance without notice.[6]

Though written from different premises, the Clark and Moynihan commentaries are in this respect sadly alike.

A second phenomenon was that the "citizen participation" requirement necessitated a review of our concepts of representation and representativeness. Shall the poor be directly involved, shall they participate directly, or shall that be accomplished through representative bodies? If the latter is the answer, as our political heritage dictates (town meetings are a subculture in American life and have been for well over a century), then how is the representative body to be chosen?

Perhaps not surprisingly, election of representatives emerged as the prototypical, though not universal, system for selection of the citizen representation component of community action programs. One quite detailed study of the process of formation of the community corporations in New York City, which were to be given authority to disperse OEO community action funds within their respective jurisdictions, reports that in the 1967 elections about 55,000 voted, or about 10 percent of those eligible to vote.[7] But this reliance on the general electorate had been preceded, in the case of some of the corporations (for example, the Brownsville Community Council), by selection of representatives through the device of allocating board positions among existing organizations rather than selection of representatives by direct election. When the city-wide Council against Poverty took issue with that means of election, the Brownsville Community Council was reconstituted with a board of 55 persons, of whom 20 were elected directly, 4 from each of 5 districts; 30 were chosen by a delegate assembly representing about 100 organizations; and 5 were chosen by these 50 and ratified by the delegate assembly.[8]

Hallman expresses some satisfaction with the elective technique generally used despite the low turnout of eligible voters. He writes:

> Even if turnout was smaller than for municipal offices, the elections served as a means of arousing interest, publicizing the concept of the community corporation, and providing more experience in the democratic process. Perhaps most important, selection by popular election has given the boards of the community corporations greater legitimacy to act on behalf of the communities' interests than if they had been appointed by city officials or various organizations.[9]

But Hallman's review of the only partly directly elected Brownsville Community Council suggests at least that election is not always superior to appointment. He points out elsewhere that the mixed appointment-election technique used for selection of the Brownsville Community Council resulted in an ethnic composition of the board that approximated that of the community as a whole.[10] The result was to avoid the unfortunate black-Puerto Rican confrontation that characterized the direct election in the South Bronx Community Corporations and seriously impaired their formation and performance.[11]

It is not surprising that two issues would arise in the creation of such a new institution: its composition and the parameters of its functions. What might not be anticipated is the apparent contraction of the power of the agency thus formed; a contraction which limited it largely to service functions and penalized it for political activity deemed contrary to the interests of the existing power structure. Even more surprising is the reliance on elective techniques which had failed previously to act as a power-equalizing force for the poor in coping with the larger community and its institutions.

It is clear that citizen participation in community action programs has meant employment for some of the poor and decision making within a narrow range for those of the poor who had developed or could develop rather conventional political skills to gain power within the programs. It is also clear that, in general, such forms of participation had little impact on either poverty or the inability of the poor to control significantly decisions about the allocation of society's resources and burdens. For some participants in community action programs, the experience may lead to further political activity in institutions with larger potential, but there is little evidence to suggest that such benefits will be widespread.

WORKABLE PROGRAM

A "Workable Program" is a multifaceted plan submitted to the Department of Housing and Urban Development by a community seeking urban renewal. Acceptance of the Workable Program by HUD is a prerequisite to receipt of urban renewal and model cities funds and, until recently, public housing funds as well. In a "Program Guide" [12] published by the Department of Housing and Urban Development in 1966, the department sought to clarify its requirement that a Workable Program include as one of its components provision for citizen participation. This component dates back to 1954, when the Workable Program requirement was first imposed.

In the 1966 Program Guide, HUD explained what was required to meet the citizen-participation component:

> Experience has demonstrated that effective citizen participation over the extended period necessary to carry out a successful workable program is based on an active citizens advisory committee. This is community-wide and representative in scope, officially designated by the mayor and/or council, in accordance with local custom.... [T]he overall advisory committee ... should have minority group representation. [13]

The Program Guide also attempted an explanation of what was meant by "representative": "The members of the citizens advisory committee should be able to speak on behalf of established groups in the community." [14] The job of the citizens advisory committee, as visualized by the Guide, is illuminating:

The primary functions of the committee and its members are:

(1) to learn about the nature and extent of deficiencies and the means and methods for remedying them;

(2) to make recommendations for improvement; and

(3) to help inform other citizens and groups as to the need for the improvements and thus develop united community understanding of this need.[15]

But the description of how members are to be selected is even clearer in its message about the function of the citizens advisory committee:

These persons should be able to communicate the interests of their group or organization to the committee and to public officials concerned with the improvement programs of the community. They should also be capable of explaining to their group or organization the policies and programs put forward by the official bodies concerned with planning, housing, urban renewal, etc.[16]

However limited the functions of this committee, and however compromised its view of representativeness (particularly from the point of view of the poor minorities who were the principal losers in most urban renewal programs), it is notable as a requirement imposed administratively and not statutorily. While Section 101(c) of the Housing Act of 1949 (Urban Renewal) does impose a Workable Program requirement, nowhere in its specific demands is mention to be found of citizen participation.

The Workable Program requirements have now been reduced to four categories, but one remains citizen participation, both in the formulation of the Workable Program and in all programs that have as a prerequisite a Workable Program certification by HUD.

HUD does not establish specific requirements for either the form or function of citizen participation for an acceptable Workable Program. But as of 1970, according to Sherman Unger, the General Counsel of HUD, the department established "certain principles and objectives which are expected to underlie the community's effort." [17]

A community could establish a community-wide advisory committee embracing all major interests as the mechanism for enlisting citizen participation. Alternatively, it could establish special purpose groups; a third possibility is that it utilize existing organizations.

In addition to suggesting organizational means, HUD suggests other steps which a community can take to achieve an adequate level of citizen involvement. First, it can develop specific functions for citizens committees, such as having them hold public hearings, prepare comments on Workable Program applications, evaluate project plans, or conduct surveys of neighborhood views on current and future projects. Secondly, it can develop specific methods to insure that the advisory committees provide fair and reasonable representation of the community. Third, it can establish a planning group to help develop new ideas and techniques for generating greater involvement among poor and disadvantaged groups. Fourth, it can provide funds and technical assistance to advisory groups to help them become better informed and equipped to deal with complex redevelopment problems.[18]

Despite the scarcity of evidence regarding the operations under this expanded view of citizen participation, it is probably fair to conclude that city-wide participation is more likely to produce an honorific committee selected by the mayor to approve executive decisions than an independent body different in its representativeness of the community from the mayor himself. The same constituency is likely to dominate each. That was surely the experience under the old Workable Program requirement. If it does not prove to be true of the new, it will be because a coalition of citizen participation committees formed to meet specific urban renewal and model cities' requirements displaces the more traditional mayor's committee. That development, if it occurs, seems to lie largely in the future.

URBAN RENEWAL

Few programs of the federal government have aroused as much fear and hatred among the poor as did urban renewal until its partial turnabout in the 1960s. This reaction was partly due to the nature of the urban renewal program, which paid cities to demolish deteriorated housing, largely occupied by the poor.

The housing was replaced, not so incidentally, by commercial buildings, institutional buildings, or luxury apartment houses. Additional sources of resentment, however, were two other characteristics of urban renewal: its failure to take into account the views, values, or aspirations of the residents of renewal areas; and its failure to accept an obligation, imposed by statute but ignored in fact, to find, or if necessary create, decent, safe, and sanitary housing for those whose homes were demolished under the program. The citizens advisory committee contemplated by the Workable Program requirement did not begin to serve as a basis for communication between the city and residents of renewal areas, let alone succeed as a means for residents to influence planning.

In 1968 HUD, acting either out of recognition that increasing opposition by renewal area residents could bring the program to a halt or out of a growing philosophic position that it was right to provide a role for residents in renewal planning, adopted a requirement of Project Area Committees (PAC) in certain kinds of urban renewal areas. Considering the significance—or potential significance—of such committees, the Urban Renewal Handbook is remarkably unspecific about the composition and function of Project Area Committees.

The Handbook[19] requires creation of a PAC made up of residents of the project "for each urban renewal project in which residential rehabilitation activities are contemplated." For other project areas PACs are encouraged but are not required as a condition of federal funding. The Local Public Agency (LPA) established by state and local law to administer urban renewal is required to: "work closely with the PAC to assure that project residents participate in the formulation and execution of plans for renewal of the area and improvement of the condition of its residents." A second Handbook requirement is that: "sufficient information about the project shall be made available to project residents to enable them to participate knowledgeably." This second requirement is not, of course, necessarily directed to the operation of the PAC. The third and fourth descriptions of "Relationship between LPA and PAC" do relate directly to the PAC function. The third, however, is constructed only partly in mandatory terms and the fourth is entirely discretionary with the LPA. The third states that the LPA may provide technical assistance to the PAC but must "assure that the PAC has the capacity to participate in the formulation and execution of plans for renewal of the area and improvement of the condition of its residents." The fourth provides that the LPA may arrange with the PAC for employment of residents in connection with the project.

What it comes down to, then, is this: the Handbook requires the LPA to work closely with a PAC which has the capacity to work closely with the LPA on the formulation and execution of plans. Given the past ambiguities of citizen participation programs, one could have hoped for greater specificity. The situation is distinctly not aided by the fact that the Handbook nowhere states the time at which formation of and working with the PAC becomes a requirement; rather, it notes only that the PAC is to be formed sometime between the designation of the urban renewal area and the submission of the application for federal funding of the plan.

The Handbook provides considerable leeway to the LPA about how the PAC members are chosen. The chief requirement is that it be "representative of a fair cross section of the residents." It states that an existing neighborhood organization may be designated as PAC, but it must, apparently, satisfy the "representative" criteria.

Perhaps the chief contribution of the PAC provisions of the Handbook is to characterize expenditures by the LPA to provide technical assistance to the PAC for the performance of its functions as eligible costs of urban renewal with the consequence that such expenditures become part of net project costs, of which the federal government pays two-thirds (or three-quarters in smaller towns).

The Project Area Committee device may prove to be an effective vehicle for the expression of community views, but the Urban Renewal Handbook provisions hardly seem designed to move citizen participation beyond an advisory role, albeit an informed advisory role. As in the case of citizen involvement in Workable Program, emphasis seems to be placed on the planning function. Consequently, the limitation of the PAC requirement to residential rehabilitation projects may be justified on the ground that it makes little sense to require area residents to be involved in projects which call for clearance or for nonresidential rehabilitation. On the other hand, from the point of view of residents in a clearance or nonresidential reuse area, one aspect of the planning does involve their interests quite crucially—planning for the relocation of dislocated persons. Indeed, the history of resident demands for participation in poverty areas is principally characterized by demands of persons who will be dislocated by the city's plans—the slum clearance face of urban renewal, which was dominant until recently and may still be so.

It must be pointed out that the Neighborhood Development Program (NDP) variation on traditional urban renewal may have a significant impact on PAC activity in NDP areas. Under the NDP approach, planning and execution are accomplished for one-year periods; rather than planning for an entire project—an enterprise likely to be six to eleven years in execution—the NDP planning is for the next year. If only because the PAC may have the capacity to block the next year's funding, this year-to-year approach augments PAC power over its status in conventional urban renewal, in which the federal funding commitment is made for the entire project, however long its accomplishment may take.

It has been said that a review of some citizen participation efforts in urban renewal (all before the PAC requirement was imposed) suggests that collaborative planning, which seems to be the model the designers of the PAC had in mind, will work well only where the residents and the city planners have basically similar goals. Therefore, where planners want land for nonresidential uses, or for residential uses above the income level of existing residents, but residents want to avoid dislocation, it is not likely that collaborative planning between the LPA and the PAC will be productive.[20] On the other hand, if the PAC is constructed in a way which appears to give it the legitimacy of representativeness, its opposition may have at least a marginal impact on the urban renewal plan. That impact will depend in part, as do most political decisions, on a balancing of forces pressing for various plans, but in urban renewal the decisional process is also influenced by the professional technical personnel within the LPA, who not unnaturally have a vested interest in implementation of the plan as originally designed by them. This factor of the professionalization of decision making adds further complexity to citizen participation in the setting of urban renewal.

MODEL CITIES

Unlike citizen participation in the PAC or its predecessor, the city-wide advisory committee, citizen participation is a statutorily required element in so-called model cities under Title 1 of the Demonstration Cities and Metropolitan Development Act of 1966.[21] As a condition of eligibility for federal funding of a "comprehensive city demonstration program" (the statute's name for a "model city" program), that Act (in Section 103 [a]) requires, among other things, "widespread citizen participation in the program."

In 1967 HUD promulgated City Demonstration Agency Letter No. 3 (October 30, 1967), which elaborated upon this statutory language. The CDA letter required that there be established in each model neighborhood an "organization structure . . . which embodies neighborhood residents in the process of policy and program planning. . . ." It provided that the "leadership of that structure must consist of persons whom neighborhood residents accept as representing their interests." "That structure must have sufficient information about any matter to be decided . . . so that it can initiate proposals and react knowledgeably to proposals from others." In order to assure such knowledgeable reactions, the CDA letter provided that "some form of professional technical assistance in a manner agreed to by neighborhood residents shall be provided." The CDA letter also provided for financial assistance to neighborhood residents to facilitate their participation and for the employment of neighborhood residents in planning activities.

The CDA letter was later elaborated upon by Technical Assistance Bulletin No. 3, issued in December 1968.[22] This Bulletin reiterated the provisions of CDA letter No. 3 and described issues that had arisen in the course of its implementation. It is notable for its frankness in acknowledging the difficulty of the undertaking it imposed upon the designated model cities. It selected technical assistance as the key aspect of the relationship between the city and neighborhood residents, but recommended only a combination of assignment of city staff and grant of some funds to the residents' organization to retain consultants. The function of these consultants, as perceived by the Bulletin, would be "to help the citizens understand options and alternatives, or to advise them of options and alternatives and innovations that city or institutional staffs may have overlooked." But, states the Bulletin, this does not mean use of Model Cities planning funds "to hire duplicate and competitive planning staffs." The Bulletin also makes clear, lest there be any doubt, that although there is a "partnership" contemplated between the city and the residents, "city government is clearly the dominant partner in the Model Cities Program," and it is the city that has the "ultimate power of final decision," though the Bulletin warns that the partnership concept must not be "reduced to rhetoric, thus defeating the objectives of citizen participation." In what ought to be viewed as a masterpiece of ironic understatement but was apparently intended as a sincere and direct statement of a truth, the Bulletin states, "in many ventures, some partners are more equal than others."

It is in the light of these provisions that the Department of Housing and Urban Development's explanation of its view of the meaning of the statutory mandate of widespread citizen participation must be understood: "The quality of life in American cities cannot be improved unless people of all classes, races and ethnic groups, and public officials on all levels of government, create process and mechanisms for assessing problems, developing strategies and planning and implementing corrective actions together." [23]

The internal contradiction apparent in the Bulletin's treatment of provision of technical capability to the resident group is manifested also in a statement made in January of 1969 by a HUD Model Cities official:

The residents of the Model Neighorhood are required by Model Cities policy to have access to and capability in decision-making. Any local Model Cities effort which does not afford an effective role to persons affected by the program does not meet Model Cities standards. Any local effort, however, which results in abdication by local government of its administrative and policy-making responsibility also fails to meet program standards.[24]

Of course, the CDA letter, the Bulletin, and the remarks in the above quotation all preceded experience in implementing Model Cities plans, as does the best known of the evaluations of the planning process in Model Cities.[25]

In the process of implementation, the relationship of the city to the group formed to carry out citizen participation has become intertwined with the relationship of various city agencies to the Mayor. The basic purpose of the Model Cities program was to assist cities in achieving coordination of all their functions directed at particular areas of the city most in need of assistance. Thus police, sanitation, health, education, job training, housing, and many other city services were to be coordinated toward a specified set of goals included in the plan created by joint effort of the city and affected citizens. The hope, presumably, was that the leverage of additional federal funds could achieve the coordinated planning and execution in deteriorating areas where it had not been achieved through the existing political processes. It is possible that the hope may yet prove to be justified, but the addition of the residents' Model Cities committee to the already badly coordinated and highly self-centered city bureaucracies gives little reason for optimism. The effort in some cities to bypass existing city agencies in order to achieve some concrete results from Model Cities has generally been rebuffed by a Washington bureaucracy intent upon forcing local coordination and prepared to accept inaction and lack of results if that coordination is not forthcoming. It is not clear that the citizen participation in Model Cities has been a further obstacle in their struggle—more likely it is rather neutral.

In any event, the current administration in Washington appears committed to broadening Model Cities from a deteriorated neighborhood focus to a city-wide focus. Already twenty of the one hundred fifty Model Cities have been designated as "planned variation cities," meaning that the program will operate throughout each city. Whatever impact this may have on the coordination objective, it is bound to compromise severely the effectiveness of existing model neighborhood citizen participation structures. And for the phrase "compromise severely" it may be better to read "destroy." What has happened is that President Nixon has seized upon Model Cities (which for a while his administration had contemplated destroying) as a testing ground for "revenue sharing." From the point of view of citizen participation, there is a considerable irony in this development. The essence of revenue sharing is presumably the grant of federal funds to state and local governments without the kinds of restrictions and conditions that typify categorical grant programs. But the early imposition of citizen participation requirements in federal law, not excluding Model Cities, emerged from a conclusion that local government would not, without external compulsion, create effective political mechanisms to give the poor a voice in programs that affected their well being, or, one should say, affected their margin of survival.

Although these later developments may render moot much of the debate that surrounded the creation of the Model Cities citizen participation organizations, reference to it remains relevant to a general inquiry into citizen participation. The same options existed as have already been noted—reliance on election in the area or on appointment from among existing community leadership. In many of the Model Cities elections were employed—and in most the turn-out of the electorate was small. As was the case in community action elections, the number of candidates was frequently large, their political organization minimal, and the electorate's understanding of the function of the Model Cities committee incomplete. Once in operation, many of these citizen participation structures appear to have established little in the way of regular communication to and consultation with their constituency.

In many of the Model Cities communities the nascent political organization of the poor, begun with the community action programs, found itself confronted by a confusion of boundaries as definition of the area for the purposes of the community action program failed to coincide with the Model Cities neighborhood.

OTHER PROGRAMS

The foregoing constitute the significant grant programs in which the federal government has imposed—by statute or administrative action—the requirement of some form of citizen participation. But they are not exhaustive.

Another example of special interest is to be found in the requirement of parent councils in connection with the administration of funds under Title 1 of the Elementary and Secondary Education Act (ESEA). That Title provides for grant funds to assist school districts ("Local Education Agencies" or LEA) in the education of children from poverty-stricken families. The LEA is required to establish "a system-wide council composed of parents of children to be served in public and nonpublic schools participating in Title I Activities." [26]

The memorandum confronts the two basic issues of how such a group is to be formed and what are to be its functions. As to the first, the memorandum requires that: "members of such a council must be chosen in such a manner as to ensure that they are broadly representative of the group to be served. In addition, each local educational agency is encouraged to form similar councils at each school participating in Title I activities." As to the function of the council or councils, the memorandum reflects the same uncertainty as the earlier administrative materials I have reviewed. It is clear that the councils must be informed concerning the uses of Title I funds in general and each project applied for in particular. Beyond this requirement of information, the memorandum provides that the LEA must "involve its parent council in the planning and development of the Title I project application." But in explaining the meaning of involvement, the memorandum lists activities that give it less than its potential sweep. Thus, the parents council must have access to school officials to comment on Title I projects, a procedure must be established to respond to parent council questions about Title I projects, the parent council must have the right to inspect official documents connected with Title I projects, views of the parent council about the unmet needs of children in Title I project areas must be "incorporated into the local educational agency's planning process" and the views of the parent council concerning the concentration of Title I funds in particular schools and grade levels must be incorporated into the LEA's development activities.

Thus, the function of parent councils is to advise. They are without power to decide. Their advice is based solely on information provided them. They lack the leverage they might gain if their advice were based upon independent technical assistance.

Still other citizen participation programs have been created by local government. For example, in the City of New York there are local planning boards, members of which are appointed by borough presidents, which have the function of advising the City Planning Commission as to community views of proposed action on such matters as zoning and capital budget. The boards are advisory only, but their views must be sought.

New York City has also established community health boards composed of doctors, hospital personnel, and representatives of community organizations to determine community health needs. Eight experimental boards were established in 1969, largely in poverty areas. The future of the community health planning boards —both their structure and function—remains uncertain. It appears, however, that like virtually every other citizen participation program, the basic thrust would be to permit a citizen group to advise central agencies in connection with the planning processes of the central agencies.

NEW FORMS OF CITIZEN PARTICIPATION IN TRADITIONAL GOVERNMENTAL FUNCTIONS

As I indicated at the outset, citizen participation in emerging social institutions may prove to be less significant than emerging citizen participation in existing social institutions. The most spectacular development in this area has been the pressure for neighborhood government, particularly in poverty areas. Thus far this has achieved a concrete result in the form of a reformation of the New York City School System into thirty-one community school boards which function, more or less, as the local school boards for the elementary and intermediate schools within their jurisdiction. These boards are not, of course, limited to the poverty areas but encompass the entire city.

This is not the place to review the history of school decentralization in New York City. A few essential generalizations will be helpful to this discussion. First, the stated initial thrust of school decentralization and community control was to increase the accountability of the system to those the system was organized to serve. The very statement of such a proposition suggests that there was a view that the school system was not accountable to parents, children, or the community as a whole. This view is distinguishable, for the purposes of analysis at least, from the view that the schools were failing to accomplish their assigned task—the education of the city's children.

Second, the decentralization of the system into thirty-one elected boards represented a failure of the techniques of advice and consultation as a mode for citizen participation. Decentralization had followed approximately ten years of action by advisory local school boards appointed by the central Board of Education from lists drawn up for each school district by organizational leaders from that district. This experience, together with what was believed to be the general unresponsiveness to citizen views of the central Board and headquarters professional organization, made joint planning and operation of the system an unacceptable alternative to proponents of change (persons largely but not exclusively from poverty areas).

Third, the functions that were retained centrally in the face of considerable decentralization reflected the ultimate power of existing city-wide institutions to retain essential elements under their control. Thus, in the areas of resource allocation, capital construction, and collective bargaining, the powers of the community boards are minimal, and in matters of hiring, promotion, transfer, and discipline of personnel the functions of the community boards are rather narrowly circumscribed.

Fourth, the techniques of selecting community board members— a district-wide election carried out by proportional representation —engendered a mix of confusion and apathy. Although the turnout of about 14 percent of eligible voters compares favorably with Model Cities and Community Action elections, it was not impressively large. It would not be unfair to say that, in general, control of community boards went not to those who had most actively favored community control, nor to parents for whom a shift in control over schools seems most important, but to religious organizations (concerned with allocation of Title I ESEA funds for parochial schools), to the teachers and other school professionals, and to existing political organizations (largely political parties).

Nevertheless, the decentralization of New York City's school system deserves to be viewed as an indication of citizen dissatisfaction in our large cities with the degree to which existing institutions are capable of responding or do respond to locally felt needs and priorities. New York City is about to undertake a further experiment in neighborhood government. The functions to be assigned to it and the manner of its composition when these become known may be viewed in the light of experience both with community school boards and the citizen participation elements in the federal grant programs.

Still another and different form of citizen participation changing the face and function of an existing social institution is to be found in the broadening by the courts of the concept of standing to sue, particularly in the federal courts. In urban renewal and in environmental matters particularly, the courts have permitted interested citizen groups to invoke judicial review of the legality of governmental (usually administrative) action. This has at times resulted in a judicial order that an administrative agency permit submission of data to the agency before it reaches a decision affecting the citizens complaining of anticipated administrative action;[27] at other times it has resulted in forcing a significant change in the administrative decision already reached.[28] It is important to note, however, that all the expanded willingness of courts to hear citizen complaints can achieve is more rigorous compliance with the constitution, statutes, and applicable administrative regulations. It cannot reach the most basic allocational decisions nor test the wisdom of most governmental programs nor alter the manner of performance of most governmental services.

SUMMARY AND CONCLUSIONS

Concerning the community action programs, Moynihan has written:

> It may be the poor are never ready to assume power in an advanced society: the exercise of power in an effective manner is an ability acquired through apprenticeship and seasoning. Thrust on an individual or a group, the results are often painful to observe, and when what in fact is conveyed is not power, but a kind of play-acting at power, the results can be absurd.[29]

Although it is too early to reach final judgments about the various forms of citizen participation undertaken since the mid-1960s, Moynihan's conclusion may hold for most of the citizen structures in most of the programs. But his statement must not close discussion but serve rather to reopen the issues for further examination.

Judged from the point of view of conduct rather than rhetoric, the past six years have demonstrated that a decision to involve the poor in decision making by constituting committees that are essentially advisory on general policy matters achieves little but frustration for those involved in the effort. To the poor it seems that there is only, in Moynihan's phrase "playacting at power." To the city officials, there is at best simply one more bit of red tape, one more bureaucratic obstacle; at worst, the result as seen by city officials is the creation of a lobbying group which, while not powerful enough to create decisions, may have the power to frustrate the decisions of the city planners.

It must be noted that with far fewer formal mechanisms at hand than those created by HUD, OEO, and others, various groups around the United States have, over the years, had considerable impact on federal, state, and local governmental decision making. Efforts such as those led by Nader have significantly altered the posture of all levels of government toward consumer protection issues; efforts by the Sierra Club, the Environmental Defense Fund, and other conservationist groups have forced great changes both in statutes and in administrative action on environmental issues. These experiences and others of the last decade are but later analogues of the power demonstrated in earlier years by regulated industries: it is, under certain power configurations, possible to influence administrative action utilizing only a right to comment on proposed regulations or sometimes to testify at public hearings. Both of these participatory devices are ridiculed by militants for "citizen participation" and "community control," who say they are meaningless. And they are of course largely meaningless when used by or for the poor of our society: years of public hearings on urban renewal plans produced few if any changes for the protesting poor.

The fault, then, may lie not in the devices chosen—whether hearings, advisory committees, or even joint planning structures—but in the distribution of power in our society. The powerful person or group finds many devices useful—the poor person may find none.

In writing about the poverty program, sociologist Nathan Glazer said that:

> My reservations about the anti-poverty program are much like those of the critic who says the subject of the play should have been different. . . . I think we still have to take on the jobs which the anti-poverty program, as set up under the Act, did not address itself to—reducing the unemployment rate, increasing the number of jobs, expanding and revising the social security and social welfare systems, improving the systems of job training, job counseling and job placement, attacking the failures of school systems and police systems. . . . In the end . . . a democratic polity cannot take the position that the major way to improve its institutions of government and welfare is to finance guerrilla warfare against them. It must take up the job of directly improving and transforming them.[30]

It is not difficult to draw up a list of the kinds of structural changes that might make a fundamental difference in the life of the poor in our society. On the political side, recent judicial decisions and legislative enactments have moved somewhat further toward making participation in the existing political institutions more meaningful and less burdensome—the reapportionment decisions by the Supreme Court, the invalidation of the poll tax, the enforcement of reasonable rules for voter registration, limitations on campaign expenditures, establishing a kind of semipublic fund for campaign expenses—all these may ease access to existing political structures. In the future, use of cable TV systems in local elections may further this same objective.

If political power in this nation were based purely on voter behavior at election time, these developments might raise great expectations. But such expectations must be tempered by the fact that wealth weighs at the very least equally in the scales of political power. How then can the poor gain political power when the very characterization of their economic status seems to assure their political weakness? Must participation in governmental decision making for the poor remain, to borrow Justice Jackson's memorable phrase, a munificent bequest in a pauper's will? Since there is little hope of changing the formula of political power that gives economic capacity so large a role, it is necessary instead to deal directly with the roots of powerlessness—poverty itself.

That, as we are learning, is more easily promised than achieved. Token categorical grant programs with citizen participation structures are clearly inadequate for the task. Although, as a law professor, I probably speak out of turn on the matter, let me hazard a few suggestions. In a capitalist society, which despite the allegations of some conservatives we still are, participation in economic rewards is dependent upon productivity. Although we have distorted that relationship through perpetuation of oligopolies in both business and labor, the relationship persists. The poor are poor in part at least because they do not produce, or produce that to which society attaches little economic value. As for those who are infirm, or for other reasons unable to increase their productivity, society can only undertake to ease their burdens by contributing funds for their lifetimes. The responsibility of society to those poor whose capacity to produce can be enlarged, however, is to provide realistic and believable opportunities to increase that capacity. We have accepted this challenge in the institution of public education. But even if that education were of sufficient quality, it would be of little use if the student did not believe the societal promise of an opportunity to produce at the end of schooling. We wish everyone in our society to have faith in it—but after too many years of unfulfilled promises there can be faith only where there is reasonable hope. Working hard in school is an act of faith. We can expect it when there is hope. There can be no hope until we undertake all of those institutional changes that will be needed to achieve not only a virtual full-employment economy, but one in which race and class prejudice do not preclude opportunities for increased productivity and increased economic rewards. Even at that point, governmental intervention may be required if the economic rewards of certain kinds of work are inadequate to provide a decent standard of living.

An act of faith likewise underlies participation in the political process. Only if one believes that that participation may influence governmental decisions, will desire to participate continue and grow. Thus the circle is complete—poverty, alienation, stasis.

It is not my intention to communicate a sense of lack of merit in the developments summarized in this essay. A number of potential benefits inhere in programs such as community action, PAC, Model Cities committees, and the like. The political experience gained by the leadership of the new citizen participation organizations may be applied to the larger political scene where crucial decisions about the redistribution of wealth are made. The economic and social programs, while grossly inadequate, may bring some improvement in the lives of the poor and with it some renewed faith in the system as a whole and willingness to participate in it. Those among the poor who have direct responsibility for making decisions on economic issues within the community (though those decisions may be ignored by the city) may develop economic expertise which will be of continuing benefit to them when applied to the general functions of our economy.

On the other hand, our citizen participation efforts thus far undertaken entail potential dangers. Perhaps most fundamental, if attention be focused primarily on the poor, is the possibility that political energies will be employed on the wrong stage. We will have induced the exhaustion of limited political energy (reflecting little political faith) in the side rings while the center ring of major societal conduct goes unwatched and unaffected. This is a sophisticated form of leading the poor to accept a political ghetto, as their economic circumstance has confined them within a racial ghetto.

Still another danger—perhaps in the long run an even more serious one—is that the theory of community self-determination (perhaps the logical end point of the doctrine of citizen participation as we have been developing it) may lead to unjust and unwise results viewed from a larger perspective. Thus it is clear that by-and-large middle-class white Americans will, if they have the choice, prevent the construction of public housing in their communities (unless perhaps it is exclusively for the aged). Somewhat wealthier Americans, living in the suburbs, make land-use decisions that result in a high land cost to unit ratio which in turn makes housing construction for the poor or even the middle class impossible. Indeed, probably the most crucial political question of our day is how and whether we will terminate the autonomy of the suburban governments whose economic and land-use decisions have created so many difficulties for our cities. In turn, in urban renewal areas and model cities areas in which the citizen participation organization has prevailed on some decisions, the same egocentric phenomena may be observed. There is no reason to believe that economic and social selfishness observes class bounds.

While we continue to examine what we may do to create direct involvement of all citizens—and particularly the alienated poor—in matters pertaining to particular neighborhoods, we must more clearly focus on the goals we have often stated but not pursued—a redistribution of wealth and political power to achieve greater equality of access to our political, economic, and social institutions. As we accomplish that great goal, we may discover that many existing political and social institutions will work better than many of our citizens now believe possible.

NOTES AND REFERENCES

1. K. G. Clark and J. Hopkins, *A Relevant War Against Poverty* (New York: Harper & Row, 1969).
2. See D. Moynihan, *Maximum Feasible Misunderstanding* (1969).
3. H. Spiegel and S. Mittenthal, *Neighborhood Power and Control: Im-*

plications for Planning (A Report Prepared for the Department of Housing and Urban Development; Institute of Urban Environment, School of Architecture, Columbia U., 1968), pp. 30-34.

4. Clark and Hopkins, *Relevant War*, pp. 152-156.
5. *Ibid.*, p. 156.
6. Moynihan, *Misunderstanding*, pp. 134-135.
7. H. Hallman, *Neighborhood Control of Public Programs* (New York: Praeger, 1970), p. 18.
8. *Ibid.*, pp. 32-33.
9. *Ibid.*, p. 40.
10. *Ibid.*, p. 33.
11. *Ibid.*, pp. 28-31.
12. Department of Housing and Urban Development, *Workable Program for Community Improvement, Program Guide No. 7* (Washington, D.C.: Government Printing Office, 1966).
13. *Ibid.*, p. 1.
14. *Ibid.*, p. 2.
15. *Ibid.*
16. *Ibid.*
17. S. Unger, "Citizen Participation: A Challenge to HUD and the Community," *Urban Lawyer*, 2 (1970), 29, 34.
18. *Ibid.*
19. Urban Renewal Handbook, RHA 7217.2, Chapter 5, Section 2. Compare the Michigan statutory provision for citizen participation in urban renewal, *Mich. Stat. Ann.*, Section 3504(2) (Supp. 1970).
20. Hallman, "Neighborhood Control," pp. 185-186.
21. Public Law 89-754, 80 Stat. 1255, 42 U.S.C. 3301.
22. HUD MCGR 3110.3.
23. *Ibid.*
24. Remarks of Mr. Bernard Russell, HUD Assistant Administrator of Model Cities, Proceedings of the National Conference on Advocacy and Pluralistic Planning, January 10 and 11, 1969, at p. 83 (Mann ed).
25. See "The Model Cities Program: A History and Analysis of the Planning Process in Three Cities: Atlanta, Georgia; Seattle, Washington; Dayton, Ohio." (Prepared by Marshall Kaplan, Gans, & Kahn, printed by U.S. Government Printing Office for HUD, May 1969.)
26. Memorandum from T. H. Fall, Acting U.S. Commissioner of Education, to Chief, State School Offices, entitled "Advisory Statement on Development of Policy on Parental Involvement in Title 1, ESEA Projects," October 26, 1970.
27. *Powelton Civic Home Owners Association v. HUD*, 284 F. Supp. 809 (E.D. Pa. 1968); *Western Addition Community Organization v. Weaver*, 294 F. Supp. 433 (N.D. Calif. 1968), injuction dissolved, 320 F. Supp. 308 (N.D. Calif. 1969).
28. *Shannon v. HUD*, 436 F. 2d 809 (3d Cir. 1970); *North City Area Council, Inc. v. Romney*, 428 F. 2d 754 (3rd Cir. 1970); *Gautreaux v. Chicago Housing Authority*, 296 F. Supp. 907, 304 F. Supp. 736 (N.D. 111. 1969).
29. *Maximum Feasible Misunderstanding*, pp. 136-137.
30. Glazer, "The Grand Design of the Poverty Program," from *Poverty, Power and Politics*, ed. Chaim Waxman (1968), pp. 291-292.

9

EXPERT AND LAY PARTICIPATION IN DECISION MAKING

STEPHEN WEXLER

Each man's right to participate in the decisions that affect him has been seriously compromised by an excessive reliance on professionals and experts. Our right to participate directly in personal decisions and our right to participate through political mechanisms in group decisions are both affected. We do not understand how and when to use professionals and experts, and so we have come to rely on them when we should not and they have gained power that they should not have. Computers are giving experts greater and greater access to information. This enhances their claims to power and increases our reliance on them.

I wish to suggest that there is a kind of question that an expert can answer for us, and another kind of question that we must answer for ourselves. Experts can *help* us with questions of the latter sort, and I shall try to outline some of the ways in which they can do so. But, though an expert can help us with such questions, they call finally for a decision that only we can make.

Without some information we cannot answer even the easiest (nonanalytic) questions. If we are trying to find a way of crossing a stream and someone calls out "Will this log reach across?" we would surely want to look at both the log and the stream. We would be unable to answer even easy questions if we did not have a little information, and, therefore, when we cannot answer hard questions, we tend to think it is because we do not have enough information. We believe that getting more information always puts us in a better position to answer any question.

It is true that some information is needed to answer any question. It is not true, however, that more information is always useful. Some questions are hard to answer only because we do not have enough information. Once we have enough information the question is an easy one. But some questions are altogether different: it is not a lack of information that makes them hard to answer, and therefore, more information cannot help one answer them. There is no such thing as enough information to make such questions easy.

The distinction is important and corresponds, I believe, to a distinction made along the following lines. Simplex questions are those in which all relevant factors can be measured in the same units.[1] "Will the log reach across the stream?" is a simplex question; it turns on the length of the log and the width of the stream, both of which can be stated in the same units.

If the log is eight feet long and the stream is twenty feet wide, "Will the log reach across?" is an easy question; it is also easy if the log is twenty feet long and the stream is eight feet wide. To answer easy questions like these we need only approximate information; a glance at the log and the stream is enough. Not all simplex questions are easy ones, however; if the log is about as long as the stream is wide, "Will the log reach across?" is a difficult question. We will want more than just a glance at the log and the stream. We will want to measure and, given the proper question, we may want to measure quite precisely.

The point to notice is that what makes a simplex question difficult is precisely that we lack information. More information is exactly what is needed to answer difficult questions of this kind.

Complex questions are those in which all the factors cannot be measured in the same units. "Should we wade across or fell a tree to bridge the stream?" is a complex question; it involves, at least, our feelings about getting wet and our feelings about work, and these cannot be stated in the same terms. Complex questions can be reduced to simplex ones by ignoring relevant factors. Thus, "Will it take longer to wade across or bridge the stream?" is a simplex question but it ignores wetness, coldness, the difficulty of different tasks, etc.

Complex questions can be easy. Thus, if the water is very cold and we have a power saw, it is easy to decide whether to wade or bridge the stream; it is also easy if the water is pleasant and we have only hatchets. For easy complex questions as for easy simplex ones, approximate information is enough. We do not need to know the exact temperature of the water or the precise difficulty of felling a tree.

But if the water is fairly cold and bridging the stream is a fairly hard job, whether to wade or bridge is a difficult question. The important point is that a lack of information is not what makes this a difficult question, and more information will not help us answer it. Once we have said the water is *fairly* cold and felling a tree will be *fairly* hard, we have all the information that is useful. More precise information may seem to be useful, but that is illusory. What good does it do to know that the water is 56°? Suppose it had been 58°? The difficulty in this question rests not on lack of information but on having no way, in close cases, of measuring getting wet and cold against working hard.

We need no help with easy questions, simplex or complex. It is with difficult questions that we need help. It is with difficult questions that we go to experts. An expert's license indicates that he has certain information or the skill to obtain it,[2] and so, given the proper instructions, an expert is the person best suited to answer difficult simplex questions. These questions are difficult for us because we do not have or cannot obtain certain information; for an expert this difficulty does not exist.

Can an expert "answer" our difficult complex questions? It would seem not. These questions are not difficult for lack of information: they are difficult because we must compare two or more different values and we can do so only in the grossest cases.

Can an expert decide whether we would rather be fairly wet or fairly tired? Though experts are regularly asked to answer such questions and regularly answer them, it seems to me that their licenses do not really entitle them to do so. They can be very helpful in a number of ways when we decide difficult complex questions, but they cannot decide them for us, as they can answer difficult simplex questions. Let me point out some of the ways they can help us.

1. Difficult simplex questions often underlie difficult complex ones. Thus, "Should I bring suit?" is a complex question, behind which one finds simplex questions such as "Have I a cause of action?"—precisely the sort of question a lawyer is licensed to answer. But that simplex question is not equivalent to "Should I sue?" "Should I sue?" requires a personal decision in which one must compare the advisability of suing with the hassle involved, the personal feelings between the parties, one's trust in one's lawyer, etc. A lawyer is in no special position to decide that question. In some ways, he is in a very bad position: his training leads him to ignore all the factors that make the question complex.

If both the lawyer and I know what to expect of experts, the lawyer can be useful. Complex questions often appear to be difficult only because we have not answered simplex ones. Thus, "Should I sue (if I know there will be bad publicity)?" may seem a difficult complex question until I find out that I have no chance of winning, at which point it becomes an easy question.

We all tend to treat experts in other fields as wise men. Thus, we might be tempted to ask a doctor, "Should I tell my friend that his illness is very serious?" But how can the doctor decide whether I should obey my friend's wish that I tell him or do what is medically best? As with the lawyer, I should ask, "Is it likely to be medically bad if I tell him that his illness is serious?" If the answer is no, then what looked like a difficult decision is in fact an easy one. If the answer is yes, then I, and not the doctor, must decide what to do.

The danger is that the doctor will say "You must not tell him." And professionals often say just this sort of thing. One day, at lunch, a friend of mine who is a lawyer talked about a problem he was having:

I don't know what to do. I've a criminal trial this afternoon and

I can't decide whether to put my man on the stand. He says that the policemen who arrested him are lying about what they saw him do. I don't think the lie means much because even if he did what they said, I don't think they have a case. But my man says he wants to tell the truth. More important, if he says the police are lying, the judge is likely not to believe anything he says. I just can't decide whether he should testify or not.

It seems to me that my friend has no business making this decision. He may be able, as I have said, to help his client make the decision, by clarifying questions about evidence and judicial tendencies, but nothing in a lawyer's special training or skill entitles him to decide how important it is to tell the truth.

2. There is another way in which experts can help us decide difficult complex questions. Often, the expert will have seen other people make similar decisions, or he may have access to statistics on prior decisions. Thus, a trail guide might know that, of the people he has been out with, most of those who chose to wade the stream regretted their decision, while few of those who chose to bridge it regretted theirs. An expert may have experience as well as knowledge.[3]

This experience can be useful if the expert has seen many cases, if they have been substantially the same, and if the results have not been the product of the expert's biases. However, there is no reason why the expert cannot give us the details of his experience rather than summary advice. Instead of telling me what to do, he should tell me what he knows and let me decide what to do. The expert's experience only answers the simplex question "What percentage of the people have regretted wading?"—i.e., "How likely is it that I will regret wading?"

But "How likely is it that I will regret wading?" is not the same as "Should I wade?" I might sensibly say, "Well, though it is likely that I will regret wading, nevertheless I will do so."

Let me illustrate: "Is Jones lying about what he did Friday night?" is a complex question (unless I know for certain what Jones did Friday night).[4] To answer this question I must weigh Jones' past record for telling the truth against his demeanor, against his reasons for lying, against the plausibility of his story, etc. A psychologist may be able to tell me that people like Jones are, in his experience, very likely to lie in cases such as this, but he cannot answer the question "Is Jones lying?"

It seems quite clear to me that even after I have heard the psychologist, I will still want to talk to Jones: I will want to talk to Jones because I might conclude, "Though it seems likely that a man like Jones would lie in a case like this, nevertheless I believe him."

3. An expert may help us decide complex questions by pointing out relevant factors that we have neglected. Thus, if we are trying to decide whether to encourage small farmers to move to the cities, and we are weighing the loss of rural life styles against increased farm yield, an expert might tell us that we have forgotten to note the increased welfare costs entailed by forcing workers into a tight economy.

4. An expert can help us to know that the complex question we face is a difficult one. In some cases only an expert will be able to give us the approximation we need to see the problem. Thus, we may not know that felling a tree is *fairly* hard work. Or that putting a road through a town will cause *fairly* serious social upheavals.

We do need *some* information to know that there is a real question, and experts can often give that to us. But more information will not help to decide it.

If we face a simplex question and an expert tells us the tree is about eight feet long and the stream is about eight feet wide, we can usefully send him back for a closer measurement. If he returns and says, "The tree is eight feet plus a little less than one inch long and the stream is eight feet plus a little less than one inch wide" we can send him back again. We can push him back through as many decimal places as is necessary to get an answer. Approximations will not do.

But if the expert tells us the road will be *fairly* useful and the number of families up-rooted will be *about* 400, he has served his purpose. If we ask for, and he obtains, more accurate information, he has given us something useless. So it is exactly 396 families. So what?

Now I wish to raise and deal with a very important objection.

If the information that experts bring us is sometimes useful and at worst useless, why not get as much of it as we can? There are at least four good reasons not to do so—four good reasons why we should remember that information, and therefore experts, can play only a very limited role in the decision of difficult complex questions.

1. If we neglect to distinguish between questions an expert can answer and questions we must decide ourselves, we may inadvertently ask the expert the wrong one and he may answer it, thereby preempting our decision. So, if we ask an economist whether we should encourage small farmers to move to the cities, he may compute the costs and the profits and say "Yes," and we will forget to count the loss of the rural life style.

2. If we forget that there are some questions we must decide for ourselves, we will come to rely on experts too much. They will become wise men for us. The Pentagon Papers reveal that Lyndon Johnson gave away the American people's ability to participate through their elected officials in deciding whether to make war in Vietnam. And he did so because he developed an improper reliance on body counts, kill-ratios, and cost-benefit analyses and the people who prepared them.

3, If we remember that precise information is not always essential in making decisions, we foreclose one of the arguments of those who would take away our right to participate. "Do you know exactly how many megatons the bomb on Amchitka will be?" "Don't tell me lots of people get killed, tell me how many get killed." "Can you be sure that putting mercury in the lake will kill the fish? Professor so-and-so is not sure." "When were you in Cambodia last?" When we are deciding difficult complex questions, an argument that rests on the other fellow's lack of precise information is spurious.

4. Most important, once we have invested time and money to get information we will be tempted to use it. A friend of mine once decided to build a brick wall. She ordered the bricks, and by the time they came she was no longer sure she wanted the wall. But she had spent a lot of money on the bricks and so she *decided*

to build the wall. If an expert tells us that the water is 57.3°, we are likely to say, "Well, it's more than 57°, so let's wade."

I would like to make one final point. There is a difference between "answering a question" and "deciding a question." "Answer" and "decide" may be used interchangeably in some cases, but they are clearly not interchangeable in other cases. I suggest that where "answer" and "decide" cannot be used interchangeably it is generally true that "answer" goes with simplex questions and "decide" with complex ones.

Much of the characteristic talk surrounding "answer" and "decide" seems to me to bolster the main point I have tried to make above. Here then, briefly noted, are some interesting differences between "answering" and "deciding" a question:

1. I am less upset if someone "answers for me" than if someone "decides for me."

2. If X was hurt in a car accident with Y, and X was not wearing his seat belt, can Y set up the defense of contributory negligence? A lawyer goes to the library and *answers* this question; a judge hears argument and *decides* it.

3. An "answer" is characteristically "right" or "wrong"—a decision is "sound" or "unsound" but rarely "right" or "wrong."

4. An answer is "wrong" because it is not *the* answer. If a decision is wrong, it is not wrong for that reason.

5. An answer can be said to be wrong *before* one acts on it; if one says a decision is wrong, it is usually in retrospect, *after* acting on it. If we decide to wade the stream, find we don't like it, and see our friends have bridged it easily and happily, we will say, "We made the wrong decision." (The question "Should we wade or bridge?" calls for a decision. But the question "Should we have waded or bridged?" calls for an answer, and it is the existence of a right answer that makes our decision wrong in retrospect.)

6. One can "regret a decision" but not an answer (at least not in the same way).

7. An answer can be wrong by 25 percent; a decision cannot.

8. A question that has been decided is different from a question that has been answered.

NOTES AND REFERENCES

1. "Measurable in the same units" obviously begs all sorts of questions about measuring, sameness, and units. Professor Donald Brown has suggested that what I am after is "capable in principle of being definitely settled by available methods of investigation." That too is close but not without problems. In any case, the real distinction is between questions that are difficult because we lack information and questions that are difficult for other reasons. "Measurable in the same units" is offered only as an aid and not as a test, and I think what I mean by it is clear. I also want to avoid questions about whether we can measure pleasures and pains. If we cannot get an answer in close questions where the factors are "measurable" in "utiles" only, then such questions are complex and we must decide them. And if we can in close cases measure or rank pleasures and pains, then the questions are simplex, but we are the "experts" on them; we must look inside ourselves and not to experts for answers.

2. Experts are also licensed on the basis of their skills to perform certain operations. Typically these skills, insofar as they are not used for gathering information, are applied after a question has been decided, simply to give effect to the decision. Thus, surgery is performed sometimes to see if further surgery is necessary and sometimes to remove something the doctor has decided must be removed. One need not suggest that the patient participate in the operation just because one suggests that he participate in the decision about whether there should be an operation.

3. There are times (for instance, when it is important to make a *quick* choice) when we can reasonably rely on an expert to decide a question we could decide. Also, making a decision may consume a great deal of time, and so we might in certain circumstances reasonably delegate it to someone else. Finally, an expert may have what is sometimes called a trained intuition; he may know something in a way he cannot explain. It sometimes makes sense to trust an expert's intuition. I believe we rely on experts too much, but that is not really the point here. Whether we increase, decrease, or continue our reliance on experts, we should know why we rely on them and whether we have good grounds for doing so.

4. If I know for certain what Jones did, then "Is Jones lying about what he did?" is a simplex question and I am an expert on the matter; I have all the information needed to decide.

10

PARTICIPATION WITHOUT RESPONSIBILITY: CODETERMINATION IN INDUSTRY AND UNIVERSITY

CARL J. FRIEDRICH

"The idea of participation remains fuzzy. . . . For to participate can mean several things." Thus starts a discussion of workers' participation in industrial management in a recent French work of these problems.[1] In Germany, the practical thrust of participation in industry and university—two focal points of modern industrial society—is the notion of codetermination *(Mitbestimmung)*. The notion of *Mitbestimmung* often is associated with ideas reminiscent of those popular in the American Left of an "industrial democracy."[2] Generally speaking, it denotes an organizational arrangement under which those customarily seen as *not* participating in the running of the organization, but part of it under the direction of others who are in charge, acquire the right (and the duty) to *participate* in the making of policy decisions. The notion is not

195

popular among British and American organized labor; here it is felt that such participation confuses the lines of responsibility and involves labor in decisions that might inhibit a union's effective defense and promotion of the workers' interest. The parallel notion that students should participate in the running of universities, that they should share in making policy for a university and in selecting its teaching staff, has had a much wider range of practical application, especially in the United States. One key difficulty in both cases lies in the fact that workers in a plant and students in a university constitute fairly numerous collectives who could participate only by representatives, presumably chosen by those represented. Something more will be said about these difficulties later on.

Factories and universities are organizations with a technical goal. The achievement of the goal—the manufacture of a certain product, the provision of a certain education—presupposes technical knowledge. To illustrate the obvious: one cannot teach mathematics, and one cannot manufacture an automobile without knowing automotive engineering or employing those who do. To put it more generally, one cannot run a business without knowing how to market its products at a profit. The opposite view, widespread among protesters, is that for a variety of philosophical reasons people may effectively participate in decision making on such technical operations without possessing the knowledge of the operations involved in the particular undertaking. The growth of modern democracy has promoted this sort of outlook; for, the argument runs, if people can effectively participate in government, a difficult and complex process, they surely can do so in other less demanding operations. However, the implied analogy between government and such activities as business and education is unsound, for a basic reason. Government is a multipurpose undertaking, and the participation of nonexperts is arguable in terms of choosing the purposes and their rank order.

A recent Brookings publication deals with the setting of national alternatives.[3] At the start, the authors affirm that "the federal budget is more than a collection of numbers . . . the budget is a means of determining how national resources should be allocated"; for "the size of the budget and the way it is financed strongly influence national output, employment, and the rate of inflation." It is evident that the people at large should have some voice in how the priorities that so vitally affect them are decided upon. The massive expertise that is involved should be "on tap and not on top," to use a hackneyed phrase. But in single-purpose organizations, such as health, education, or profit, there is no need for such participation in order to determine what the purpose should be. And even in organizations with several fixed purposes, such participation would serve only a very limited purpose. So-called policy decisions are not directed toward choosing alternative purposes, but are concerned with ways of achieving them.

An experienced and successful executive, Chester I. Barnard, argued some years ago that the term "policy" was meaningless—an overstatement of a significant point, namely, that "policy" may mean different things under varying circumstances.[4] Workers' participation in industrial management is concerned primarily with those decisions that affect labor's well-being. Industrial democracy means that the trade unions participate in all decisions, within enterprises and beyond them, that are concerned with the economy.[5] Since the workers themselves cannot all participate, they must be represented, and such participation is structured by their unions. The unions play a role similar to that of parties in the political process at large. It is not surprising that the unions have been in the forefront of the agitation favoring *Mitbestimmung,* while the two leading German parties, the SPD and the CDU[6] are split on the subject and the liberals are opposed. The latter have kept the SPD from moving on this front; it is one of the weak points in their coalition. Basically, the present issue is whether to extend the provisions of a 20-year-old law establishing *Mitbestimmung* for the coal and steel industry. The labor unions claim that it has worked well, whereas industry questions this assertion. Labor has shown some dissatisfaction over abuses incidental to the administration of the law. But what counts is, of course, that a policy that runs counter to the general principles of a free market economy (even when qualified as "social") may be feasible within a small sector of the system but would be impracticable when applied to the entire economy. Hence even if *Mitbestimmung* in the coal and steel industry could be proved to have been entirely successful—and no one has been able to show this so far—it would not allow one to conclude that it would be desirable for industry as a whole. There are other complicating factors, notably the effect of such a system upon the competitive position of German industry within the European Common Market, the other members of which do not prac-

tice *Mitbestimmung*—Labor in Britain, France, and Belgium is
opposed to it. The rapid decline in the coal industry must also be
taken into account, since the workers' situation is very unstable;
many are threatened with losing their place of work as a result of
the coal crisis.[7]

The extension of the existing *Mitbestimmung* in the coal and
steel industry is linked to a proposed alteration in the German law
for industrial corporations, the *Betriebsverfassungsgesetz*. Under
this law, a constitution for commercial enterprises, it is provided
that in companies over a certain size labor is represented on the
supervisory board by one of its three members (besides having
shop councils). The opinion prevailing among those concerned is
that this arrangement has been successful. It has increased the
workers' understanding of managerial problems; it has helped communication among managers (owners as well as employees), and
has provided important knowledge for the making of sound policy
decisions. Whether a gain would be realized by expanding it as far
as the *Mitbestimmung* in coal and steel may well be doubted. Some
degree of "democratizing" by granting representatives of labor a
real voice in the management of industry and other business seems a
natural extension of democracy in highly industrialized economies.
It means the application of the basic ideas of *constitutional* democracy to the governing of the great organisms of an advanced industrial society. But it is often forgotten in these discussions that
constitutional democracy calls for the restraining of power under
law. Many of the advocates of industrial democracy, i.e., of *Mitbestimmung,* write as if democracy necessarily means unlimited
power for the people.[8] It does not. Rather, it calls for the careful
delimitation of such popular power. In line with this approach, the
workers' participation in industry requires an analysis to determine
to which fields and functions such participation should extend. The
same approach applies to student participation in the governing of
universities. Students have a significant contribution to make to
functions related to living arrangements, curricular structure, and
priorities as to what is to be taught. There are other functions,
such as personnel (e.g., selection of professors) and the requirements for achieving the goal of professional competence through
the appropriate training, in which students' potential contributions
are limited, so that they can fill only a consultative or advisory
role. Unfortunately, the moralizing approach, which views the is-

sue not in terms of functions and potential contributions to the goal but of psychologizing generalities, tends to lose sight of such considerations. The fierce partisanship that prevails does not generate the suspicion of the potential abuse of all power that promoted the development of constitutionalism in modern government.[9] On the contrary, there is a pronounced tendency to question the existence of such a danger. It would take a detailed analysis of all the votes (including votes *not* taken) to offer conclusive empirical proof; one notes in the absence of such a study that the Biedenkopf Commission Report fails to deal with this vital question.

The heart of the problem is that of responsibility. To whom are labor's representatives responsible in crucial situations? The grave decisions called for in response to the coal crisis were presumably sound. But sound from what point of view? In a sense, the identical issue arises in situations in which student participation in university administration is advocated or practiced. To whom are these representatives responsible?[10] Quite apart from the aspect of responsibility that implies accountability,[11] responsible conduct by power-handlers has been brought about by religious belief as well as by political, administrative, and judicial sanctions. More recently, ideological outlook has replaced religious belief for many people. The representative quality of a person is much affected by his being responsible to those with whom he shares a common ideological outlook. This fact has decided relevance for workers' codetermination, for a widespread anticapitalist outlook would seem to exclude the possibility of workers' representatives on supervisory boards and management boards.[12] But the German law provides for their effective participation, and a resulting confusion as to who is responsible to whom and for what. It is probably the fact that Anglo-American constitutional tradition has imbued many with an almost instinctive sense of the relation of representation and responsibility that accounts for the hostility of British and American organized labor toward codetermination schemes. It is likewise probable that the hostility of the Communists to such a plan of codetermination is ideologically motivated. For effective responsibility cannot in their perspective be expected from a workers' representative on the board of an industrial company in a capitalist system. Though they do not express themselves in these terms, what they do say makes it quite clear that responsibility is at the core of their objections.

It seems relevant to our analysis of codetermination to elaborate upon the issue of responsibility, political responsibility. The responsibility of representatives affects their legitimacy; for it determines the belief of those concerned in the title of such representatives. In the working out of Workers' Codetermination in Germany it appears that such legitimacy has been accorded the workers' representatives,[13] which in turn has led to the demands for its extension to all large enterprises in Germany (and maybe Europe). Representation is legitimate when those affected believe it to be rightful. Those affected are not only those represented but also those confronted by the representative, such as the owners and managers of codetermined companies. The links among representation, legitimacy, authority, and power provide the basis for a more rounded judgment on responsibility. For even a legitimate representative may be irresponsible. This is certainly true of certain student representatives. If, as at Heidelberg, fewer than 20 percent of the students in a particular institute participate in electing their representatives, and if these elected representatives then boycott the body to which they were elected, this is assuredly highly irresponsible conduct. It is noteworthy that in the working out of codetermination in industry there were few such occasions.[14] This is apparently due to the fact that the mature and experienced trade union men who were elected by large percentages of the working force knew not only from their practical work but also as a result of their familiarity with the particular enterprise or industry what was expected of them. It may be well to mention here that one of the points of sharp disagreement between the opponents and some of the advocates of *Mitbestimmung* is over the question of whether representatives of labor on these boards should be members of the factory's work force, or at least of that particular branch of industry, or whether they should be selected by central labor organizations. Without entering into the pros and cons of this argument, it is evident that the legitimacy of such representatives, as well as their responsibility, would be augmented if they did belong to the working force of the enterprise. Hence much opposition to codetermination would be reduced, if not eliminated, if labor did not demand that the central unions share in the representation on the supervisory and managing boards. This issue of maintaining the cohesion of the enterprise is little understood by the general public. It is an issue that also affects the university situation, but in a different way. The greatest obstacle to student representation is the fluid nature of student bodies. The students of a university do not constitute a constituency, except in an ephemeral way. Many of the issues with which university authorities are confronted are very long range, and students will never see the results of the decisions they have participated in. It follows naturally that responsibility is greatly reduced: a group of students cannot assume that part of responsibility which consists in accountability. The natural link of representation and responsibility is therefore fractured, which means that such representatives will be tempted to engage in arbitrary decision making and, more particularly, to indulge their ideological and personal prejudices. Unobjective (*sachfremde*) decisions will result. Such a constellation will also increase the danger of intrigue, for representatives who are not responsible are readily exposed to bribery—in its refined forms—and other types of deviation from what a rational decision in the public interest would call for. To return to codetermination of workers, it has been authoritatively reported that such deviation is infrequent in that field. Although a good deal of envy is engendered by the posh treatment of labor representatives on the boards of companies, there is relatively little concrete detailed evidence of wrong-doing.[15] In the course of their work many of these labor representatives have established a truly impressive record of objectivity and dedication. They have shown that workers can effectively participate in the responsibilities of management and yet fulfill their functions as workers' representatives. They have shown by their conduct that the Marxian theories about class struggle and the inevitable conflict of the interests of owners and workers are incorrect and exaggerate the antagonism. They have shown that they can "participate" in the genuine sense. An American scholar was able to demonstrate and became convinced that "without codetermination, those of them [workers] who are labor managers would not have had opportunities to work as industrial executives, to become acquainted with other industrialists, to get an understanding of the economy based on practical business experience, and to make more money than any of their colleagues."[16] It is, of course, precisely this assimilation of labor's representatives to the establishment of industrial capitalism which British and American Labor fears and the Communists wish to prevent. At this point, rational argument cannot resolve the divergence of views; it turns upon the basic approach to labor relations in industry, to teacher-student relations in the university. Whoever believes in harmony and cooperation will respond favorably to the German scheme of codetermination (*Mitbestimmung*); whoever believes in competition and conflict will suspect trickery and a sell-out. The detached observer will not want to exclude either aspect but will conclude that both may be, and usually are, present in codetermination schemes. Such schemes are no panacea, but codetermination whether in industry or the university can help in shaping the authoritative relations between manager-owner and workers, between professor and students in such a way that coercion is replaced by consensus. In that sense, codetermination is implementing political democracy in the broader sense. What now exists in Germany is only a beginning. Significant improvements are needed to make this beginning into a constitutional democracy.

Very interesting proposals for the constitutionalizing of the German scheme were put forward by the commission that studied the working of the legislation for coal and steel.[17] Therefore, in conclusion, we shall analyze these proposals here. The proposals are grounded in the notion that workers' participation cannot be satisfactorily provided by their taking part in the work of merely a single institution, such as the board of supervisory directors. It must be based on balanced sharing in the responsibility of several institutional arrangements within the enterprise. The proposals insist that such balanced sharing means that no single part of the sharing may be altered without upsetting the entire scheme. Hence they urge that workers' representatives be members of the supervisory council (but not a majority), that a separate member of the management board handle personnel and social problems, that management and the works council cooperate effectively, and that this cooperation and related matters be more widely publicized (fairly strict rules of secrecy prevail in German industry). There is no need to go into the complicated technical details of the proposed law. Only certain features related to the present analysis of representation and responsibility will be taken up. The discussion of much concrete detail presupposes a thorough knowledge of German industrial organization, more especially the law of the constitution of German enterprises (*Betriebsverfassungsgesetz*). We are faced here with a distinctive feature of European political culture. The propensity of the Germans and other Europeans living under the tradition of Roman law has often come in for severe criticism from people accustomed to the traditions of the common law. In a sense, the entire idea of workers' participation in industrial management is an outgrowth of German legalism and formalism. Yet it should occasion no surprise to anyone familiar with the history of Anglo-American constitutionalism, for constitutionalism is politics according to law. Legalism is an integral part of constitutionalism, and such institutions as the separation of powers and the protection of human rights can be handled only by legal means. A careful study of the proposals demonstrates that the experience with the existing codetermination, institutionalized in coal and steel, has given rise to numerous legal difficulties which the Germans seek to remedy. Among these difficulties, some are directly the outgrowth of the problem under discussion here, namely, granting participation without fixing responsibility for the consequences of mistaken decisions.

Everyone agrees, we learn, that the management of an industrial enterprise or commercial organization presupposes that the body charged with handling such management must be "homogeneous," and can only act effectively if it is. Under the law of codetermination of 1951 (Coal and Steel), a director (manager), called *Arbeitsdirektor,* was added to the management board. It had been feared that he might destroy the necessary homogeneity, but these apprehensions have proved mistaken. In most cases, this "labor director" has become integrated into the management board. Even so, the commission took the view that it was more appropriate for codetermination to be focused on the supervisory board; for its function is to *supervise* the management, but supervisors are not limited to supervision. This supervisory board is centrally concerned with selecting top managerial personnel, especially the members of the board of management, known as *Vorstand* (and its members as directors). Nonetheless, the supervisory board is primarily a controlling and not an initiating and managing group. It is fairly obvious that the participation of the workers in the governing of industrial enterprises can be worked out most readily in the field of supervision, when implemented by participation in the selection of top personnel.

The commission was much concerned with the problem of avoiding a split in the supervisory board by organizing it in terms of a dualistic conception of interest. Not a dualism, but an integrated monism of interest was their goal, and the report makes a considerable effort to explain and justify the rather complicated arrangements that are to serve this purpose. They rejected the principle of parity much advocated in labor circles, giving the owners half of the twelve members and labor four. They also provided two outsiders in addition to the one who had been provided in the old law of 1951. Since the Commission's investigations showed that the practice of codetermination in coal and steel had produced, to an overwhelming extent, unanimous decisions of the supervisory board, they felt that the increase of the number of outsiders would also have an integrating effect. The principle of parity,[18] based on the equal right of capital and labor, was seen by the commission as transcendental and hence an unprovable premise of social ethics. Allowing that both capital and labor are essential parts of an industrial enterprise, the commission did not feel that it had any conclusive evidence for giving weight to their relative importance. In the perspective of responsibility (and representation), it would appear that in a market economy the responsibility toward the owners is more weighty, and the responsibility toward the public is entitled to some recognition. Three outsiders who are not directly identified with the enterprise and its interests, but only indirectly via the public interest, are more likely to uphold this responsibility. The situation differs from governmental set-ups where the public interest is in fact represented by the public service and advisory bodies may well contain an equal number of capital and labor representatives since they are counterbalanced by public officials. In the case of codetermination, the participation of outside members prevents the owners from abusing their majority, yet it enables the supervisory board to fulfill its functions within the enterprise effectively; that is to say, responsible conduct can be expected from them.

Under such an arrangement, six members of the supervisory board would be elected by the shareholders and four by the employees. The latter would be nominated by unions having members in the enterprise, but they should not be delegates of central unions. The outsiders should be coopted by the board, but the management board should have the right to nominate them. Evidently, the prevailing opinion in the commission was that the management board (*Vorstand*) should have such a role in the procedure. Again one might ask whether this does not confuse responsibilities, for if the supervisory board is meant to supervise the *Vorstand,* it would seem a mistake to have the *Vorstand* participate in the selection of even some members of the board. But the commission did not consider this objection as protection against possible abuse, the commission suggested that the selection of these particular board members be subject to approval by a majority of both the representatives of capital and of the workers—a cumbersome procedure, to say the least, and one likely to lead to the selection of top men to these positions. It would seem that, in the last analysis, these public members of the supervisory board would not know whom they represented or to whom they were responsible! One can appreciate and sympathize with the commission's desire not to disturb the balance of power between labor and capital in the decision-making process, and yet one wonders whether these complicated arrangements do not introduce an element of irresponsibility.

The problem of balance presents further difficulties in connection with the selection of the *Vorstand.* Customarily, under German corporation law, a job for the supervisory council, and subject to variations in detail in different kinds of corporations,[19] the selection of the *Vorstand* (managers) is a key issue in the field of codetermination. Here at least, parity of the representatives of capital and labor seemed necessary. But the commission rejected this solution, which involved enlarging the supervisory board for such purposes, and adopted a scheme which in cases of conflict makes it possible for the majority of shareholders to prevail. The real decision is made in preparatory talks, and what the president or a special committee proposes is accepted by the supervisory council. Hence it seemed important to make sure that the representatives of labor are involved at an early stage. The commission therefore wants to require that a representative of labor (on the supervisory board) is made a member of any selection committee, or is made vice-chairman of the board, where the board chairman is in charge of preparing the selection. "It is decisive that there be an early participation of the employees' representative in the selection process."[20] Only in this way are the workers enabled to develop an initiative of their own in the selection process and to nominate persons they consider well suited for a position in the *Vorstand.* Upward movement has become easier in German industry, and unusual managerial talent may be made available to an enterprise by such a procedure.

Clearly any firm adherent of Communist ideology will look upon these proposals with particular hostility, for they are evidently calculated to attenuate the class conflict by involving workers through their own representatives in the management of the enterprise. In our own perspective here, we are led to ask to whom such a manager will feel responsible. Only experience will show what the answer is going to be, though the general experience of politics would suggest, and political theory would confirm, that such a person will feel himself at least in part responsible to the workers who proposed and eventually succeeded in electing him. How the homogeneity of the *Vorstand* can be preserved under such conditions seems unclear to me.

This issue has its parallel in the insistence of student radicals that students' representatives must participate in the selection of professors (permanent members of the faculty). The academic situation however, is not the same as that in industry in two very important respects, both vitally related to participation without responsibility. Owing to the permanency of higher academic appointments, a mistake made in the selection of a professor may have long-range disastrous consequences in the misdirection of future students and research. Nor do professors have the kind of policy control exercised by the *Vorstand* of an industrial enterprise. To be sure, they participate as faculty members in the making of certain policy decisions. But not only are these faculties (now *Fachbereiche* or disciplines) usually larger groups than the management board *(Vorstand)* of an industrial enterprise, but their prime function is quite different from those of a *Vorstand*. It is teaching and research in a particular discipline. So the analogy is mainly negative: participation is even more likely to lead to irresponsible decision making.

To insure a reasonable degree of responsibility in the decision making of supervisory boards, the members coming from outside the enterprise, being neither representatives of owners nor of workers, are to be coopted by the supervisory board itself. They are seen as representatives of the public interest who should look out for such matters as pollution of air and water as well as the interests of customers and suppliers, but it is deemed unnecessary for the enterprise to have more than two or three such members. The difficulty of determining objectively what is the public interest,[21] and the fact that such public interest is in fact represented by public authorities, makes it seem improbable that two or three members of the board would be effective. This argumentation seems correct, but it overlooks the key point that the "public" has no control such as an election or appointment by public authorities (which is excluded for other reasons, obviously) would give, so the participants would have no enforceable responsibility, let alone accountability.[22] A better appreciation of the requirements of *constitutional* democracy, and its stress on the limitation of power, would have persuaded the commission to avoid this pitfall. It is true, of course, that the market mechanism and governmental supervision (in the case, e.g., of pollution) protect the general interest; some of these need strengthening.

A final point, related to what has just been said, is an improvement in public information. The commission voiced the opinion that minutes should be kept of all meetings of the supervisory council, and that the reasons for all decision making should be articulated so that the minutes should reflect the grounds on which the majority took its position, especially when the representatives of labor are outvoted. It was hoped that this required publicity would compensate somewhat for the minority status of labor in the council.[23] Since most of these decisions are likely to be discretionary and concerned with objective issues *(sachorientierte Ermessensentscheidungen)*, it was felt that the requirement is not unduly burdensome and that it may even lead to more careful consideration. From the standpoint of this analysis, these decisions are apt to be more responsible.[24] Public information has an effect similar to that of representation.

In this connection, the commission pleaded for a relaxation of the requirement that all that occurs be kept secret. This requirement has been very burdensome for the representatives of labor. It prevents them from justifying their votes on the board, thus interfering with their responsibility and even more with their accountability. Americans are familiar with the problem, from the US Senate Committee on Foreign Affairs; it became an aspect of the controversies over who is responsible for the Tonkin resolution and other senatorial decisions on the war in Vietnam. As in that case, the freeing of representatives from their obligation to be discreet makes it difficult, and perhaps dangerous, for management to communicate certain kinds of information to the supervisory board, and that in turn reduces their ability to fulfill their function of supervision. However, in the case of basic decisions, such as the closing of a plant, the advantages of public information outweigh those of secrecy.[25] A third recommendation with respect to better public information is advocating more detailed reporting about the relationship between management and labor representatives, especially the shop council. The annual report should contain a section dealing with these relations and should not only contain the customary pious phrases about how thankful management is for the cooperation of the workers *(Arbeitnehmer);* this information would also be helpful to the shareholders.

The National Association of Employers' Associations has protested against these proposals because, with the others reported above, they would nullify the pretended effort to maintain a slight preponderance of the owners.[26] They stress the power that the trade unions as mass organizations have in a democratic society in influencing public opinion and through the political process. Furthermore, the shop councils exert a not inconsiderable influence. As a result, the equality *(Paritaet),* which the commission claimed to have aimed at, is in fact jeopardized. This argument, the employers feel, applies even more pointedly to the selection of members of the management board *(Vorstand),* which they feel is supposed to be running the enterprise for the owners who are in law and fact responsible for the enterprise, and should therefore be selected by the owners. Along the same lines of reasoning, the employers object to the cooptation recommended by the commission; they forewarn against the disagreeable struggle over the selection of such coopted members. But they fail to point out that such cooptation obscures the lines of responsibility. To whom are these coopted members responsible? It is difficult to see how such a process is to be understood in combination with participation of the workers in the control of industrial enterprises. Such coopting eliminates the annual meeting as well as the workers as constituencies of the supervisory board and of the management, and thus runs directly contrary to workers' participation, as well as to a pattern of clear responsibility.

The last observation raises the question of these electoral processes. "The effect of codetermination of the workers in industrial enterprises decisively depends on the selection of persons who are charged with participating in the decision making in the enterprise."[27] The commission was much concerned with how the workers' constituency *(Wahlgremium)* would be formed.[28] It is an issue vitally related to the problem we are concerned with here, namely, participation without responsibility. The commission opted for what I have called "objective" responsibility in a study of the modern civil servant whose qualifications for a particular kind of work are looked upon as a better guarantee of responsible work than any kind of electoral process *(Leistungsprinzip)*. It is an issue lately popularized by the term "meritocracy," and the commission favored an effective combination of the two viewpoints.[29] It argued that the suggestion of a right of the central trade union to nominate the candidates, and the suggested requirement of the consent of the majority of workers, would provide the needed combination of selection by majority vote and by qualification—*Mehrheitsprinzip* and *Leistungsprinzip*. In this connection they consider it important, especially in large enterprises, that a *Vorauswahl* or preliminary selection be provided in which the recognized groups of workers could be activated. These groups are provided for in the law on the constitution of enterprises.[30] Should the elections call for proportional or majoritarian representation? The Commission would like to see both permitted so that the workers and employees could choose which method they prefer. Leaving aside further interesting detailed points as not especially important for the perspective of this paper, it remains to be noted that the electoral process envisaged under the proposed law is the classic scheme of traditional Western democracy, and subject to all those criticisms that question the assumed rational attitude of represented and representer. In view of the awareness of workers and employees, they are less valid, and hence a greater degree of actual responsibility may be expected. The basic difference between industrial enterprises and universities is particularly striking at this point, for the workers and employees constitute a relatively stable constituency which can enforce a measure of responsible conduct on the part of the representatives by the threat of not re-electing an irresponsible representative. In contrast, the student body of a university does not constitute a stable constituency, nor are the representatives likely to be interested in re-election, due to their short-lived status as students. Hence the electoral process does not serve to enforce responsibility. In a number of cases this failure has already had unfortunate consequences that have made the process a caricature of democratic procedures. The instability of the constituency and the temporary participation of the representatives in the university suggest that codetermination is considerably more questionable in academic institutions than in industrial enterprises. For both, it can be said that codetermination brings about a situation in which elected representatives are given substantial power without the restraint of effective responsibility. Participation of this kind, far from being democratic in the tradition of Western constitutional democracy, is in fact a kind of privileging of special groups of persons, reminiscent of feudalism. It was to eliminate precisely such group privileges that democracy was developed. Workers in Britain, France, and Scandinavia, among whom the tradition of constitutional democracy is strong, have therefore fairly generally rejected workers' participation, if not student participation. The plan of extending the German scheme throughout the Common Market has encountered bitter opposition and is not likely to succeed.

NOTES AND REFERENCES

1. François Bloch-Lainé, *Pour une réforme de l'entreprise,* 1963 (Paris: Editions du Seuil), p. 96.
2. See for this my *Constitutional Government and Democracy,* 4th ed. 1968, chap. XXII, and the bibliography in which this material is selectively reviewed.
3. The full title is *Setting National Alternatives—the 1973 Budget,* by Charles L. Schultze, Edward R. Friend, Alice M. Rivlin, and Nancy H. Teeters (Washington, D.C.: The Brookings Institution, 1972). The quotes are on p. 1.
4. Chester I. Barnard, *The Functions of the Executive* (Cambridge, Mass.: Harvard University Press, 1938). See also his article "Comments on the Job of the Executive," *Harvard Business Review* (Spring 1940), 295-308.
5. *Mitbestimmung in der Bundesrepublik Deutschland—Tatsachen und Forderungen* (p. 55)—a pamphlet recently issued by the Deutsche Industrieinstitut, Koeln. This body, financed by industry, is of course partisan in its outlook and opposed to worker participation. It stresses the trade union aspect, but so does the official report "Mitbestimmung im Unternehmen," prepared by an official expert commission on the basis of a resolution of the German parliament; cf. Drucksache VI/334, *Deutscher Bundestag,* 6. Wahlperiode, 4.II. 1970. It is usually referred to as the Biedenkopf report, because Professor Kurt H. Biedenkopf was the chairman of this commission, which was to evaluate the results of a law providing for workers' participation in the coal and steel industry from May 21, 1951. This commission's report defined *Mitbestimmung* as follows: *die institutionelle Teilnahme der Arbeitnehmer oder ihrer Vertreter an der Gestaltung und inhaltlichen Festlegung des Wil-*

lensbildungs- und Entscheidungs-prozesses im Unternehmen ... " loc. cit., p. 8.

6. The familiar abbreviations for *Sozialdemokratische Partei Deutschlands* and *Christlich-demokratische Union* which will be used hereafter. LDP is the abbreviation for the small party in coalition with the SPD—the Liberal Democratic Party.

7. All these matters were fully explored by the Commission Report cited in note 5. See also the study by Herbert Spiro, *The Politics of German Co-determination* (Cambridge, Mass.: Harvard University Press, 1958). Spiro is primarily concerned with analyzing another German law, different from that for coal and steel, which provides for a carefully circumscribed amount of workers' participation in management, the *Betriebverfassungsgesetz* (law for the constitution of an enterprise).

8. For this basic distinction between constitutional and unlimited democracy, which has been known since Aristotle, see my *Constitutional Government,* especially chap I, and my *Comparative Constitutionalism,* 1973.

9. Cf. my *Constitutional Government.*

10. My study (with Taylor Cole) of *Responsible Bureaucracy—A Study of the Swiss Civil Service,* 1934, later questioned by Herman Finer and elaborated by Herbert Spiro in his searching study *Responsibility in Government: Theory and Practice,* 1969, contains numerous references to the large literature—philosophical, politological, and legal—on the issue of responsibility.

11. For this important distinction, cf. Spiro, *Responsibility in Government,* p. 14 and chap. 4.

12. For the meaning of these terms in German corporation law see Spiro, *Politics,* p. 28. We cite: "Under the German Corporation law of January 30, 1937, a corporation has three governing bodies: the general stockholders' meeting, the supervisory board of directors, and the managing board of directors." See for further detail pp. 28ff. It is important to know that the supervisory board (*Aufsichtsrat*) is not a board of directors in the American sense; its function is not to direct, that is to say to determine the policies of the corporation, but to supervise the management board which is in charge.

13. Cf. the Biedenkopf Commission Report, Part III, pp. 29ff.

14. *Ibid.,* pp. 78ff.

15. *Ibid.,* p. 26, para. 36; and p. 50.

16. Spiro, *Politics,* p. 148.

17. Biedenkopf Commission Report, pp. 96ff. The reasons given for the proposed changes are particularly interesting from the theoretical viewpoint developed here.

18. See *ibid.,* pp. 101ff.

19. There are at least four major kinds: share companies (*Aktiengesellschaft*), companies of limited liability (*Gesellschaft mit beschraenkter Haftung*), limited partnership (*Kommanditgesellschaft*), and the ordinary company with unlimited liability (*Handelsgesselschaft*). Cf. for this Karl Geiler, *Gesellschaftliche Organisationsformen,* 1922; the comparative aspects in Walter Hallstein, *Die Aktienrechte der Gegenwart,* 1931.

20. Biedenkopf Commission Report, p. 105.

21. Cf. for this *The Public Interest (Nomos V),* 1962, and my paper in the forthcoming *Festschrift* for Prof. Schilpp (Open Court Publishing Co.).

22. One member of the commission, a Professor Fritz Voigt, was of the opposite opinion and wanted the law to charge these members with the

duty to raise issues of public interest. Biedenkopf Commission Report, p. 108.

23. *Ibid.*, p. 106.

24. It may be recalled in this connection that both Kant and Bentham, in arguing for radical publicity of all decisions involving the public interest, stressed this point.

25. For a fuller discussion of the problems of secrecy, see my *Pathology of Politics* (New York: Harper & Row, 1969), chap. 11.

26. Bundesvereinigung der deutschen Arbeitgeberverbaende, *Stellungnahme des Arbeitskreises Mitbestimmung zum Bericht der Sachverstaendigen-kommission: Mitbestimmung im Unternehmen,* Cologne, November 1970, p. 86.

27. Biedenkopf Commission Report, p. 111. The sentence is an obvious tautology, and does not in fact state what the effect is; what is meant is that it is implied.

28. *Ibid.*, pp. 112ff.

29. We read in the Report, "dass bei der Ausgestaltung des Auswahlverfahrens in erster Linie die Gewaehrleistung einer moeglichst breiten Zustimmungsbasis anzustreben und die Beruecksichtigung der Sachqualifikation im Rahmen eines dieser Bedingung entsprechenden Wahlverfahrens erfolgen muss." It seems to be equivocal, to say the least, for the term meritocracy (*Sachqualifikation*) has popularized the idea of disregarding electoral preference by sticking a new label on it.

30. Cf. above, note 7; (the provision is found in paragraph 76). The most important traditional grouping is the distinction between workers and employees (*Angestellten*). They both would nominate candidates.

11

PROFESSIONAL RESPONSIBILITY AND POLITICAL PARTICIPATION

DAVID G. SMITH

An important development in contemporary America lies in the increasing extent of political awareness and participation by professionals, especially those engaged in public or semi-public activities.[1] At times, political consciousness has been expressed dramatically by New Left professors, by "advocate" planners and social workers, and by "public interest" lawyers who have occupied buildings, organized the poor, and sued officials and businessmen. Though less visible, an equally pervasive concern is felt by other representative professionals, in practice and in the academy, about the social and political contributions they might be making or about the ends for which their professional skills are being used.

American commitments, both military and social, insure that

professional responsibility is likely to be a lasting political issue. For in this era of the administrative state, of military research and development, and of the provision of social services, professionals and public officials must collaborate. They need each other, whether the symbiosis is happy or not. This relationship implicates the professional and provides him with political access and political resources. He (or she) is impelled as well as invited to act.

The contemporary upsurge of professional concern and political activism appears to be a distinctive phenomenon. Historically, educators, social service professionals, and public health doctors were often "in politics," seeking to badger local and state governments into raising their budgets, adopting a sanitary code, and so forth. But for this older group, political participation was typically incidental to an established professional aim, such as improving public health practice or social casework. Today's professional activists differ in that they emphasize self-conscious participation and aim their activities at specific political ends. Thus, they seek to turn science toward humanitarian goals or to promote equality and racial justice through law or social casework. Today's professionals function with an awareness of the politics of science, education, and medicine. And new professional roles give specific expression to political concerns or aims, such as the "advocate" planner or the public interest lawyer.[2] Where formerly the professional occasionally used politics to further a professional aim, many contemporary professionals seek to use their professions to gain political ends.

An increase of professionalism may help to account for this trend toward activism. We live in a period of professionalization— if not of everyone, certainly of a great many.[3] Professionals worry about objectives, and having more professionals increases the amount of worrying.[4] Also, for many busy professionals, especially those in public or semipublic roles, their organizational base can provide, and may best provide, their main opportunity for civic-spirited contributions.

The nature of administration increases professional involvement and the exigency of the moral and political dilemmas associated with it. Especially since 1960, administrators have relied heavily on the use of government contract and project grant and, as a consequence, on professionals within and outside government. Professionals staff the programs within government; they plan and consult about them; and they implement them in local communities or as part of university or corporate outreach. Thus, one must note the obvious importance of professional participation for administration. Equally noteworthy is the creation of a system of "private federalism" with a characteristic politics of its own. Those knowledgeable in this field sometimes distinguish "administrative" or "governmental" politics from electoral politics.[5] And professionals themselves know from experience that more of the "politics" of programs may occur after legislation and authorization than before. Conscientious professionals find themselves in difficulty, for participation and leadership are not merely invited but virtually thrust upon them. With participation and leadership come the usual dilemmas of power, but for the professional they are compounded by a sense for his craft and his vocation of service to clients and to mankind.

Professional response tends to be either to withhold services from objectionable governmental use[6] or to attempt to increase the social or political benefit of their professional activity. A good example of the first type of response is that of the scientist who objects to working on life-destroying technology, e.g., atomic bombs or poison gas. The second is typical of the professional supplying individuated services to a clientele.[7] Historically, one of the most familiar examples is the casework movement among social workers.[8] Contemporary examples are the advocate planner or social worker, the public interest lawyer, and especially academics, many of them of the New Left, concerned with the social and political relevance of their disciplines and the state of the nation.

Whatever their lasting result, both responses have stirred up considerable controversy. When the ideological smoke has lifted and the issues can be seen more clearly, many of the fundamental concerns will, I believe, prove to have been real ones, correctly identified and described by the more activist professionals and academics. Yet, as I will also argue, they partly mistake the issues and, in consequence, propose the wrong remedies.

I

One way to begin an examination of the political philosophy of professional activism is to set forth what appear to be the key propositions of this philosophy and to elucidate or expound

them briefly. Since much of the writing associated with this movement is occasional and partisan, separating and articulating these
basic propositions is necessarily a work of interpretation. Furthermore, insofar as a coherent philosophy exists, it has been most
forcefully and coherently stated by the liberal to radical and New
Left members of the various professions, not the average or typical
ones.[9] Nevertheless, professional journals attest to a sharing of
similar concerns and a consensus about action broad enough to
say that a phenomenon approaching a "movement" and some more
or less articulated and shared propositions resembling a doctrine do
exist. But the following exposition should be subject to the caveat
that this doctrine is "more or less" of a shared and coherent unity,
variously representative of the views of many professionals, and
subscribed to wholly by only a few.

The Professional Realizes Himself
through Professional Activity

To overstate only slightly, we (professionals) work in
"institutions" (universities, hospitals, welfare agencies, charitable
foundations) and are engaged, vocationally and avocationally,
mostly in professional or professionally related activities. Our world
is not that of corporations, managers, or blue-collar workers, but
that of the educated middle class for whom the "institution" is more
representative than the corporation, services more important than
manufacturing, and development or process more typical than re-
petitive operation. Some writers draw upon existentialist doctrine
and philosophers like Sartre or Merleau-Ponty to make an elegant
argument about activity preceding essence and the need for an
existential definition of self.[10] For the professional, though, the
point must seem upon a moment's reflection to be pretty obvious.
For him, personal and professional growth are closely related,
sometimes almost identical. The golf-playing dentist or the time-
serving bureaucrat may almost completely separate private and professional activity. But they are atypical. Most professionals carry
into their socializing, avocations, or civic endeavor the acquaintances established through professional activities and a variety of
professional attitudes or concerns.[11] Occupational demands upon
time and energy encourage such a channeling of activities. Also,
the professional is often most effective and happiest with himself—

gets the most positive reinforcement from such activities—when he does so.

The Professional Must Be Committed

"Commitment" generally means dedication to the humane ends of the profession. Thus, it is moral commitment. And the thesis being advanced is that the professional who merely does his job or practices a craft is less than a fully moral person. To be sure, skill and the purpose for which it is used are not the same. The professional performs an operation competently or advises his client accurately regardless of his own social morality or politics. But without dedication, he is less than a "good" doctor or a "good" lawyer, so that we speak of a man as being a "good technician," but, nevertheless, not a credit to or an ornament of his profession. The thesis seems plausible, for the professional fills a role that is both diffuse and diverse: he is a craftsman; he holds in trust the lives or interests of others; and he serves as an example to colleagues.[12] Professionalism requires extensive and continuing socialization in which an outer self or a colleague speaks to an inner self. Without commitment, this socialization is unlikely to be successful. Also, not to make this commitment would seem for most professionals to entail a tension between occupation and the mystique surrounding it and a forced separation of activity and of an acknowledged common morality. He would be, as we say, "living a lie."

The Professional Is Responsible for the Uses Made of His Professional Skills

The responsibility meant is larger than that of serving a client faithfully or sticking to the disinterested search for truth. The professional is, in this view, morally responsible for the foreseeable social consequences of his professional acts.[13] Responsibility extends to both commission and omission. The professional can be "responsible" in the sense that he helps to effect an evil, for instance, by working on the H-bomb or contributing to racial exploitation. He is like an accomplice in a crime. And while he is not legally answerable, he should be accountable to conscience. But, it is argued, not to act is also to choose; that is, to lose the issue by default.[14] Thus, the professional is "responsible" also in a more

positive sense, for the dedicated and effective use of his trained
abilities. Like a steward or trustee, he is responsible both for the
prudent use of his resources and for his most conscientious endeavors. Responsibility includes not simply the immediate welfare
of the patient or the integrity of scientific investigation, but serving positively the ends for which science and the professions exist:
truth in the larger sense or the humane values of equality and justice. Thus, he must concern himself both with preventing the mis-
use of his professional skills and with assuring their beneficial use.

Upon initial inspection, this last proposition seems hard to defend. Obviously, it is not true in any simple way. The professional
is *not* ordinarily accountable for the consequences of his (professional) acts.[15] He is responsible for malpractice. Also, in liberal
countries—the United States, for instance, as opposed to dictator-
ships—he is free to practice without being answerable for social
or political consequences. If the proposition means only that the
professional ought himself to be greatly concerned about consequences, it would still seem dubious. The professional is not an
especially good judge of third-party as against second-party consequences. His most important concern is his client. He may, if he
likes, practice in the ghetto and be a better man for it. But if he
does, he will do best to practice his profession, not worry about
consequences.

Nevertheless, the concern for consequences of professional activities is solidly grounded. What makes it so is the "socialization"
of professions—including science and academia as well as law,
medicine, and others. By "socialization" is here meant both the
employment of professionals in organizational settings and the direction of professional activities to collective ends, not just individual ones; examples include Cold War uses of science, the hiring of
professionals by government, the practice of law and medicine in
large organizations. In these situations, it is possible to argue that
moral responsibility for third-party relations is virtually thrust upon the professional.

Large-scale organization and technological interdependence can
give rise to social responsibility. Most of us would agree that the
concerned atomic scientists *ought* to have been concerned because
they were indispensable participants in events of enormous social
consequence. Their responsibility to act was greater not only because they were influential and would be heard but also because of

a kind of "historic" responsibility: a march of events that made them both strategically and symbolically important. Without the scientists, no (American) bomb. They also represented or epitomized the terrible dilemmas that confronted conscientious men. If they let the issue go by default, the conscience of mankind would be the weaker.[16] Thus, they had responsibility thrust upon them.

In a less dramatic way, social responsibility arises for many professionals in everyday affairs. The doctor, the lawyer, or the scientist is the one with the knowledge, the skills, or the reputation to move people in matters of public health, urban planning, or scientific research and development. He may plead previous commitments or let George do it, but he will, usually, recognize a special obligation and feel that refusal needs more of a justification than that owed by an ordinary citizen.[17] He feels "responsible" and gives up some of his leisure time to help organize a group or to appear at a hearing.

Professional activity also takes place within a social context. It always has, for that matter. But today the social context is both more deliberately organized and more relevant to practice. Thus, a good doctor concerns himself with activities both within and outside the hospital that support his therapy. Similarly, in serving their clients' interests social workers, educators, and other professionals must go beyond their "core" professional skills to the supplementary services and even the social milieu in which the professional services are rendered. In essence, the "social" component of professional services has increased. If the professional is not, strictly speaking, concerned with third-party consequences, he must at least be concerned with relations to third parties and the social milieu of his practice.[18]

Neither of the two arguments presented here amounts to saying that the professional is responsible for the social or political consequences of his actions. That statement is surely too sweeping and too vague. It also appears to bury the otherwise useful concepts of responsibility and accountability beneath murky sociology and existentialist philosophy. But a good case, it seems, can be made for the bare proposition that professionals do have both negative and positive duties with respect to some of the social uses made of their professional skills, especially where they have involved themselves in an exogenous process or in a number of socially related procedures.

The Professional Should Reform the
Social and Political System

According to this proposition, professional responsibility leads directly into political participation: working for the reform of political institutions or the reordering of governmental priorities. Participation is a natural outgrowth of concern for the social context of professional activity. The professionals—more typically, the politically liberal to radical ones—are simply arguing in one sense that better professional results depend on institutional reform. Thus, the advocate social worker or planner attacks the "power structure," [19] the "public interest" lawyer seeks precedent-setting cases,[20] doctors want to change health delivery systems in order, as they see the situation, to increase the quantity and quality of services to clients. Much could be said about their view of the facts and the viable alternatives. But the reason for political intervention seems valid. Indeed, except for the shrillness of the rhetoric and the egregious implausibility of some of the propositions supporting political intervention, the position of the professionals today seems to differ in but one important respect from that taken traditionally by doctors, lawyers, educators, and other professionals who have turned to the state to advance professional aims.

That difference, especially among activist and left-wing professionals, is the insistence that the vocation of the professional (or the intellectual) extends beyond professional activities as traditionally conceived, even in the wider sense of concern with the social environment of that practice, to include the criticism and reform of existing institutions generally. The professional, it is argued, cannot escape responsibility for his actions. He is involved. Furthermore, *not* to act *is* to act, to make a choice: letting the issue go by default and accepting complicity in an evil outcome. To be a good man as well as a good craftsman, the professional must pursue his vocation more fully, by living and exemplifying its humane values,[21] working to reform the profession itself,[22] challenging power,[23] and criticizing the government and its acts. Making an opportunity from a dilemma, many see for professionals—especially the scientists and academics—a role similar to that of the eighteenth-century *philosophes:* critics of and advisers to government and advocates for humane concerns.[24]

This last conception of professional responsibility produces most of the controversy—rising to peaks of intensity over such issues as the Vietnam war, peaceful uses of science, poverty in the urban ghetto, and governance of universities and professional associations. Conservatives fear the "politicizing" of the professions: corruption of professional practice or philosophy, factional controversy, and the capture of association offices by extremists. The liberal or radical argues that the profession already is politicized, the only choice being whether or not to redress existing biases.

It does not seem unduly harsh to say that the views of the activists and the radicals are in some ways elitist, pretentious, and even silly. The elitist overtones are obvious, especially in the professionals' self-nomination for roles of leadership and their dedication to social change even when it is detrimental to clients' interests or contrary to popular preferences.[25] Some pretentiousness is present in the academic's or professional's claim that he speaks for or represents the whole, moral man[26] or the public interest advocate; that he has full knowledge of the public good.[27] And there is sometimes silliness in the irrelevance or the inappropriateness of the professional's policy recommendations. [28]

Nevertheless, if we relate the issue of professional participation to the nature of contemporary governmental or administrative politics, a case can be made for the activist position. In part, the activist is arguing against professional neutrality for the same reasons that earlier political scientists or social theorists challenged the neutrality of the state,[29] the separation of expert and populace,[30] or the validity of the policy-administration distinction.[31] Contemporary trends in public administration, especially since 1960, provide additional support for the activist's case. Vietnam and the urban ghetto have sharpened the issues, but the basic problems developed independently and will persist into the future. The important administrative developments are the extensive fusion of public and private activities; the increased significance of research, planning, and development in administrative activities; and the organizational employment or "bureaucratization" of professionals.

A vast amount has been said about government by contract and grant and the development of a public-private continuum merging and mixing governmental and nongovernmental activities.[32] What ought to be fairly obvious, but is seldom specifically discussed, is that the professional is the key actor both in creating this continuum or partnership and in sustaining activities with it.[33] Also, the more this relationship approaches a true partnership, as contrasted with an arms-length contractual relationship, the more the professional finds himself involved in conflicts of interest, enthusiastically "doing his own thing" and encouraged to do it, but troubled about what is owed to the government, what to his institution or profession, and what to himself. Participation is also complicity, made palpable by such devices as the project grant and the prime contract and by need for continuing participation in the public-private subculture.[34] The professional could choose to opt out entirely. But if he participates, even minimally, he is likely to be "engaged" and faced with dilemmas that he can confront more or less strenuously and honestly.

Once in any way engaged, the conscientious professional finds it hard to be neutral. One reason is that government is so extensively interventionist.[35] With continuing and pervasive intervention come research, development, and planning, not only in defense or health, but also in education, housing, urban renewal, transportation, resources management, land use, intergovernmental relations, etc. For these activities, the professional is vital, for he, especially, relates knowledge to new circumstances or rule to discretion. His problem is not really that he is being coopted by, or selling out to, the military-industrial complex or the "technostructure," but that he is inevitably involved in collaborative activities aimed at deciding, explicitly and implicitly, the alternatives for the future. Typically, research and development involve lead time, intermediate steps, and irreversibility. Thus, the professional may indeed find himself in situations in which his decisions affect more than he intended and in which not to act is to let issues go by default, for his own acts foreclose future possibilities. To mention briefly one example, urban renewal plans require great momentum to succeed and therefore should not be lightly upset. To postpone intervention on behalf of the poor is, then, very likely to decide the issue against them. For the urban affairs professional, in a very real sense, not to decide is to decide.

The organizational employment or "bureaucratization" of professions—in army, industry, and academia as well as in the government—is significant because of its relation to professional responsibility. Professions putatively set standards and discipline themselves, but an organization creates an artificial environment, insulating the professional from peers and clients, often from his own conscience. At the same time, because he is a professional and is expected to employ discretion, he is not easily held accountable by administrative controls. Nor do professional restraints effectively check administration itself. A hiatus exists. On the one hand, able and conscientious professionals may be led to pursue collectively an absurd or immoral purpose, for instance, in Vietnam.[36] On the other, they often enjoy material benefits or power "illegitimately"—beyond that intended and without effective accountability, e.g., the so-called poverty establishment.[37] One observation about this situation is that traditional professional codes provide inadequate regulation, which is to say that the remedy must be at least partially governmental. Furthermore, from the nature of the case, the professional must collaborate in developing remedies. Putting the matter in other words, as conscientious individuals, professionals should participate and they should concern themselves not just with the exercise of power but also with the ultimate ends pursued by fellow professionals.

II

There would appear to be a case for political participation of professionals, not just as informed and resourceful citizens but as professionals.[38] This case can be made mainly be drawing out the implications of the changed situation of today's professionals, especially the social and organizational environment in which they now act. That environment has entailed an increased responsibility of professionals for their actions and, at the same time, weakened checks upon professional activities. Professions and professionals have an obligation to help develop the necessary guidance and control. Professionals also have an increased responsibility for their clients or those they serve. This is so because the possession of power creates an obligation of responsible use and because of the special role and capabilities of the professional. Inevitably, improving the professions involves government and, almost certainly, increased political participation by professionals.

The issue of political participation, though, is how much? And how should that participation be controlled? The activist wishes to extend the professional role to include reform of the political system or at least alteration of collective priorities. I will argue a more moderate position: that professionals should restrict them-

selves to proximate goals, especially those related to the integrity
of the profession or professional practice, or client interests in a
fairly immediate sense. Political advocacy in this restricted sense
is part of the obligation of professionals; more widely, it is not.

The activist case rests substantially upon joining two aspects of
responsibility that are usually separate, responsibility as complicity
and responsibility as stewardship. It may be that we should feel
responsibility for or be held morally or legally responsible for participation in an evil enterprise. Of itself, this kind of responsibility
does not entail an obligation to reform the enterprise or alter its
priorities. A teacher in a segregated school may feel guilty and
may be guilty of immoral complicity. He or she should teach well.
But these two considerations may or may not create an obligation
to change the system. For most professionals—engaged in their
own segment and comparatively isolated enterprises in university
or government—complicity is likely to be small,[39] though there
are exceptions as noted. Often, it is the professional with *no* involvement who is alarmed at his colleague's complicity.[40] As for
the professional's stewardship, his obligation to make good use of
his talent and training, he can do that in most situations. He can
work creatively, perhaps even more creatively, in a prison or a
madhouse.

Practically, the activist philosophy may be counterproductive.
What is meant is not the destruction of institutions and programs
—though this to many people seems a part of the consequences
for which a professional should be responsible. Nor is it adverse
political reaction by Middle America to the "pointy-head" meritocracy, still perhaps a possibility. As T. C. Schelling has said, the
activists have approached the issues as though engaged in a populistic crusade against a conspiracy of evil-doers. One effect is to
convict the enemy, including colleagues who have "sold out," of
a "complete wrongness of a deeply personal, highly shameful
kind."[41] Such an approach may relieve the conscience of troubled
professionals, but probably at the expense of alienating colleagues
and potential allies.

Stating the issue so as to confuse guilt and opportunity also
produces a biased approach to issues of public policy. Dissociation
from an evil purpose and ritual purification seem more important
than positive results. A case in point is that of military research
on campuses, for instance, that of Charles Stark Draper and the

M.I.T. Instrumentation Laboratory. Following demonstrations, a "research strike," and a commission report, the I-Lab was banished from the campus. The I-Lab continues to work on weapons, e.g., MIRV, now untroubled by importunate colleagues from the university. Separation provides moral satisfaction for the academic but is unlikely to affect either the military-industrial complex or professional practice.[42] Also, it may foreclose alternate solutions, such as the transformation of scientific endeavors to peaceful uses. This alternative, though, will almost certainly involve "complicity": consultation, sharing of purposes, and development of alternatives.[43] But to pursue the example one further step, swords may not make good ploughshares. Many dislike the idea of converting the aerospace or missile industry into planners and organizers of pollution control or health care "systems," or at least see the issue as fraught with many perplexities, particularly conflicts over who will build these new systems and who will control them.

One basis for the professional activist's animus would appear to be a view of policymaking as antiquated as the populistic outrage that stems from it. This is the view, like older conceptions of policy and administration, line and staff, that "they" decide matters upon counsel of their advisers or "mandarins."[44] Mostly, "they" do not "decide," at least in the discrete way that term suggests. They struggle to create and bring together the elements of a common solution, which is to say that administration is largely a matter of stimulating and persuading others, not "deciding" to do something.[45] The intellectualized view of administration makes the academic or professional more important than in fact he is and thereby his alleged prostitution a greater offense.[46] Like Faust, he can elect evil. But for most, the devil does not so clearly reveal himself. One reason is that the administrative scheme and its elements are almost always in process of becoming—at least in the areas of heavy professional involvement. Neither the parts nor the whole exist in blueprint but are yet to be determined, both physically and conceptually.[47] Thus, for the conscientious professional, the issue is more typically not whether the government is evil, but what contribution to a developing alternative he will make, how long he will stick with a project, and at what point the worthwhile alternatives have been exhausted.[48] He may choose wrongly or delude himself, but it seems both more charitable and more descriptive to say that he has risked his professional soul and may have lost it—

perhaps in a good cause—than to say that he has sold out.

If the argument so far is valid, what does it suggest about the role of the professional and the extent of his participation in public or quasi-public affairs? I should like to argue that the professional as such has three legitimate concerns: the interests of a reasonably determinate body of clients (or students); the integrity of his profession; and the expert information needed by the community in reaching decisions. Thus, the advocacy or political participation that is appropriate goes to these areas, not to the wider concerns of collective priorities or the political system.

What of the atomic scientist, the public interest lawyer, the advocate social worker, the concerned physician or academic? Should they do nothing? Drift with the times? Clearly not. For reasons already stated, more active protection of both professional integrity and client interests is desirable. These interests, rightly understood, may be enough to worry about. They are legitimately at issue in most current disputes over professional obligation. And they are *the* concerns that professionals are uniquely qualified to champion. Thus, scientists ought to defend their professional integrity, for example, in issues arising from the doing of secret research on campuses. Physicians ought to be more actively concerned about professional integrity and specific patient interests.[49] These are areas they know. To take them up as issues may also be as good a way to beat the devil as, for example, to cry out against the military-industrial complex or the American Medical Association.

The quarrel with the activists, though, is about politics and professionals, and especially whether professionals as such should take political stands, attempt to influence priorities for collective action, or engage in "advocacy" as presently practiced. No absolute rule can be given, but I should like to argue for a presumption against such activities.

The thesis is not that professional advocacy of larger scope may not reduce good results,[50] but rather that it seems hard to justify in principle. Professionals exercise a tutored discretion, rooted in science but guided largely by experience from the past. As professionals they cannot with assurance say, for instance, that it is clearly evil to work on death-dealing weapons or obviously good to convert science to peaceful uses, especially when these choices are removed from the realm of absolute ends to that of specific limited projects. To do so, furthermore, is to abandon the prudence of experience for prophecy and the discipline of caring for specific cases for wholesale prescription, trading upon the credulity of the layman.

Probably there is no conclusive answer to the scientist who says he cannot work on military weapons or, for that matter, to the doctor who refuses to perform abortions. Similarly, an emergency or crisis[51]—such as starving welfare recipients—creates strong grounds for action regardless of professional propriety. But it ought to be observed that professionals in such situations are stepping outside professional roles and appealing to individual conscience, a version of natural law, or the vindication of "history." Furthermore, there is another way of reconciling the tension of professional role and civic obligation which, if not attractive to all, would seem at least to be more defensible on rational grounds: that would be for the professional, as such, to speak only to matters strictly within his professional competence. As a professional, he should speak the truth. As a fellow citizen, he can contribute the information that all need for collective decision.[52]

Our society might well benefit from less political involvement by professionals. Also, many professionals might be better off. Professions are spoken of as vocations or callings. Emphasis is usually put upon the commitment necessary, the dedication to professional objectives. Rather less attention is called to the need to *practice* a vocation, to work diligently in it, and to confront its own special difficulties. One danger of professional "advocacy" is that it become a way of avoiding the problems immediately at hand, and thereby neglecting individual professional development. From this direction also, the professional stands in some peril of his soul.

Finally, what of the "Party of Humanity"? Should the professional be a kind of advocate for mankind? Aside from the pretentiousness of such a notion, some of the words do not fit well together. "Party" does not conjure up the same associations as "humanity," and many of the values associated with the two ideas do not agree. Perhaps the professional best serves humanity by preaching what he practices: dispassionate appraisal, skeptical rationality, a respect for facts and figures, and a steady devotion to a working, personal synthesis of professional competence and humane values.[53]

NOTES AND REFERENCES

1. This essay applies mainly to such professionals—including lawyers, doctors, academics and other teachers, social workers, urban planners, and scientists (especially those working on government projects). Excluded from consideration are most semiprofessions and those with little or no public-relatedness, e.g., engineers in private industry, accountants, morticians, etc.

2. Lisa R. Peattie, "Reflections on Advocacy Planning," *Journal of the American Institute of Planners,* 34 (1968), 80; R. A. Cloward and R. M. Elman, "Advocacy in the Ghetto," *Transaction,* 4:2 (December 1966), 27; Note, "The New Public Interest Lawyers," *Yale Law Journal,* 79 (1970), 1069.

3. Cf. Harold L. Wilensky, "The Professionalization of Everyone?" *American Journal of Sociology,* 70 (1964), 137.

4. Often without distinguishing professional from broadly social concerns, e.g., in social work, education, or social planning.

5. Don K. Price, *The Scientific Estate* (Cambridge, Mass.: Harvard University Press, 1965); Edwin M. Epstein, *The Corporation in American Politics* (Englewood Cliffs, N.J.: Prentice-Hall, 1969), especially chap. 2.

6. Properly, one ought to say "threat of withholding," or alternate use. Research "strikes" or even collective protests are episodes of a day or two. Most seriously concerned scientists do not cease working for the government—they merely work on less objectionable grants.

7. Since he has a clientele, withholding services is a less satisfactory alternative.

8. Roy Lubove, *The Professional Altruist, The Emergence of Social Work as a Career, 1880-1930* (Cambridge, Mass.: Harvard University Press, 1965). Other similar examples from the past would be the scientific management movement among public administrators and the political activities of professional educators.

9. Some representative examples are: Theodore Roszak, ed., *The Dissenting Academy* (New York: Random House, 1968); Martin Brown, ed., *The Social Responsibility of the Scientists* (Glencoe, Ill.: The Free Press, 1971); Edgar S. and Jean Camper Cahn, "Power to the People or the Profession? The Public Interest in Public Interest Law," *Yale Law Journal,* 79 (1969), 1005; Angus Black, *A Radical's Guide to Economic Reality* (New York: Holt, Rinehart and Winston, 1970); also, more generally, *Social Welfare Forum,* especially vols. 92 and 93; and *The Health-PAC Bulletin.*

10. Marvin Surkin, "Sense and Non-Sense in Politics," in Marvin Surkin and Alan Wolfe, eds., *An End to Political Science—The Caucus Papers* (New York: Basic Books, 1970).

11. Doctors marry nurses; academics socialize with other academics; lawyers join the A.C.L.U., and so forth.

12. Thus, Staughton Lynd speaks of a profession as "an open declaration." Lynd, "Historical Past and Existential Present," in Roszak, *Dissenting Academy,* p. 92. A problem arises in applying the propounded thesis across the board to all professions and especially to those often termed "semiprofessions," such as scientific research, teaching, or social work. These semiprofessions lack, variously, a relation of "trust," a core doctrine, or a code of behavior. Thus, to ask dedication of the public assistance caseworker or the research chemist working for General Foods

seems inappropriate. On the other hand, we expect dedication on the part of the academic scientist or the social worker therapist. In their activities and objectives, the latter are more like the classic professions. But they are often working in organizational settings which frustrate professional aspirations and nourish discontent. For this latter point I am indebted to my colleague Charles E. Gilbert. Also, see A. M. Carr-Saunders and P. A. Wilson, *The Professions* (Oxford: Oxford University Press, 1933) and Amitai Etzioni, ed., *The Semi-Professions and Their Organization* (New York: Free Press, 1969).

13. Cf. Martin Brown, ed., *The Social Responsibility of the Scientists* (Glencoe, Ill.: The Free Press, 1971), p. 5; also, Roszak, *Dissenting Academy.*

14. Christian Bay, "The Cheerful Science of Dismal Politics," in Roszak, *Dissenting Academy;* Noam Chomsky, "Responsibility," in *March 4— Scientists, Students, and Society,* ed. Jonathan Allen (Cambridge, Mass.: MIT Press, 1970).

15. As Everett Hughes points out, one essential aspect of professions is that they are licensed to help and to harm and generally to interfere with the lives of others. *Men and Their Work* (Glencoe, Ill.: The Free Press, 1958), especially chap. 6, "License and Mandate."

16. R. W. Reid, *Tongues of Conscience—Weapons Research and the Scientist's Dilemma* (New York: Walker, 1969); Brown, *Social Responsibility,* especially Charles Schwartz, "Professional Organization."

17. Cf. A. C. Ewing, *The Individual, The State, and World Government* (New York: Macmillan, 1947), especially on the concept of "prima facie obligation."

18. The distinction being made is between services for clients that require the cooperation of third parties and the indirect effects of professional activities upon third parties.

19. Cloward and Elman, "Advocacy in the Ghetto."

20. Cahn and Cahn, "Power to the People."

21. Cf. Louis Kampf, "The Scandal of Literary Scholarship," in Roszak, *Dissenting Academy.*

22. E.g., the activities of the various "caucuses" within the professional associations and at the annual meetings.

23. Thus, the "movement" has popularized and, I believe, perverted the Quaker idea of "speaking truth to power."

24. Cf. Roszak, "On Academic Delinquency," in Roszak, *Dissenting Academy;* Ralf Dahrendorf, "Sociology and the Sociologist," in *Essays in the Theory of Society* (Stanford, Calif.: Stanford University Press, 1968); Peter Gay, *The Enlightenment: An Interpretation,* vol. II, *The Science of Freedom* (New York: Knopf, 1969); also *The Party of Humanity* (New York: Knopf, 1963).

25. Like the *Philosophes* or other message-proclaiming elites, the activist professionals seem dedicated to saving their fellow scientists, the urban poor, or other "masses" in spite of what they might themselves want. The advocate social worker or the public interest lawyer engaged in community practice faces such an issue directly and concretely: whether to work for the needful individual client, for a common or group concern, or for a valuable precedent for future use. (Cf. Cloward and Elman, "Advocacy in the Ghetto"; also, "The New Public Interest Lawyers" (Note in *Yale Law Journal, loc. cit.*).) In a neighborhood legal corporation, for example, how to decide the caseload? Should the legal staff work on divorce cases (which a majority of the clients pre-

fer), or on novel economic and legal remedies which the lawyers believe can establish important principles? How is this to be decided: by the legal staff or by the corporation membership? By whom and how are the legal staff held accountable? hired? fired? Not surprisingly, specific solutions to such dilemmas often tend to move between extremes of technocracy and populism (*Yale Law Journal, ibid.*)。

26. Cf. the injunctions of New Left academics to represent a moral vocation to their students and to be "critics of life" (Roszak, Kampf, in Roszak, *Dissenting Academy, op. cit.*). Some, like Max Weber, might argue that by being removed from "practical" activity, they know less of power and less, therefore, of either responsibility or of evil. It seems open to question, at least, whether they are better guides than other people, either for achieving the "whole" life or providing answers to moral dilemmas.

27. Cf. a description of the role of an advocate planner: pleading "his own and his client's view of the good society . . ." "appraising the values underlying [cost benefit] plans . . ." and pointing "out the nature of the bias underlying information presented in other plans . . ." Paul Davidoff, "Advocacy and Pluralism in Planning," *Journal of the American Institute of Planners* 31 (1965), 333.

28. Professionals, including even lawyers, are sometimes at their worst when they speak on social issues outside their professional competence: the scientists on world peace, the doctors on politics, the typical academic on corporate management, etc. The trouble, Warner Schilling has suggested, is not merely that the professional forgets the limits of his expertise, but that he is likely to interpret the unfamiliar situation by applying some of the metapropositions taken from his own field. Thus, the scientist in formulating his advice about the nuclear test ban may be unduly predisposed in his views of policy by a pessimistic view of the capabilities of science (domestic or foreign), by an optimistic faith in human rationality, or by his own commitment to the humane uses of technology. The more competent the professional, often the more steadfastly he adheres to these propositions, especially those which constitute his professional "credo." But for this reason, his views are at times both misleading and irrelevant: misleading because of their concealed biases, irrelevant because not related specifically to the dilemmas the policymaker must confront. Thus, the professional can be worse—more dangerous—than the layman. Cf. Warner Schilling, "Scientists and Foreign Policy," in *The Politics of Science,* ed. William R. Nelson (New York: Oxford University Press, 1968); and Harold K. Jacobson and Eric Stein, *Diplomats, Scientists, and Politicians—The United States and the Nuclear Test Ban Negotiations* (Ann Arbor, Mich.: Michigan University Press, 1966), especially pp. 480 ff.

29. Leon Duguit, *Law in the Modern State,* trans. Harold J. Laski (New York: Huebsch, 1919). Harold J. Laski, *Grammar of Politics* (London: Allen and Unwin, 1925).

30. John Dewey, *The Public and Its Problems* (New York: Henry Holt, 1927); Mary Parker Follett, *The New State* (New York: Longmans, Green, 1918).

31. Paul Appleby, *Policy and Administration* (University, Alabama: University of Alabama Press, 1949); Herbert A. Simon, *Administrative Behavior* (New York: Macmillan, 1947).

32. Cf. Price, *Scientific Estate.*

33. For instance, Price discusses science and government, but not profes-

sionals generally. Galbraith and others discuss industry or business and government, but again not professions and professionals.

34. As most grantsmen are aware, one must stay current, keep up contacts, and follow the action. These activities almost inevitably lead to a sharing of purpose and, if that purpose is evil, of guilt. The project grant nicely institutionalizes complicity. Where used as an umbrella for coordinating efforts it points up many problems for the morally strenuous to worry about, especially investigators' taking money for purposes not genuinely shared or which, upon conscious reflection, they might have to disavow.

35. Cf. Gunnar Myrdal, *Beyond the Welfare State* (New Haven, Conn.: Yale University Press, 1960).

36. Motion pictures and novels deal with this theme: e.g., *Dr. Strangelove* and *Catch 22.* Cf. also, Louis Ferdinand Destouches (Céline), *Journey to the End of Night,* trans. J. Marks (New York: New Directions, 1960).

37. Administrators delegate to professionals but often, for instance in group activities, are not capable of effectively auditing the results. The professionals do not discipline themselves. In consequence, while power and material benefits move downward, decisions about accountability and moral responsibility are delegated upward, and then not made. Cf. Reinhold Niebuhr, *Moral Man and Immoral Society* (New York: Scribner's, 1932).

38. As citizens, professionals, like others, would have an obligation to participate—for instance, to vote, serve in community organizations, and so forth. Their special qualifications might also argue for a large role. However, the tough issue is not whether professionals should participate *as citizens* but whether they ought to extend into the political sphere a particular conception of professional mission.

39. That is, they work separately and are seldom tightly or closely related to a common objective.

40. One is reminded of Mark Twain's comment on "tainted" money: "It's twice tainted," said he. "T'ain't mine, and t'ain't yours."

41. T. C. Schelling, "The Future of the Academic Community," in Jonathan Allen, *March 4—Scientists, Students, and Society,* p. 84. Academics are urged to "expose the lies of governments," with the implication that those who do not, condone such lies. They are also urged not to "join the team" or, for instance, "sell [their] souls for money or professional advantage to the anti-human forces in society." Cf. Roszak, *Dissenting Academy;* "Social Responsibilities Symposium," *Current Anthropology,* p. 395.

42. Dorothy Nelkin, *The University and Military Research* (Ithaca, N.Y.: Cornell University Press, 1972).

43. Cf. Irwin Hersey, "Pressing Social Problems Replace Military Research," *Engineering Opportunities* (February, 1970).

44. Cf. Surkin and Wolfe, *End to Political Science;* Irving Horowitz, *Professing Sociology* (Chicago: Aldine, 1968); Noam Chomsky, *American Power and the New Mandarins* (New York: Random House, 1967).

45. President Truman's famous examples come to mind, especially the executive saying, "Do this, do that, and nothing will happen," and "I sit here all day trying, trying to persuade people to do the things they ought to have sense enough to do without my persuading them." Cf. Richard E. Neustadt, *Presidential Power* (New York: Mentor, 1964), p. 22.

46. It has been argued that the only expert really essential to government

is the lawyer. Cf. Robert Wood, "Scientists and Politics: The Rise of an Apolitical Elite," in *Scientists and National Policy-Making,* ed. R. Gilpin and C. Wright (New York: Columbia University Press, 1964).

47. Not only in typical research and development but also in "social planning" and most areas of public-private collaboration.

48. Cf. remarks by T. C. Schilling, in Jonathan Allen, *March 4—Scientists, Students, and Society,* pp. 83-84.

49. The argument might be made that the A.M.A. already worries too much about these matters. It would seem, though, that what the A.M.A. has done is to use a legitimate interest in these matters to achieve guild-like protections for its members: that is, protection not of professional integrity or patient interests but of the members' pocketbooks.

50. In principle, though, the results are likely to be bad. Professionals usually resist novelty, are likely to respond to it defensively, and can defend the status quo effectively.

51. Cf. Leon Bramson, "Reflections on the Social and Political Responsibility of Sociologists," *The Sociological Review Monograph,* No. 16 (Keele, England: University of Keele, 1970).

52. As an illustration, the following resolution—signed by a number of scientists at the 1969 meeting of the American Physical Society—is worth pondering, both for what is right and what is wrong about it. (Quoted in Brown, *Social Responsibility,* p. 32.)

> Mr. President:
>
> We as scientists and citizens urgently seek the withdrawal of plans to build and deploy the Safeguard ABM system.
> Our concern springs from two basis sources:
> 1. As scientists, we are wholly. unconvinced that any presently proposed ABM system can defend against a determined missile attack.
> 2. As citizens, we deplore the beginning of a particularly dangerous, yet ultimately futile round of nuclear arms escalation when our expanding domestic crisis demands a reallocation of the national resources.

For my own part, I would approve the distinction of professional and citizen and the particular phrasing of ideas 1 and 2. The first sentence, though, appears to mix these roles and involve scientists as such in commenting (ignorantly) upon the negotiations and implicit "bargaining" between the United States and the Soviet Union. Three examples of advocacy that I find rather difficult to deal with are (1) the economists who denounce begger-thy-neighbor tariffs; (2) lawyers who work for model legislation, such as the Uniform Commercial Code; (3) physicians who protest health budgets as inadequate for decent patient care. Clearly, each of these activities, under some circumstances, would be appropriate. They appear to be legitimate instances of political advocacy of a larger scope. At the same time, I would argue that it is the attempt to be professional, to offer a largely disinterested, scientific view, or to defend vital and immediate client interests, which bestows the legitimacy.

53. Cf. Eugene Rabinowitz, "Responsibility of Scientists in the Atomic Age," in *The Politics of Science,* ed. William R. Nelson (New York: Oxford University Press, 1968).

12

THE COMMUNITY AND
THE CATTLE-PEN:
AN ANALYSIS OF PARTICIPATION

LISA H. NEWTON

"Community participation" was probably a hoax from the beginning. The move to include the poor residents of an urban area in the planning of their own "renewal" probably proceeded from a desire on the part of the designers to make their own job easier. "Maximum feasible participation" would put whatever resources were in the area—of materials, talents, and especially leadership—at the disposal of the planner. It would disarm local resistance by the appearance of democracy and provide the opportunity to forestall obstructionist moves of powerful local groups by indicating where those groups were and how they might be handled. Above all, it would commit a leading elite of the area to the support of the renewal program, to the city government administering it, and to the federal government funding it. Important political advantages could be expected for the administration then in office. If the program has been judged a failure, it is probably because those political advantages were not forthcoming as antici- pated. Given the limited motivation for real participation on the part of federal and especially of local officials, and the limited scope of the program to begin with, such failure was perhaps inevitable.

But the question of the possibility of the success of such a pro- gram in its participatory aspect can be approached from another standpoint, aside from all problems arising from faulty motivation or lack of funds. What, we may ask, would have counted as suc- cess? What kind of participation, by what kind of group, might have been foreseen by those who most desired that success? It is this question we consider here: Under what conditions can any agen- cy, charged with bringing a program of change to a given area, enlist the active and legitimate participation of the residents there- of? How can it secure a kind of cooperation such that it can truth- fully be said, when the program is accomplished, that the people of the area took part in the planning? The answer we will pro- pose is that the task was probably impossible even in theory—that even with the best will in the world no legitimate community par- ticipation could have been secured, owing to the associative struc- ture of the areas the program was designed for.

COMMUNITY

First of all, if participation of the "community" is under consideration, we ought to ask what we mean by "the commu- nity." Pinning down a general notion of community is notorious- ly difficult; basically, the term refers to the shared life of any num- ber of individuals, their life in common as opposed to the private life of each individual. With such a vague reference, we can speak intelligibly of communities as small as a pair of friends or as large as the world. We can restrict the meaning of the term for the pur- poses of this paper by specifying that since we are concerned with political problems, and the participation in question has at least a political component, the political community will be the focus of the analysis. Then Aristotle's characterization of the *polis,* or political association, can serve as a starting point: it is simply "the most sovereign and inclusive association," "directed to the most sovereign of all goods."[1] Aristotle's approach is particularly useful to us because it assumes that the community is one association among others, but different from all the others in that its purpose comprehends (and thereby regulates and coordinates) all the other purposes its people may have. Man is by nature an associative animal, a creature most of whose activities are normally carried on in structured association with other members of his species. Aristotle simply assumed the truth of this assertion; more recently, alarmed by the temper of the Age of Alienation, sociological theorists of various persuasions[2] have undertaken the task of spelling it out in detail and establishing it. A rich associational life appears to be necessary for the psychological (moral and emotional) well-being of an individual, as well as for the furtherance of his practical interests. Isolates, persons without associations, are by this argument not normal specimens of the species; they are distorted or deformed in some way.

Ordinarily, people will associate in order to achieve a wide range of purposes—economic, charitable, recreational, religious, etc.—in established institutions and in ad hoc groups. (If a fairly well-defined type of structured association is common and recognized as normal and good in a society—the family, say, or a church or a political party—it is known as a "practice" or "institution.") "Observation shows us . . . that all associations are instituted for the purpose of attaining some good," but all associations or institutions except one—the *polis* or, as we shall call it, the community—will be restricted to a single purpose or a narrow range of purposes, advancing the interests of their constituents in one aspect only. The community will be the association that integrates the purposes of all the others, providing indirectly for all interests, and insuring self-sufficiency for the group as a whole.

In a small town, we will recognize the community easily enough as the local government. In cities, which concern this paper, the task of finding the community may be much more difficult. Using the town (of necessity) as our model, we can see some of the necessary characteristics of the community, as opposed to the other associations to which the people belong.

The community is an association that coordinates and regulates the functioning of all other associations in its area. As this regulation necessarily involves the curbing of at least some interests, at least some of the time, the fulfillment of its function entails that membership in it be nonoptional. All command, and especially all coercion, are authorized only through the community; when the people of the area decide to agree on laws to apply to all (rather than members of special groups in pursuit of special interests), with the intent to enforce those laws by coercion if necessary, the community is the appropriate institution to supply the procedures for that purpose.

The community plays a crucial role in the associative life of its citizens. Its existence is not, unfortunately, susceptible to ontological proof, following immediately from its desirability. Like other worthy institutions, it may or may not exist. Men must belong to some associations to survive, but they can survive without a community—community is only the culmination of association, the highest form. Useful here is Wolff's division of human association into three types:[3] The lowest, and psychologically the most necessary form, he calls "affective community"; it is the shared consciousness of a common life and culture, the assurance of non-isolation. The intermediate form, geared to all the practical and material requirements of the society, he calls "productive community"; it includes all associative endeavor necessary for economic survival. With these major concerns of the society taken care of, the people will live; but their full rational potential will be largely untapped. Full humanity seems to imply autonomy, the will and ability to take responsibility for one's actions. On a societal scale, the duty of autonomy requires that individuals of any group associate themselves for self-government, in an association which will be responsible to them for actions taken in regard to them and in their name.[4] The association that ensures self-sufficiency in this sense, by ensuring that coercion and other forms of nonoptional control proceed at least in part from those falling under its jurisdiction in the area, can be correlated to Wolff's notion of "rational community," the dialogue between autonomous persons in which patterns for governance can be worked out. For practical purposes—purposes of staying healthy, gaining a living, etc.—this dialogue can easily be replaced by external control; indeed, under the best of conditions, there will always be a large percentage of the population who have no interest at all in engaging in the dialogue, in taking part in their government. Yet this institution alone, as the coordinator of the others and as the only one responsible to all the people in a given area, could legitimately represent those people to an outside agency.

PARTICIPATION

The poverty program instructed its administrators to secure the "maximum feasible participation" of the poor. What, precisely, is this activity of which they requested a maximum amount? As with "community," we will have to restrict the applicable senses of "participation." Since we are concerned with institutions, particularly political ones, we shall confine the topic to the notion of participation in an institution, as a family, a game, a church or other association.

Participation in an institution does not have to be voluntary or even terminable; one does not choose to become a member of one's family, and no matter how many actions one might take to cut oneself off from it, there will always be a residual sense in which one remains part of it. But the participant must be aware of the institution; he must know that it exists and that he is a part of it, and in most cases he must be willing to be a part of it. Since an institution is always definable in terms of rules, it follows that participation involves acceptance of the rules that define the institution. The number and complexity of these rules will vary from case to case. Very few and simple rules define the institution of the family: a small set of legal stipulations with occasional reference to biological relationships. On the other hand, a game— chess, baseball, etc.—is completely specified by all the rules in the rule book, which collectively define the activity. If one rule is not being followed, it is, strictly speaking, a different game. A club or other voluntary single-purpose association may be defined by few or many rules, depending on the sort of constitution appropriate to the organization.

These rules, the defining rules, which a participant in an institution must of necessity accept in order to be called a participant, are what H. L. A. Hart calls the "secondary rules" of any system of law.[5] Such rules specify what shall count as an instance of the practice, define roles within it, and indicate the procedures for carrying on or changing its activities and operations. Naturally, all the participants do not have to know all the secondary rules, as long as those occupying the more important roles know them and know how to apply them. Acceptance of the rules for the participants does not require conscious affirmation; ordinarily, the only criterion for "acceptance" is that, in daily practice, the participant behave appropriately toward those offices, agencies, and procedures that the rules define.

The participants' acceptance of the secondary rules must be complete: I cannot play chess with you if you insist on moving your rook diagonally, and no club can operate if some members will not allow the officers to perform. Only general, and perhaps conditional, acceptance is required for the primary rules and individual rulings, for the existence of the institution does not depend on these. Thus, a family may argue indefinitely about the reasonableness of the dating rules for the teenagers or the wisdom of the father's choice of a vacation spot without endangering the particular family or the practice of the family in general. From this feature of institutional operation follows a corollary crucial to our purpose: it is by no means required that the participants in a practice agree with one another on most issues. They can have very widely divergent interests and, often, opposed ideological viewpoints, and still be able to operate perfectly well within institutional structures. Each particular act or rule or ruling within an institution may arouse vociferous objections from some portion of the participants and even, on occasion, refusal to go along with it, without necessarily threatening the institution. (Of course, a certain degree of general acceptance is necessary to allow the institution to function at all; and consistent refusal to accept the rules on the part of one participant may very well result in the involuntary termination of his participation.)

"Active participation" in an institution is ordinarily understood in relation to primary rules; the active participant is the member who engages in certain activities of debating, framing, objecting to or enforcing the primary rules (clearly this characterization applies to some institutions more than others, but then, "active participation" is an issue only in some institutions). But participation does not require this type of activity; as above, the most important aspect of an individual's participation in an institution is simply his conscious membership in it, his recognition of its existence and its jurisdiction over him, and his acceptance of the rules that define it. Membership precedes active participation in all cases. In the family, the precedence is obviously temporal; in all others, the precedence is probably temporal and certainly logical.

PARTICIPATION IN THE COMMUNITY

The participant in the community, the sovereign governing association, is known as a citizen. Often his participation will take the form of joining actively in the governing process, and his right to do so, as Aristotle defines him, is his most essential characteristic.[6] But membership, in this case citizenship, precedes that activity. Membership in the community is not optional, although it is terminable; it involves recognition of the single association that integrates and regulates associative life for everyone, awareness of one's membership in it and acceptance of the rules, written or unwritten, that define it and declare its jurisdiction. Again, such acceptance in no way implies that each member feels a common interest with other members in matters other than the bare existence of such a community. And not only vociferous dispute but also individual refusal to obey the community's laws can be absorbed without threat as long as the resistors continue to recognize the community. Of course, as in other institutions, the individual risks termination of his membership. That is what happened to Socrates in his community: he fully accepted the claims of the secondary rules of the city, including the Athenians' rights to bring him to trial, condemn him to death, and carry out the sentence. The only objection he had was to certain primary rules of conduct which would, if articulated and enforced, have prevented him from teaching philosophy, and the Athenians deemed those rules of sufficient importance to warrant removing Socrates from the institution altogether.

So far, participation in the community is like participation in any other institution, and we may add another point of similarity which is especially crucial to community in the light of the purpose of this paper. Citizens and community, members and institutions, create each other—their existence depends upon recognition by the other. If no one believes himself to be playing baseball according to the rules of baseball, then a baseball game is not in progress. If no one accepts, as applying to himself, the definition of a member of a certain church, then that church does not exist. And where the people of an area do not feel themselves to be members of a community, and do not recognize the community or accept any rules as defining it, then it does not exist. If it does not exist, then, of course, the people in the area are not citizens of it.

It follows that "participation," in the larger sense, precedes com-

munity itself, as necessary for its existence. Individuals, by an initial
act of recognition (foundation, establishment, or constitution), can
create a community, *ex nihilo* as it were, and bring it into existence (and themselves as citizens) by the act of commitment to it
as their government. After that initial act, it exists as an institution, and their membership in it does not depend upon (although
it is enhanced by) active participation in the making and administering of primary rules.

The existence of a community is by no means an assured fact.
Without citizen participation to begin with there is no community,
and the state that results from its absence is difficult to legitimize
in political philosophy. Either the area and the population without community are not governed at all, or, more likely, are governed by another, larger government, legitimate in its own eyes (by
its own rules) and in the eyes of the populations of the surrounding areas, illegitimate in the eyes of the population in question
(since by hypothesis they have not accepted the defining rules and
jurisdiction of any community). The people in the area cannot
then, be "citizens" of anything at all; their relationship to the larger
government may be tolerant and tolerable, but it cannot be political. Basically, there is nothing they can do with the larger government except stay out of its way, and nothing it can do with
them but keep them out of the way and restricted to their own
area. They are not being "governed," if that word implies a conscious acceptance of the situation on the part of ruler and ruled;
they are being kept, like cattle in a pen, fed and calmed and
herded hither and yon when necessary, but not regarded as citizens. If man is necessarily a political animal, as Aristotle claims,
a large part of their humanity is ignored or denied.

PARTICIPATION OF THE COMMUNITY

This situation raises a multitude of questions on the
rights of resistance, rebellion, and secession. More pertinent to the
concerns of the political agency trying to encourage "maximum
participation," it raises the problem of how to involve in the agency's activities a community that isn't there. The answer to his
problem is, unfortunately, that it cannot be done. To deal with a
community is to deal with a single entity, incorporating within its
structure the articulated conclusions of its citizens in those matters

that concern them all, practical because adapted to the community of which they have practical experience. To deal with the individuals of an area in the absence of community is to deal with the competing interests of the private organizations of the area, if the individuals are members of those organizations, or with the necessarily distorted views of the isolated. The members of the private organizations—unions, political clubs, churches, welfare agencies, universities, or the numbers racket—may be very well informed on the needs of their clients, knowledgeable about the nature of the power structure of the area, and congenial to work with; often enough, the local political agency can agreeably select a representation from these local groups and play them off against one another where their interests conflict. But the net result will not be community participation.

For in this pleasant (if imperial) arrangement, representation fails. The isolates will be unrepresented. How on earth do you go about representing an isolate with any combination of associations, membership in which is optional, when he will not voluntarily join any association at all? Those belonging to organizations that are not represented but not belonging to those which are, will also be unrepresented. And those who do belong to organizations that are represented will be represented only in that aspect of themselves, be it a large or small proportion of their loyalty and energy, that is captured by that organization. "The people"—the people as they ought to be, that is, in association—will be unrepresented. But if the existing organizations are not to be utilized, or are to be utilized only in limited ways, how shall we administer the "participatory" program?

There would seem to be two approaches to a solution to the problem, neither of them very attractive. One approach is simply to forget about the political aspect of the "community participation" of the original program. Let the projects to be accomplished in each area be decided by the funding agencies themselves, with an eye toward using the building process to get as much wealth into the area as possible, and let them simply be imposed on the residents. Given no accepted and effective institutions through which all the residents can channel their objections, opposition from the area can probably be disregarded. Where there are no citizens, all the human material can safely be treated, from a political viewpoint, like the cattle in the pen. Clearly there is a Kant-

ian failure in this program, however beneficent its effects are foreseen to be, for it amounts to denying to a certain number of persons any recognition of their humanity and human rights, including the right to have a say in programs designed to affect them.

Another approach would consist in simply giving a certain
(preferably large) amount of money to each resident in the area, on
the theory that lack of money is the essential feature of poverty
and one might as well treat the disease directly. Without a community and the protection of law it could offer, the money is virtually certain to end up in the hands of a few energetic numbers
men, landlords, furniture salesmen, drug pushers, and other entre-
preneurs, but the simple increase of income in the area may do
some good anyway. Although the attitude and effect of this program and the other one appear to be radically different, they are
very similar in one important aspect; neither takes into account
the desires or interests of the residents as a whole—their public,
as opposed to their private, interests. The first program serves various interests, public or private, in the larger government and some
private interests in the area involved; the second serves only private interests in the area. The public interest is served by neither,
and cannot be, because, strictly speaking, there is none; the public good cannot be an object of interest until there is a body capable of being interested in it, or articulating and advancing that
interest—and that would be a community.

The other approach is, I think, the correct one, but it promises
no useful results for a long time after the program is initiated, and
the procedures for carrying out the program are so little understood as to make initial failure practically inevitable. Basically,
this approach requires that community be created where it is lacking before any outside agency initiates any other program at all.
This approach would, if successful, result in a legitimate representation for all the people of the area, a responsible and highly visible administrator for the programs decided upon—whatever extra technical help may be needed, the community would have the
responsibility for the results—and, not inconsequentially, a means
for the individuals so inclined to join in the activity of governing,
thus fulfilling what Aristotle, at least, felt to be one of the more
important attributes of a human being.

There can be little question that it would be desirable to have
going communities in the areas targeted by such schemes as ur-

ban renewal. There are necessary regulatory activities—supervision of the street conduct of the younger residents, for example, and policing the distribution of welfare benefits for fraud—which simply cannot be undertaken by outsiders (especially outsiders of a different color or culture) without breeding resentment, and which any group of adult residents could accomplish more effectively anyway. Pulling together the warring factions of the present partial associations, the community could eliminate the sabotage that hinders genuinely helpful projects, public and private. The community could mediate between the parents and the public schools, keeping the former informed and the latter responsible. It could mediate between the welfare protesters and the welfare agencies, keeping the former reasonable and public-spirited and the latter sensitive to the problems of life on welfare. The community could pull the passive out of their isolation and channel the protests of the activists away from senseless destruction and into effective political pressure.

And so on, if it could be done. And doubts as to how it might be done are the crux of the objection to this approach. For does it not require, in effect, that all the problems the Poverty Program (and others) were designed to solve, somehow solve themselves before the program begins to operate? Why, after all, are the people of the area in such sorry shape that the federal government must step in to help them, if not because they lack precisely the accompaniments of a going community—police protection, crime and racket control, responsible public services? We know that a kind of power proceeds from the opening of a purse, as another kind proceeds from the barrel of a gun, and that the people involved have little power of either kind. But in dealing with the agencies that actually run the lives of the poor in the cities (and in the nation), the power that proceeds from the unified and determined community, a people associated to govern themselves, ascertain their own needs, and defend their own interests, is the most effective kind of power that can be mustered. Surely, it might be argued, if community could be created in the area at all, the unhappy residents would have created it by now. How could any community organizer help the situation?

The answer to this objection is twofold. First, as has been pointed out in a number of recent works,[7] the dominant individualist trend of American thought makes it difficult for a citizen without special education or training in community organization to conceive of the *possibility* of creating a community. The only purpose of association, according to that trend of thought, is to further some private interest against competing interests, and that requires agreement on many issues among all the participants. But a community is exactly that association which equally furthers and limits all private interests and regulates the competition, so no one would join it or create it to further his private interests. Further, it is an institution that survives very well with agreement on only the most general issues: on the constitutive rules of the community itself and on the value of the freedom and equality entailed by the notion of citizenship.[8] Community is possible among warring factions so long as some common sense of justice prevails. Perhaps education as to the possibilities and advantages of this sovereign association will galvanize an area into the attempt to create it, and perhaps it will not always fail.

Second, if community is the necessary condition for the eventual success of every other effort, and self-government is a desideratum in itself, as I take it to be, then the effort to create community has to be worthwhile regardless of the initial failures that will attend the process while we learn how to make it work.[9] This consideration, along with the consideration concerning the greater ease and effectiveness of working with people organized into a community structure, suggests that we can do no better than work to create community where it is lacking. All other efforts, if this one has not succeeded, must eventually fail and defeat their own purposes. The effort to create community is the most fruitful in the long run, and it has one advantage that makes it unique among all the efforts at beneficial change for disadvantaged people: its respect for their autonomy, their natural political capability, their reason, and indeed their very basic human rights, makes it the only effort that must leave the situation better than it found it no matter what practical obstacles are deployed to block it.

NOTES AND REFERENCES

1. Book I, chapter i of the *Politics*.
2. See, among other examples of this trend, Robert Nisbet, *The Quest for*

Community (New York: Oxford. University Press, 1953) and Robert Ardrey, *The Social Contract* (New York: Atheneum, 1970). Edmond Burke's *Reflections on the Revolution in France* and Emile Durkheim's *Suicide* are two of the classic texts.

3. Robert Paul Wolff, *Poverty of Liberalism* (Boston: Beacon Press, 1968), pp. 162ff.

4. As Aristotle puts it, "in order that their association bring them self-sufficiency" (*Nicomachean Ethics,* Book V, chapter vi).

5. H. L. A. Hart, *The Concept of Law* (Oxford: Clarendon Press, 1961), chapters V and VI, specially pp. 91ff., 103ff.

6. *Politics,* Book III, chapter i.

7. The ones I like best are Philip Slater, *Pursuit of Loneliness* (Boston: Beacon Press, 1970) and Wolff, *Poverty of Liberalism.*

8. See Aristotle, *Nicomachean Ethics,* Book V, chapter vi, *Politics,* Book VII. Of course, Aristotle did not think that all men were capable of participation in political association, and some modern writers agree. (See Edward Banfield, *The Unheavenly City* [Boston: Little, Brown, 1969] for a grimly pessimistic estimate of the political potential of the "lower class.")

9. From the point of view of the city government, of course, self-government for the area may not be a desideratum. To avoid imponderables which cannot be dealt with in general and in the abstract, I have left out of account the real possibility that some city governments may just prefer penned cattle, even if they get out of hand and stampede sometimes, to vocal and well-disciplined self-governing communities.

13

THE LIMITS OF FRIENDSHIP

JANE J. MANSBRIDGE

In the last ten years, many small organizations staffed by middle-class young people of the New Left have operated as "participatory democracies." Every major city and every rural area to which young people have migrated has had its free schools, food coops, law communes, women's centers, hot lines, and health clinics organized along "participatory" lines.

The term "participatory democracy," apparently coined by Arnold Kaufman in 1960,[1] came into widespread use after 1962, when the Students for a Democratic Society (SDS) gave it a central place in their founding Port Huron Statement. What the term meant then was unclear, and has become less clear since, as it has been applied to virtually any form of organization that brings more people than usual into the decision-making process.

In many radical organizations, however, "participatory democracy" has been more than a slogan. It has implied specific mechanisms for making decisions (1) in such a way that each member sees him- or herself as equal to others in the organization; (2) by unanimity and not by majority rule; (3) by direct democracy and not through representatives; (4) in face-to-face assembly, not by referenda.

These principles began as the principles of friendship. As Aristotle suggests, friendship is an equal relation, it does not grow or maintain itself well at a distance, and its expression is in unanimity.[2] The participatory vision seeks to extend the mode of friendship to larger groups, and beyond voluntary associations to decision making on the job and in the neighborhood. It attempts to derive the formal, public procedures of government from the informal arrangements of friendship.

Yet the participatory democracy of the New Left is more than a return to familistic, "ancient" or primitive social organization. It embodies ideals—like those of political equality and individual rights—that are the result of several centuries of rational-bureaucratic thought. Participatory democrats demand that actions be taken and decisions be made according to the universalistic criteria to which they are accustomed in a public polity. In constant tension between the informal intimacy of a friendship and the formal, public nature of a government, these small democracies must also face the related tension between their members' conflicting desires for a life in common and for individual autonomy. They handle these tensions by making the same formulae—political equality, unanimity, direct democracy—carry two contradictory burdens. Each formula must, in one or another of its incarnations, both create a community in which an individual is one with others and protect the same individual against the others in that community.

As participatory democracies grow from small groups of close acquaintances to larger associations of strangers, each formula changes its function. The ideal of equality, which a small group of friends experiences as mutual respect, becomes, as the group grows larger, an insistence on exact equality of power. The ideal of unanimity, which among friends reflects similarity in goals, becomes with growth an individual's veto against actions of the majority. Face-to-face contact, which friends value for the pleasure of coming together, becomes in a larger group the insurance that no decision escapes each individual's scrutiny. Distrust replaces trust, and the natural equality, unanimity, and directness of friendship are transformed into rules whose major purpose is the protection of the individual.

Aristotle wrote that "friendship appears to hold city-states together."[3] Friendship also appears to hold participatory democracies together until they evolve into polities that only aggregate and protect individual interests. This essay examines the changes in the functions of political equality, unanimity, and direct democracy that accompany such an evolution. It concludes that, in order to achieve the goals they originally set for themselves, participatory democracies must stay small, stable, and voluntary enough to remain real groups of friends. Building participatory organizations therefore requires a federation of small friendship groups and an ideology that accepts the limitations of participation in larger polities.

POLITICAL EQUALITY

Members of a group can become interested in the equal division of power[4] for at least three reasons. They may want to shore up the group's commitment to the equal worth of each member, insuring equality of respect. They may want each member to develop responsibility, feelings of control, and political skill. And they may want to protect members equally against the impositions of others. The first goal, equal worth and equal respect, is the most closely linked to the conditions of friendship. This is usually the initial reason that a small organization self-consciously pursues social, functional, and political equality.

Equal Worth

Almost every small organization of the New Left has gone through the experience of trying to eliminate inequalities of status, interest, functional importance, and power among the jobs in the organization. In Vietnam Summer, a radical political group active in 1967, the political staff itself helped organize a "revolt of the secretaries," because "some of the members of the political staff seemed embarrassed that, often for the first time in their Movement experience, they had others to do their 'shit work' for them." [5] As a result of this upheaval, the secretaries began to advise local organizing projects while the political staff did its own typing.

Why? In the first place, as the Greeks said quite simply, "friendship is equality." [6] Children, who idolize their elders and enjoy dominating younger siblings, like best to play with others their own age. They want to be met and understood, challenged but not overwhelmed. Among adults, friendships form among those who feel in some way on a par, and any situation which puts people in clearly unequal roles is a threat to the friendship between them. Participatory democrats want the exhilaration, mutual trust, and reciprocity of working with equals. They want colleagues, not secretaries.

Second, their empathy prevents these young people from settling for an organization divided into a corps of equals and a maintenance crew. It makes them uneasy about asking others to play roles that they would not want to play themselves. They would be mistaken if they assumed that everyone else shared their own preferences in task, responsibility, or working conditions. But they are rarely mistaken in assuming that all members of an organization want at least to be regarded as equal to the others in worth, value, and dignity. [7]

Natural friendships are built on equality of respect. In would-be friendships, like Vietnam Summer, members use political equality to strengthen their commitment to each others' equal worth. They never succeed perfectly, for no one can respect all others equally. However, the constant attempt to make power more equal can keep the ideal of equal respect vividly present. Institutions devised to spread power equally guarantee some attention to each member. A goal of equal power encourages those who would otherwise concentrate only on their tasks to recognize the psychological effects of their actions on other members of the organization. Finally, the very fact that an organization cares for its individual members enough to worry about equality of power may also contribute to an individual's self-esteem. For self-respect normally depends upon the respect of others, and the ideal of equal power publicly affirms each member's worth. [8]

By concentrating on this one means of fostering equal respect, participatory democracies sometimes neglect other means. One can encourage situations in which people see each other as competent in roles they all consider important. Equal respect can also arise from moments of emotional identification. In the first flush of discovering their common history, women in the radical women's movement felt a tremendous sense of "sisterhood." To feel that all women were your sisters meant that all other differences, or inequalities, faded into insignificance beside the overwhelming understanding that you had, so to speak, grown up together—shared the same fears, troubles, ways of coping, humiliations, and joys. In the era of sisterhood, institutional reminders of the distinctions and inequalities of the larger society became intolerable. We found too much in each woman to respect.

To the extent that we feel we share experience with another, we feel alike, and hence in some sense equal. We think of this underlying experience when we say that although human beings may be unequal in "outward" qualities, they are equal "underneath." Our common experience allows us to view others as somehow independent of their social roles and titles, which are clearly unequal.[9] Blood brothers and sisters, unequal in skills, often feel these sentiments of identity and equality of respect. Workers, blacks, Jews, women, nationalists—all groups with a common past—can, in stressing that past, evoke feelings of identity and equality. "Fraternity" does not contradict the ideal of equality, as Lukas contends, but rests on a perception of underlying likeness.[10]

The shared experience that develops a perception of likeness may be deliberately and consciously created. It need not come from a distant past. War, working together under stress, a common "transcendant" experience, or self-revelation in consciousness-raising sessions and encounter groups can quickly create mutual identification, empathy, and respect.[11] In young participatory democracies, a sense of experimentation, of difference from the outside world, and even of struggle against that world, reinforces the members' points of common identity. The small size of the group allows an intense interaction that soon becomes meaningful common history. The experience of identification is a firm basis for equality of respect. When that emotional identification begins to weaken, however, participatory democracies, rather than trying to strengthen it directly, usually turn to a formal commitment to political equality.

In most participatory democracies, the commitment to political equality means a good deal more than the conventional "one person, one vote." In one women's group in New York, each member took twelve disks as a meeting began, having to spend one each time she spoke. Most participatory groups, if they do not ask a different person to chair each meeting, use a "rotating chair," by which each participant after speaking calls on the next, in order to prevent the domination of one chairperson. Large meetings break down into small groups to enable everyone to speak. Keniston reports that in Vietnam Summer,

> individuals who were not informed about the issues were sometimes included in policy-making discussions; while the "natural" leaders with the greatest experience, the best ideas, and the surest grasp of the facts sometimes deliberately refrained from voicing their opinions lest they appear to dominate.[12]

Behind such drastic departures from traditional procedures lies the attempt not only to shore up with political institutions a crumbling equality of respect, but also to allow all members to develop their faculties through political participation and to protect their interests equally in the decision-making process.

Self-development

The argument from personal development through political participation appears constantly in the theoretical literature, although it is rarely considered by participatory democrats themselves. Philosophers from Aristotle through Hegel to T. H. Green have suggested that the social and political arrangements of the state should function to help citizens develop their faculties.[13] J. S. Mill added an egalitarian twist by using this general principle as an argument for extending the suffrage. Arnold Kaufman drew on the tradition when he concluded that the main justification for participatory democracy "is and always has been . . . the contribution it can make to the development of human powers of thought, feeling and action."[14] The Port Huron Statement assumed that participatory democracy would "develop man's unfulfilled capacities for reason, freedom and love," and foster his "unrealized potential for self-cultivation, self-direction, self-understanding and creativity."[15]

Yet widespread power, rather than equal power, suffices for this purpose. According to various versions of this argument, members of a polity ought to acquire a sense of responsibility for others in the community. They ought to have the experience of control over some of the larger events that affect their lives. They ought to be able to acquire political skills through the experiences of debating, writing, finding a compromise, standing firm, trying to solve problems, thinking about public issues. None of these different forms of self-development logically requires an equal distribution of power. Individual needs inevitably vary if "need" is defined by psychic or educational benefit. Reducing political inequality helps spread the opportunity for political development. But optimal individual growth depends on flexibility, variety, and the experience of taking as much responsibility as one wants or can stand. It does not depend on an exactly equal division of power.

Equal Protection of Interests

It is when significant conflicts of interest emerge that those affected begin to worry whether the division of power is precisely equal. Liberal tradition sees political equality primarily as a means, in a situation of conflict, to the equal protection of individual interests. Locke argued that each person, giving up in civil society his natural right to defend his interests by force, acquired the right to have those interests protected by the government to the same extent as did other individuals. The right to a "fair and equal Representative" [16] became in Locke's civil society the individual's guarantee of protection.

The extension of a "right" to protect one's interests equally to all sane, mature human beings in a polity has taken generations. The first conceptual step seems to have been extending the ancient idea of equal protection of the law, in which the relevant category entitled by right to equal protection was that of all human beings within a polity, to the right of all sane, mature members of that category to participate in making the law. The second step is from the right to participate to the right to equally weighted participation.[17] The Supreme Court of the United States, without specific mandate in the Constitution and presumably following the logic implicit in the right to vote, itself began this last step when it decided that votes in state and federal elections must be votes of equal weight.[18]

Once competing interests have arisen, the Liberal argument from equal protection of interests leads participatory democrats to seek mechanisms—such as direct democracy, speaking quotas, even the self-censorship of influential members—that give each participant not just an equally weighted vote, but, as far as possible, equal power throughout the decision-making process.[19] A vote of equal weight will not suffice to protect an individual's interests if that individual is deprived of power in spheres other than the ballot box. If the objective is to benefit the poor as much as the rich and the shy as much as the aggressive, provision must be made for the poor or shy to have as much power, electoral and nonelectoral, as the rich and the aggressive.

A major problem with this argument from equal protection of interests is that the standard analogy with voting poses the issue as one of "rights." This suggests an absolute ideal that is neither intuitively appealing nor, in most cases, practical. A democrat might prefer to conclude that if the exercise of power confers benefits, a just society would provide those benefits equally to everyone unless there were compelling reasons to do otherwise. This is not the same as saying that there is an absolute right to equal power, but it does imply that equal power is a goal of importance to be weighed against other competing goals.

Weighing the Costs

Most people assume that the costs of a more equal distribution of power are prohibitively high, whatever the benefits of bolstered equal respect, increased political education, and the equal protection of interests. They fear that more equal participation in decision making will impair the quality of the final product and the efficiency of production.

We do not have a great deal of empirical evidence about how equalizing power within organizations affects their level of efficiency. Warren Bennis and Philip Slater suggest that when creativity, innovation, adaptability, and responsiveness are at a premium, more equal influence in decision making produces a better product.[20] The experiences of Israeli kibbutzim suggest that it is possible to have much more equality in economic and political structures than we now have in the United States without impairing either the quality or the quantity of the goods and services produced.[21] Just as we can probably redistribute income quite a lot without reducing incentives to work,[22] so we may be able to redistribute power far more than we usually imagine without having an adverse effect on the quality or quantity of the product.

Beyond a certain point in any process, attempts to ensure absolutely equal power in every decision will reduce output. The higher the value one puts on the benefits of equal respect, political education and equal protection, the higher the price one will be willing to pay in output. Many participatory democrats are willing to reduce the quantity and perhaps also the quality of production quite dramatically in order to increase equality. Responding to Isaiah Berlin's example of a symphony,[23] some participatory democrats would certainly argue that if the roles of conductor and players could not be rotated or the prestige of the jobs made more equal, the musicians should consider playing music that does not require a conductor, such as chamber music or some forms of jazz.

Yet even for those participatory democrats who are not especially concerned about output, the pursuit of absolute equality has high costs. By denying the existence of any inequality of power, participatory democrats lose accountability. Minimal inequalities in power do exist in all groups because all groups evolve norms and sanctions. As soon as two human beings come together, they set up rules that allow them to predict and control each other's behavior. In various ways they punish disapproved behavior and reward the approved.[24] Through this process any society or group, no matter how free of formal hierarchy,[25] comes to have its most and least favored members, with corresponding inequalities in the sanctions these individuals can threaten and the rewards they can bestow. One can alter the character and magnitudes of these distinctions, but pretending that none exist only obscures their effects.

Inequalities in energy, in interest, in available time and expertise, or in any other quality valued by a group, always result in de facto inequalities in power. If this inequality is not acknowledged, and a group has grown so large that each member does not have an intimate acquaintance with all its operations, it becomes difficult to know who has had a major impact on a decision, to hold that person to account, and to replace him or her if necessary. Informal social connections and informal sources of information become more important in determining influence than do either the amount of time spent in the organization or the considered opinions of the membership. No one knows where to go for accurate information; those without inside knowledge feel manipulated. Eliminating formal leadership, and therefore accountability, does not eliminate inequality, but drives it underground.

Every society or group also requires a division of labor, no matter how elementary. In a friendship group, in spite of some division of labor, each member is in one sense irreplaceable. The loss of that member makes a great hole in the group, changing its meaning for the others. As the group grows, different kinds of work usually become differentially important. Some members become less replaceable and therefore more "equal" than others. Participatory democracies consequently try to avoid the division of labor or rotate jobs to make such division temporary. When specialization becomes absolutely necessary, they try to insure that all specialties have equal prestige.

In practice, this often means that participatory groups unconsciously focus on areas in which none of the members has any special expertise. The radical women's movement, for example, has a strong norm of referring whenever possible to personal experience. One function of this norm is to place all members on an equal footing by eliminating the advantage of those who have learned from books or from research. While such an emphasis promotes equal respect, it also makes less likely any enterprise that demands technical expertise and makes large long-term projects almost impossible.

Participatory groups' eagerness to make space for the timid and inexperienced, letting them try their wings without the numbing comparison to others who can do it better, can also make those with skills reluctant to develop them. Members may begin to devalue their skills and therefore themselves. An extremely able and energetic woman in one participatory organization concluded dubiously of herself, "I don't think that I think that I am more competent than people in any sense—well, in some sense I do, in terms of organizing things, I guess, . . ." and later reflected about competence that "It's no longer something that you can go on feeling good about." [26]

Any calculation of the costs and benefits of trying to achieve strict political equality has to take account of a group's real reasons for wanting such equality. If the goal is primarily to promote equal respect among the members, equal political power in every decision will sometimes be less effective than shared experience and the opportunity for members to know each other on more than one functional level. If the goal is to promote the individual political growth of members of the group, a distribution according to need of the opportunity to exercise responsibility and control will almost always be more effective than a quantitatively equal apportionment of power. A plethora of small responsibilities, the rotation of office, specific training, and the general encouragement of competence give the experience of citizenship and control and teach political skills. The precisely equal distribution of power makes most sense as an ideal in a polity where decisions are made and are perceived as being made to the benefit or detriment of sets of individuals, under the assumption that the interests of those individuals ought to be protected equally. This conception of a polity is not that of a friendship.

UNANIMITY

Just as the growth of a group and the divergence of its goals change the meaning of equality from natural mutual respect to a defensive insistence on equal power, so too growth and divergence change the procedure of unanimity or "consensus" from a device for knitting a friendship together into a public weapon against coercion.

The institution of unanimity in decision making was not invented by modern participatory democrats. It is the traditional method for making decisions in communities that conceive of themselves as one body, without faction. Aristotle said of the Greek city-states that "unanimity, which seems akin to friendship, is the principal aim of legislators. They will not tolerate faction at any cost." [27] Mike, one of William Foote Whyte's "corner boys" in Boston's North End in the 1930s, echoes:

> It is better not to have a constitution and vote on all these things. As soon as you begin deciding questions by taking a vote, you'll see that some fellows are for you and some are against you, and in that way factions develop. It's best to get everybody to agree first, and then you don't have to vote. [28]

And an SDS article on draft resistance exhorts:

You are a serious resistance: don't vote on issues, discuss them until you can agree. All the pain of long meetings amounts to a group which knows itself well, [and] holds together with a serious, human spirit. . . .[29]

Rousseau saw majority vote as the hallmark of a polity where "in every heart the social bond is broken:"

As long as several men in assembly regard themselves as a single body, they have only a single will. . . . But when the social bond begins to be relaxed and the State to grow weak, . . . opinion is no longer unanimous. . . .[30]

Those traditional societies that stress group cohesion—the Indian, Japanese, or Javan village councils, for example—make their decisions without a vote. Early New England town meetings rarely tabulated their votes and did not enter the results in the minutes, preferring to maintain the fiction of unanimity. Committees, political caucuses, street gangs, and experimental small groups tend to make their decisions by consensus.[31]

In traditional societies, insistence on consensus often works not so much to resolve conflicts as to prevent them from arising. Maintaining the unity of the group is more important than the benefits of open conflict resolution. Participatory groups value this unity. They assume that the group can be fundamentally of one mind and that differences can be worked out either by rational discussion[32] or by emotional transcendence. One food coop member suggested as an answer to his group's problems, "Just put an ounce of grass in each order," and expected conflicts to be resolved in the emotional unity of the group.

Moments of consensual unity do make a profound impression on the participants. One woman describes a crisis meeting in a radical newspaper as "the first political meeting I ever went to where I really understood consensus."

It was such an exciting meeting—almost everybody talked—there were about thirty women in the room—and it went from about a total split to finally someone saying, "Listen, if we can't do that we don't deserve the paper," and then everybody saying, "Right on!" It was one of the few meetings where it

goes around and then people just really come together and say
"Far out!" You know it's right. It was such a *high* . . . it was
wonderful. It was such a high.

In a small friendship group, unanimity expresses the desire of
the group to act as one. As the group extends its boundaries but
still remains a small and homogeneous community, it preserves
the procedures of unanimous consensus in order to preserve its
unity. This is the point at which Mike, of Boston's North End,
worried about the effect of a vote. It is the point at which Aristotle's legislators tried to bring about unanimity. It is also, however, the point at which the procedure of unanimity comes to
protect the rights of the less aggressive, less verbal, or the minority,
by giving them a potential veto, making it more likely that others
will listen to them and try to understand their points of view. One
woman argued for consensus rather than majority rule within her
organization on the grounds that:

> Minority groups get trashed * so easily. . . . One thing about
> consensus is that in order to reach it, you need to have discus-
> sion and really go over things so that people understand them.
> The trouble with majority rule is that it's so easy just to make
> the decision, and nobody understands.

Consensus protects the minority from being "trashed" by allowing
it to command sufficient attention from the majority to make its
position understood. Consensus guarantees respect and listening,
by right.[33]

Finally, as the group becomes a public polity and important
conflicts of interest develop, the *liberum veto* of consensus turns
into a negative weapon, allowing every member of the association
to carve out his or her own bill of rights, a minimum area of non-
interference. In a debate on consensus as one radical constitution
was hammered out, I heard most often as an argument for the
procedure of unanimity, "I don't trust anyone except myself!"

This bitter, self-protective refusal to be coerced by a majority
has the most force when the potential harm to the minority is most
immediately obvious, as it would be if the group were going to take

---

*"Trashing," which originally meant looting and breaking windows in a
riot, involves hurting a person in a way that treats him with disrespect. Here
it refers to the way a dominant majority within the group might callously
ignore the interests and feelings of a minority.

illegal action.[34] But within an organization, a specific subgroup like lesbians, who have had the experience of being in a permanent minority,[35] may also fear the slow, subtle process of having their interests in that organization consistently weakened. They see themselves in the position of the South before 1860, and like Calhoun they want a constitution that gives them a veto. Given their generally left wing politics, most members of a participatory organization have had the experience of being in a permanent minority on national issues, and thus suspicion of majority rule is widespread.

Yet consensus, while encouraging some minorities to talk, subdues others. One meeting that I considered a triumph of consensus broke into small groups for half a day at the beginning to give everyone a chance to speak, took an entire weekend to go over each issue carefully, and eventually brought potentially irreconcilable positions into harmony. The final decisions were made unanimously. Months afterwards, however, one of the participants could say, "I found myself agreeing with things at the first mass meeting that if I'd been voting I certainly wouldn't have agreed to. Consensus is often bullying unless it's a clear consensus."

Voting by secret ballot rather than oral consensus protects the more insecure members of the community. As a participant in a town meeting reported, "If you vote by ballot you haven't got to get up and voice your opinion, you haven't got to,—ah—you can vote yes or no and nobody's going to know the difference." When middle-class students met with working- and lower-class people in assemblies of more than twenty in Chicago's JOIN, "voting was more democratic [than the process of reaching oral unanimity] . . . because the community people, intimidated by the verbalism of the student organizers, felt free to cast ballots as they wished."[36]

When unanimity comes to be used in a public and formal manner to protect the individual rights of those participants who dare to use it as a veto, it also has the contradictory effects of creating deadlock and forcing other participants into positions contrary to their wishes. In this incarnation, it may not be the most effective protection against coercion.

FACE-TO-FACE DIRECT DEMOCRACY

Growth also brings changes in the meaning of direct, face-to-face decision making. A small group gains much of its energy from the pleasure its members take in face-to-face contact. Because face-to-face relations are the cement of friendship,[37] when a group grows or begins to diverge in its goals, its members institute face-to-face meetings as a way to correct inaccuracies of perception, iron out differences, and create a spirit of community. They oppose referenda, for referenda do not allow the discussion that brings about a real consensus. They oppose representation, for it deprives the membership of the experience of citizenship. Finally, when major conflicts of interest develop, members demand face-to-face meetings as a protection against the potential coercion of an elite. They now perceive referenda as giving them control at only one stage of the process, when a question has been formulated, discussed, worded and placed, perhaps manipulatively, on the ballot. They now perceive representation as allowing a small group to make decisions in its own interest rather than in the interest of the members.

At this last stage, the legacy of Liberal consent theory provides a rationale for the requirements of both direct democracy and unanimity,[38] for in Locke's nature every man is presumptively free and thus bound in civil society only by laws to which he has given his consent. English consent theorists in fact never thought direct democracy practicable,[39] but Rousseau pushed further in the logic of consent. "Sovereignty," he wrote, "does not admit of representation. . . . Every law the people has not ratified in person is null and void. . . . The moment a people allows itself to be represented, it is no longer free." [40]

To young Americans brought up on consent theory, who lived most of their lives with a war to which they in no way consented, such words could strike home. The authors of the Port Huron Statement believed that "the felt powerlessness of ordinary people" depended on "the actual structural separation of the people from power." [41] The Statement did not explicitly recommend direct democracy,[42] but members of SDS, following its implicit logic, rejected representation in their internal governmental structure. Wave after wave of leaders in the New Left soon became willing to mix direct democracy with representation.[43] However, the continuation of the Vietnam War and other bitter disappointments in national politics intensified the distrust of representative institutions from below. As one young woman put it, "Everyone just has so much experience with representative democracy not working. The only

way to influence anything is to be directly in on it." The traditional Anglo-American fear of power, the suspicion that in elections
a voter is only a means to an end he may not suspect,[44] the homely
knowledge that people who run for office are not like those they
claim to represent,[45] the proud conviction of individual uniqueness
—all make representation suspect once the group grows beyond
the bounds of mutual trust.

Yet direct democracy is not the perfect instrument either for
producing cohesion or for preventing coercion. Unless there is
practically no conflict, face-to-face assembles, designed to produce
feelings of community, can backfire and intimidate the less self-
reliant. Face-to-face communication, despite its many advantages,
usually increases the level of emotional tension.[46] Where there
are persistent conflicts, open hostility may develop. Because the fear
of such hostility and disagreement is, at least in American society,
an important cause of nonparticipation in politics,[47] some citizens
will forgo their chance to participate in face-to-face politics rather
than expose themselves to what they feel is a frightening experience.

Residents of a Vermont town say again and again of the town
meeting that "all it is is more or less a fight, a big argument,"
observe that there are "too damn many arguments," or sum it up
by exclaiming, "I just don't like disagreeable situations!"[48] A
woman in the radical women's movement reports, "I don't go to
meetings anymore. They depress me." The causes are the same.
Face-to-face participation in political decisions, rather than creating community, may frighten away the very people it is supposed
to bring into more active participation.

When conflicts become extreme, direct democracy is used to
guard against the domination of a few. However, replacing representative with direct democracy does not eliminate differences in
power. Electing a representative may visibly deprive a voter of
day-to-day control, but the unregulated marketplace of time and
energy in a direct democracy often creates an even greater distance
between the active and the ordinary members.

The Chicago high-school student who wants a direct democracy because "No one can represent me. I'm the only one who
knows what I'm thinking and no one else can present my views,"[49]
fears for his individuality. Representation forces him into anonym-
ity, identified only with an interest or set of interests. But for most

people the practical effect of a mass meeting is worse—it results in complete invisibility.

Small groups allow each person to communicate his or her views, either through speaking or through general demeanor. In large assemblies, however most people express themselves only by voting after the discussion has come to an end.[50] They can contribute to the emotional tone of the discussion by murmuring, cracking jokes with their neighbors, shuffling their feet, or in other ways indicating their approbation or discontent, but as individuals they are not likely to make an impression on the assembled body. They might decide that their views have been expressed adequately by others, thus turning the mass meeting into another form of representative democracy. But because participants have no way of selecting speakers to represent them, their views may not be represented at all.

COERCION AND COMMUNITY

No one of the principles of participatory democracy inevitably requires the others. A polity may have political equality without unanimity, unanimity without equality, and face-to-face direct democracy without either unanimity or equality. Yet in participatory democracies these three principles do serve many of the same ends, depending on where the organization lies on a spectrum from unity to diversity, informality to formality. In the small friendship group, equality, unanimity, and direct contact work to create a feeling of community, a sense of mutual claim. In the larger polity with diverse goals, the same procedures work to protect the individual members of the group against coercion. In most real participatory democracies (no longer friendships but not yet universalistic polities) equality, unanimity, and direct democracy must at the same time knit the group together and protect individuals against the group.

This double function derives from the underlying hope of all participatory organizations, small and large, to create a society which is at once unitary and noncoercive. Like the otherwise dissimilar ideals of suburban "good government" and the "withering away of the state," the participatory ideal implies that some process, whether emotional or rational, can bring about solutions that are best for all and untainted by coercion.

This ideal can never be fully realized. No two people have identical interests. Nor can an individual in contact with others fully escape the coercive effects of their expectations and the sanctions they may impose. Friends are able to compromise their interests and submit to group norms in a way they *feel* is free and spontaneous. They do not perceive costs in the relationship as costs; they do not perceive mutual sanctions held against each other as sanctions.[51]

"When the social bond is broken," however, conflicts sometimes require that one party explicitly win or lose, rather than those conflicts being compromised, transfigured, or their implications ignored in the warmth of friendship. At the same time the "free rider" who takes no responsibility must be subjected to overt rather than covert coercion.[52] As a group grows larger, it becomes necessary either to bear unresolved conflicts and the strain of greatly disparate contributions or to find a substitute for friendship's "spontaneous," "costless" compromise and compliance. The two possible substitutes are intensified social pressure or the institution of rational-legal rules and sanctions. Most participatory groups, still modeling themselves on friendships, choose intensified social pressure. To recognize explicitly that the nature of their group had changed would lead them to consider more formal standards.

Although the unitary polity is seductive to the imagination and at times immensely fulfilling to its members, such a system does not always meet everyone's needs. Small size itself is often more coercive than large, for a small group can exert more intense pressure on its members, and in a large group the dissident can more easily find an ally.[53] The small group is a powerful instrument of behavior change.[54] In a nonparticipatory society, individuals, like those who join encounter or consciousness-raising groups, may use a group's pressure to change themselves in ways they have freely chosen. But if membership is no longer fully voluntary, the small group can become an instrument for inculcating the values of a particular political system, in the manner of Hitler's Jugendbund or of a corporation that employs "participative" techniques. Even in the absence of conscious state or corporate direction, if every member of a society or workplace were expected to participate politically through such a group, individuals might no longer feel or be free to use participation for their own ends. They might easily be drawn into groups whose ends they did not share and find themselves manipulated in ways they did not intend.

The assumption of one common interest is not, in fact, as appropriate to a neighborhood or workplace group as to a small voluntary association. In the 1970s in the United States most groups that operate on a participatory basis have a membership self-selected from a small group of friends or potential friends, similar in age, life style, and aspiration. They are usually young, unencumbered by children or ties to a given geographical area. They are relatively free to leave the association if it does not fill their needs. Most actual neighborhoods and jobs, however, attract individuals who have no such prior attachment or common goals, who may not want to make the commitment to any group, or to a new group, and who are also, once established, less able to leave. A unitary community may not be what they want or need. At least in the United States labor unions that have preserved a fictional unanimity turn out to be more coercive than those few that have legitimated conflict and faction.[55]

Within a large workplace or neighborhood, small groups may be able to form on the basis of common values, aspirations, and personal liking. But since the small group is such a powerful force, the option of leaving and joining another group must always be open, and any organization composed of small groups will require a mechanism for helping people shift from group to group. For most people, getting together with new people, learning to trust them, committing oneself to them, and then leaving for either work or personal reasons is a traumatic process. A system of small groups, if it is to include mobility, almost demands the self-reliant, autonomous personality it hopes to create.

DECENTRALIZATION

While members of large participatory democracies use participatory procedures to protect themselves from coercion, their more deeply held goal is a society in which coercion will seem nonexistent—a friendship. They are trying to create in their participatory democracies what Robert Redfield called a "folk society." This is a society with little division of labor, direct and consensual in nature. It is a society so small that everybody knows everybody well, in which "all human beings admitted to the society are treated as persons; one does not deal impersonally ('thing fashion') with any other participant in the little world of that society." [56]

A sound instinct for self-preservation draws people to such associations, where they can find refuge from an intensely competitive society in mutual respect. It is not strange that when their associations grow beyond the bounds of a close-knit friendship group, members should try to retain the equality of respect, the directness and the unanimity that marked their earlier experience.

Yet when a participatory organization expands and its members' goals diverge, mechanisms that at one time served to maintain the sense of community come to be used by individuals against the group. The principles of equality, unanimity and direct, face-to-face democracy, applied in a changed context may not always serve their new purpose of protection well, and may make it difficult for the less aggressive, or those without the right social contacts, to develop and grow within the organization. The principle of equal power can paralyze an organization, hide the real dynamics of decision making, drive competent people out, and promote a sense of lassitude and irresponsibility. The principle of unanimity can intimidate the nonverbal and the insecure, and produce immobility. The principle of direct, face-to-face democracy can work to benefit those with the time for meetings, the social contacts that make those meetings enjoyable, and the self-confidence to speak in them.

If the goal of a more participatory society is to provide its members with a context of equal respect, direct control over events that affect them and the opportunity for self-development, it must be based on groups small enough to work as friendships. The small group, like a true friendship, can come to accept its members as they are and can give them support for growing in ways they choose. It can serve as a buffer against the pressures of a manipulative society, allowing its members to choose their own pace and direction of development.

If, however, the goal of a participatory society is to protect individual interests equally, that society has already grown beyond the point of "selfless" friendship. New institutions are required in keeping with the new purpose. The most common response at this point is to establish a system in which the members periodically elect decision-makers to represent their interests. This may be a good system for ensuring equal protection, but, aside from the obvious difficulties in guaranteeing accountability and equality of representation, it does not provide the psychological or developmental benefits of participatory democracy.

Perhaps what we need are organizations that combine small participatory groups as primary units with a reformed representative democracy for making larger-scale decisions. Such organizations could probably do more than traditional representative ones to ensure that all their members' interests were protected equally, since they would bring more people into watchful, active participation.[57] A mixture of small groups and representative democracy could also do more for individual psychological development, as small participatory groups would give their members opportunities to work with others, take responsibility for others, and gain a prouder sense of themselves. Finally, the small groups in such a "mixed" organization could provide their members with a refuge of equal respect.

The problems of arranging genuinely supportive small groups and designing representative institutions which can tie them together make the enterprise I suggest difficult. The real obstacle, however, is that no one now wants such organizations. Most reformers seek only to expand the right to representation, e.g., by having workers elect their managers or by having neighborhoods elect their school boards. Participatory activists, seduced by the experiences they have tasted on a smaller scale and perhaps by the power that accrues to activists in a large "unitary" group, envision the ideal large organization and even the ideal nation-state as friendships. Yet both solutions remain fatally flawed. Traditional representative structures seldom help people to develop their faculties or to reduce their sense of powerlessness. Participatory systems based on mass assemblies fail when they try to stretch the principles of direct, face-to-face, consensual, egalitarian democracy beyond the bounds of friendship.

NOTES AND REFERENCES

1. Arnold Kaufman, "Human Nature and Participatory Democracy," in *Responsibility (Nomos III)*, ed. Carl J. Friedrich (New York: Liberal Arts Press, 1960), pp. 266-289.
2. See Aristotle, *Ethics*, trans. John Warrington (New York: Everyman's Library, 1963). On equality, pp. 174, 179, 202 (1157b, 1159b, 1168b); on direct association, pp. 173, 211 (1157b, 1171b-1172a); on unanimity, pp. 167, 199-200 (1155a, 1167a-1167b).
3. Aristotle, *Ethics*, p. 167 (1155a). Later he added that such a city could not feasibly hold more than 100,000 inhabitants, p. 208 (1170b).
4. The definition of power used throughout this essay combines Bachrach and Baratz' "power" (a relationship that exists when there is a conflict of interest between two or more persons and groups, when B actually bows to A's wishes, and when A can threaten to invoke sanctions), his "force" (when A achieves his goal in the face of B's noncompliance) and his "manipulation" (a subcategory of "force"). It specifically excludes what he terms "influence" (when one person causes the other to change his course of action without resorting to either a tacit or an overt threat of severe deprivation). See Peter Bachrach and Morton Baratz, "Decisions and Nondecisions: An Analytical Framework," *American Political Science Review*, 57 (1963), 632-639. See also Roderick Bell, David Edwards, and Harrison Wagner, *Political Power* (New York: The Free Press, 1969).
5. Kenneth Keniston, *The Young Radicals* (New York: Harcourt, Brace and World, 1968), p. 160.
6. "Philotes isotes legetai," Aristotle, *Ethics*, p. 174 (1157b).
7. See James C. Davies, *Human Nature in Politics* (New York: Wiley, 1963), p. 45. John Rawls, in *A Theory of Justice* (Cambridge, Mass.: Harvard University Press, 1971), pp. 178, 337, prefers "mutual" to "equal" respect. This formulation has the advantage of avoiding an implied requirement of absolute, mathematical equality while retaining the notions of a meaningful minimum level of respect and the recognition of self by other. I have kept the traditional "equality of respect" because when "mutual" implies "given and received in *equal* amount" or "the *same* feelings one for another" (*Webster's Third New International Dictionary*, 1961, my emphasis), the notion of equality has slipped in again unannounced. When "mutual" implies mere reciprocity and allows great unevenness among the parties, it does not meet the needs I describe.

When Robert Lane's New Haven working men say, "The rich guy—because he's got money he's no better than I am," or "I think I'm just as good as anybody else, I don't think there's any of them that I would say are better," they want more than to be treated humanely, just because they are human beings (see *per contra*, J. R. Lucas, "Against Equality," *Philosophy*, 40 [1965], 298). They want more than the moral equality that Stoics extended to all men by virtue of man's capacity to reason, and more than the spiritual equality the Christians extended to all men as children of God. They want respect, and on some level they want as much respect as anyone else. They want equal respect. Lane himself asserts that "it seems probable that when men assert their own equality in this vague sense . . . something other than moral or spiritual equality is at issue." (Robert E. Lane, *Political Ideology* [New York: The Free Press, 1962], p. 67.) The Quakers, who define their doctrine of equality as "equality of respect," believe that it should result in the "absence of all words and behavior based on class, racial or social distinctions." Howard Brinton, *Friends for 300 Years* (New York: Harper, 1952), pp. 131, 133.

For an analysis of different derivations of the concept of equality of respect and a brief criticism of Kant's derivation from man's capacity to reason, see Bernard Williams, "The Idea of Equality," *Philosophy, Politics and Society,* eds. Peter Laslett and W. G. Runciman (Oxford: Basil Blackwell, 1969), pp. 115-116. The concept is problematic. Williams, in the best philosophical discussion of the idea to date, "confesses" to "rather hazy notions" and to "vague and inconclusive conclusions" (Williams, "Idea," pp. 44 and 42), while Runciman concludes that "no formulation of the idea, including Kant's famous precept about treating men as ends but not means, has been found to be satisfactory" (W. G. Runciman, *Relative Deprivation and Social Justice* [London: Routledge and Kegan Paul, 1966], p. 275).

8. Compare Rawls, *Justice,* p. 178.

9. See Williams, "Idea," pp. 117-118, and Runciman, *Deprivation,* p. 275. Williams suggests that "each man is owed an effort at identification," at seeing the world "from his point of view" (p. 117). To the extent that it is possible to conjure up empathy by an effort of the will, this would seem to be our natural obligation. However, the more common situation is that an unwilled, perhaps unwillable, empathy produces equality of respect.

John Plamenatz and Stanley Benn also see the origins of equality of respect in identification. Plamenatz writes that equality of respect is "at bottom an indifference to all social distinctions, an indifference born of sympathy and respect for what every human creature inevitably feels. . . . I know that what I am to myself, they are to themselves, and there is therefore a sense in which all talk of superiorities and inferiorities between us is trivial and absurd." (John P. Plamenatz, "Equality of Opportunity," *Aspects of Human Equality,* ed. Lyman Bryson et al. [New York: Harper & Row, 1957], reprinted in William T. Blackstone, ed. *The Concept of Equality* [Minneapolis: Burgess Publishing Co., 1969], p. 95). On the origins of equal respect for the interests of all men, Benn writes, "possibly . . . each of us sees in other men the image of himself. So he recognizes in them what he knows in his own experience. . . ." (Stanley I. Benn, "Egalitarianism and the Equal Consideration of Interests," in *Equality* [Nomos IX], eds. J. Roland Pennock and John W. Chapman [New York: Atherton Press, 1967], p. 70.) However, Benn's final conception of equality of respect is different from the one I suggest here, and Plamenatz concludes, in an argument that would not, I think, convince Lane's working men, Brinton's Quakers, or my participatory democrats, that equality of respect "perhaps ought not to be called equality. . . . We must not confuse a moral (perhaps even a religious) feeling with a social condition." John Schaar agrees with Plamenatz that the sentiment of equality of respect lies in the "realm of relations among men where notions of equality have no relevance" (John H. Schaar, "Equality of Opportunity, and Beyond," in *Equality* [Nomos IX], pp. 248-249).

10. "Fraternity" does demand that we treat each person "as a person for him- or herself and not simply as the bearer of certain characteristics" (Lucas, "Against Equality," pp. 306-307). However, the process of being recognized for oneself must begin with others' empathy, their having had to some extent the same experiences themselves.

The term "fraternity" belongs to a time when the only conceivable citizenry was male, and the public virtues (as the word "virtue" itself suggests) were thought to derive from the quality of being male. It has an implication of male bonding which I do not intend here. Unfortunately, the term "community," with its implications of place, does not capture the depth of a one-to-one relationship, and "sisterhood" has no history of meaning on which to call.

11. See, for example, Muzafer Sherif, *In Common Predicament* (Boston: Houghton Mifflin, 1966), pp. 71-93. Shared experience is a necessary, not a sufficient, condition for equality of respect. Participants in a shared experience can earn opprobrium as well as respect.

12. Keniston, *Young Radicals,* p. 166.

13. Although for the Greeks participation in the polity developed the true nature of man, Christianity tended to separate the spiritual and secular functions. Rousseau revived the pre-Christian vision of a state that would make men moral, virtuous, and free, and in so doing touched off a nineteenth-century fascination with the goal of the development of human faculties that attracted socialists and conservatives alike. St. Simon, Feuerbach, minor social writers like Mattaï (caricatured by Marx in *The German Ideology*), Marx himself, James Mill, J. S. Mill, T. H. Green, and in America John C. Calhoun all preached in different ways the "development of the faculties."

14. Kaufman, "Human Nature," p. 272. See also Carole Pateman, *Participation and Democratic Theory* (Cambridge: Cambridge University Press, 1970), p. 27: "the major function of participation is an educative one."

15. "The Port Huron Statement," in Paul Jacobs and Saul Landau, eds. *The New Radicals* (New York: Vintage Books, 1966), p. 154. The Statement's full formulation suggests in its wording that the polity should function as a therapeutic community, following the standard of the full development of one's creative powers set by psychologists and psychiatrists like Abraham Maslow, Carl Rogers, Erich Fromm and Gordon Allport. (See Marie Jahoda, *Current Concepts of Mental Health* [New York: Basic Books, 1956], pp. 24-35.)

16. John Locke, *Two Treatises of Government,* ed. Peter Laslett (New York: New American Library), pp. 346, 419 (II 54, 158). In a more modern formulation that does not deal explicitly with political equality, Stanley Benn argues that the principle of formal equality (treat equal cases equally) combines with that of universal humanity (respect for persons *qua* persons) to produce "a fundamental equality of *claim*," resulting in the obligation to respect the interests of all persons equally. (Benn, "Egalitarianism," p. 67.)

17. On the distinction between "equal right to" and "right to equal," see Richard Wollheim, "Equality and Equal Rights," *Proceedings of the Aristotelian Society* (1955-1956), reprinted in *Justice and Social Policy,* ed. Frederick A. Olafson (Englewood Cliffs, N.J.: Prentice-Hall, 1961), p. 111.

18. *Wesberry v. Sanders,* 376 U.S. 1 at 7 (1963). The Court based its newly created right to an equal vote neither on Locke nor on considerations of outcome, but on Article I, section 2 of the Constitution of the United States, which states simply that Representatives to Congress shall be chosen "by the People of the several States."

19. Throughout this essay I have assumed that the institutions of participatory democracy were designed to achieve the equal distribution of power.

Some participatory democrats speak and write as if this indeed were their goal (e.g., Pateman, *Participation*, pp. 43, 69; Peter Bachrach, *The Theory of Democratic Elitism* [Boston: Little, Brown, 1967], p. 89), and I have adopted this assumption for the sake of simplicity.

In fact, however, people do not usually want to exercise equal power in every decision that in any way affects them. They want potential power, or, as Robert Dahl once defined political equality, "the indefinitely enduring opportunity to exercise as much power as any other citizen." (Robert A. Dahl, "Power, Pluralism and Democracy: A Modest Proposal," paper delivered at the American Political Science Association meeting, Chicago, September 9-12, 1964, cited in Bachrach, *Theory*, pp. 83-92.) This formulation, if applied seriously, would result in practice in most of the devices participatory democrats now use to curb the unequal accumulation of power. However, it opens the door, as does any wording involving "opportunity," to controversy about the reasons for nonparticipation.

Traditional notions of equal opportunity are closely bound up with notions about what people "deserve." Under the auspices of desert, "equality of opportunity" can mask a simple acceptance of the marketplace of supply and demand at any given time. But even John Rawls, who in the economic realm looks for a "conception of justice that nullifies the accidents of natural endowment" including "even the willingness to make an effort, to try, and so to be deserving in the ordinary sense" (Rawls, *Justice,* pp. 15, 74), calls only for "fair access to participation" in the political realm. His analysis is based in part on the incorrect assumption that if we were to eliminate only the financial obstacles to equal access, making access "fair" (p. 225), then the small fraction of persons who devote most of their time to politics would be "drawn more or less equally from all sectors in society" (p. 228). Bernard Williams' suggestion that equal opportunity is not fair if any of the unsuccessful sections of society is "under a disadvantage which could be removed by further reform or social action" (Williams, "Idea," p. 127) itself leaves open two problems. First, in a situation of relative reward, removing disadvantages entails removing advantages, and creates equal result. Second, it does not indicate why "sections of society" should be defined economically rather than psychologically or culturally. Transferring the debate between equal opportunity and equal result to the political realm, however, requires a detailed analysis which is not central to this essay.

20. Warren G. Bennis and Philip E. Slater, *The Temporary Society* (New York: Harper & Row, 1969). For discussion of the "participation hypothesis" that people will accept change more easily if they participate in the decision to make the change, see Sidney Verba, *Small Groups and Political Behavior* (Princeton, N.J.: Princeton University Press, 1961), pp. 206-243. For studies on the greater accuracy of group over individual decision making, see Dean C. Barnlund, "A Comparative Study of Individual, Majority and Group Judgement," *Journal of Abnormal and Social Psychology,* 58 (January 1959), 55-60. For the "contingency theory" argument that democratic decision making is effective only on some tasks and among some individuals, see Paul R. Lawrence and Jay W. Lorsch, *Organization and Environment* (Boston: Division of Research, Harvard University Graduate School of Business Administration, 1967).

21. Haim Barkai, "The Kibbutz as a Social Institution," *Dissent,* 19 (Spring 1972), 354-370.

22. George F. Break, "Income Taxes and Incentives to Work," *American Economic Review,* 47 (September 1957), 529-549.
23. Isaiah Berlin, "Equality," *Proceedings of the Aristotelian Society* 56 (1955-1956), in Blackstone, *Concept,* pp. 23-24.
24. For this general point and a brief history of the debate on the "functional" theory of stratification, see Ralf Dahrendorf, "On the Origin of Social Inequality," in *Philosophy, Politics and Society,* eds. Peter Laslett and W. G. Runciman, (Oxford: Basil Blackwell, 1969), pp. 97-108. Also, Dennis Wrong, "The Functional Theory of Stratification: Some Neglected Considerations," and Wilbert E. Moore, "But Some Are More Equal Than Others," both in *The Logic of Social Hierarchies,* ed. Edward O. Laumann *et al.* (Chicago: Markham, 1970), pp. 132-142, 143-148.
25. Walter B. Miller, "Two Concepts of Authority," *The American Anthropologist* (April 1955), reprinted in *Comparative Studies in Administration,* ed. James D. Thompson *et al.* (Pittsburgh: University of Pittsburgh Press, 1963), pp. 93-115, discusses tribes that operate without hierarchy.
26. Women's liberation interview, July 1972. Further quotations from interviews will not be footnoted. I conducted these interviews in participatory democracies of the New Left and in a Vermont town meeting between September 1971 and July 1972.
27. Aristotle, *Ethics,* p. 167 [1155a]; see also pp. 199-200 [1167a-1167b].
28. William F. Whyte, *Street Corner Society* (Chicago: University of Chicago Press, 1943), p. 96.
29. Dee Jacobsen, "We've Got to Reach Our Own People" (1967), quoted in Staughton Lynd, "Prospects for the New Left," *Liberation* 13 (January 1971), 22.
30. Jean-Jacques Rousseau, *The Social Contract,* trans. G. D. H. Cole (New York: Dutton, 1950), p. 102. Rousseau assumed that a city as large as Rome, at 400,000, could act as a single body (pp. 89-90).
31. For India and Japan, see F. G. Bailey, "Decisions by Consensus in Councils and Committees," *Political Systems and the Distribution of Power,* ed. Michael Banton (London: Tavistock, 1965), pp. 1-20, Yasumasa Kuroda, "Psychological Aspects of Community Power Structure: Leaders and Rank-and-File Citizens in Reed Town, Japan" *(Southwestern) Social Science Quarterly,* 48 (December 1967), 434, n. 4, and Verba, *Small Groups,* p. 27.

For New England town meetings, see Michael Zuckerman, *Peaceable Kingdoms* (New York: Knopf, 1970). For committees, see James David Barber, *Power in Committee* (Chicago: Rand McNally, 1966). For political caucuses, see R. T. McKenzie, *British Political Parties* (New York: St. Martin's Press, 1955), pp. 52-54, and Verba, *Small Groups,* pp. 28-29. For street gangs, see Gerald D. Suttles, *The Social Order of the Slum* (Chicago: University of Chicago Press, 1968), p. 194. On consensus in small groups, see Verba, *Small Groups,* p. 27, Robert A. Dahl, *After the Revolution?* (New Haven: Yale University Press, 1970), pp. 74-75, and Keniston, *Young Radicals,* p. 158. For a specifically religious form of consensus, see Brinton, *Friends,* pp. 100, 106, 109, and Benjamin Zablocki, *The Joyful Community* (Baltimore: Penguin Books, 1971), pp. 155-157, 175, 315-317.

Heinz Eulau, in "Logics of Rationality in Unanimous Decision-Making," *(Rational Decision* [Nomos VII] ed. Carl J. Friedrich [New York: Atherton Press, 1964]), advances a typology of the uses of unanimity roughly parallel to mine. This typology ranges from "spontaneous unanimity," which "has the effect of making each participant equal in

272   JANE J. MANSBRIDGE

status and power to every other participant, and ... assures him membership in the decisive group" (p. 48) to "injunctive unanimity," in
which "the individual participant ... uses his dissent whenever collective
action seems to threaten his interests" (p. 50).

32. See Verba, *Small Groups,* p. 224 on the "no-conflict assumption."
33. This care for the feelings of others in the group is a marked feature of
    participatory democracies. Jacobs and Landau, *New Radicals* (p. 30),
    write of the 1965 Cleveland SDS, "they exhibit great tolerance, and no
    speaker is silenced, no matter how irrelevant or repetitious." Keniston,
    Young Radicals (p. 167), reports on the 1967 Vietnam Summer radicals
    that "everyone is to be completely honest, open, and direct with every-
    one else, and ... all are to have a full say regardless of experience and
    competence." A radical women's newspaper exhorts its readers to "com-
    mit ourselves to respecting each other (really listening to a problem
    stated and hearing the person struggle with that problem)." Lore Ham-
    mond, "On Community," *It Ain't Me Babe,* 1 (September 4-17, 1970), 9.
34. See the analysis of consensus in draft resistance groups in Michael Ferber
    and Staughton Lynd, *The Resistance* (Boston: Beacon Press, 1971),
    p. 158.
35. Michael Walzer argues that by participating in the process of majority
    decision making, minorities agree to the legitimacy of the final decision,
    "hoping that one day they will not lose out and will be deferred to in
    turn." Michael Walzer, "The Obligations of Oppressed Minorities," *Ob-
    ligations* (Cambridge: Mass.: Harvard University Press, 1970), p. 47.
    This is the gamble participatory democrats refuse to take.
36. Lynd, "Prospects," p. 22.
37. Aristotle, *Ethics,* pp. 173, 211 (1157b, 1171b-1172a). See also George
    Homans, *The Human Group* (New York: Harcourt, Brace and World,
    1950), pp. 111-118.
38. Robert Paul Wolff, in *In Defense of Anarchism* (New York: Harper &
    Row, 1970), argues for direct unanimous democracy on the Kantian
    grounds that since man has the capacity to choose and to reason about
    his choices, he is under a continuing moral obligation to take respon-
    sibility for those choices. Therefore, "the primary obligation of man is
    autonomy, the refusal to be ruled" (p. 18). Even if one accepts the
    Kantian derivation of morality from reason upon which these linkages
    depend, Wolff's theory seems to reduce the concept of legitimacy to lit-
    tle more than personal self-determination. Laws turn out to have no oth-
    er source of authority than our own desires. And strangely, under Wolff's
    own terms, even direct unanimous democracy cannot produce a law that
    must be obeyed, for after the unanimous, direct decision takes place,
    people and circumstances change. To obey a law later simply because one
    has made it oneself at an earlier time is still a form of being ruled—
    this time by a younger self.
        One of the appeals of direct democracy is, nevertheless, its perceived
    greater legitimacy. If laws are more or less legitimate as they compel
    obedience through one's sense of the justice of the procedure by which
    they were made, laws to which one gives one's personal assent will in
    almost every circumstance be accepted as legitimate. In an era when
    most models of authority are considered illegitimate and laws are sus-
    pect, organizations must rely on the most obvious legitimating tech-
    niques. Direct unanimous democracy is one of these.
39. In the Putney Debates, William Petty argued only for the right to "an
    equal voice in elections" (A. S. P. Woodhouse, *Puritanism and Liberty*

[Chicago: University of Chicago Press, 1951], p. 53). He assumed that "men when they were in so great numbers that every man could not give his voice" (p. 62) chose representatives as a practical matter. Petty even saw the choosing of representatives as taking place at the moment of man's entrance into the state of government: "Whereas before there was a government every man had such a voice, and afterwards . . . they did choose representatives, and put themselves into forms of government . . ." *(Idem.).*

John Locke also assumed no difference in kind between direct consent and consent through a representative. He wrote that political judgments "indeed are [man's] *own* Judgments, they being made by himself, or his Representative" (Locke, *Two Treatises,* p. 368) and "it must be with his *own* Consent, i.e., the Consent of the Majority, giving it either by themselves, or their Representatives chosen by them" (p. 408). (Both emphases mine.)

In the Debates it was Ireton, who, to further his case against extension of the suffrage, had phrased the question, "Whether a man can be bound by any law that he doth not consent to?" The more radical Wildman carefully used the phrasing, "Whether any person can justly be bound by law, who doth not give his consent that such persons should make laws for him?" (Woodhouse, *Puritanism,* p. 66.)

40. Rousseau, *Social Contract,* pp. 94, 96. Rousseau was referring to "sovereignty," the framing of general laws, not day-to-day "government." See Judith N. Shklar, *Men and Citizens* (Cambridge: Cambridge University Press, 1969), pp. 19-20.

41. "The Port Huron Statement," in Jacobs and Landau, *New Radicals,* p. 159.

42. The Statement says, "In a participatory democracy, the political life would be based in several root principles: [1] that decision-making of basic social consequence be carried on by public groupings . . ." (p. 155). "Public groupings" may have meant not mass assemblies, but decision making by the public, as opposed to private enterprise. The rest of the Statement suggests improvements in a basic representative structure.

43. See Lynd, "Prospects"; Richard Rothstein, "Representative Democracy in SDS," *Liberation,* 16 (February 1972), 10; Norman Fruchter, "SDS: In and Out of Context," *Liberation,* 16 (February 1972), 19; Edward Greer, "The New American Movement," *The Nation,* 214 (January 17, 1972), 83; see also Christopher Lasch, "Can the Left Rise Again?" *New York Review of Books,* 17 (October 21, 1971), 36; Michael Walzer, "Notes for Whoever's Left," *Dissent,* 19 (Spring 1972), 312-313; Arnold S. Kaufman, "Participatory Democracy: Ten Years Later," *La Table Ronde,* No. 251-252 (December-January, 1968), 216, reprinted in *The Bias of Pluralism,* ed. William E. Connolly (New York: Atherton Press, 1971). Jo Freeman, "The Tyranny of Structurelessness," *Berkeley Journal of Sociology,* 17 (1972-73), 151-165.

44. By its nature, the representative system encourages the representative to view his voters as means to his own advancement, and they to view him as a means. In a small-scale direct democracy each person must pay attention, if not to the others' whole personalities, at least to a larger part of them than their votes.

45. The experience of young participatory democrats with student government has convinced many that "student government types" are different in personality and interest from those they claim to represent. Evidence

from my own case studies indicates that this is also true of activists in a direct democracy.

46. Harold J. Leavitt, *Managerial Psychology* (Chicago: University of Chicago Press, 1964), pp. 141-150.

47. Morris Rosenberg, "Some Determinants of Political Apathy," *Public Opinion Quarterly* 18 (1954-55), 349, 351.

48. Almost a quarter of the townspeople interviewed mentioned their aversion to arguments, although the open-ended interview was not designed to elicit this response. See Jane Mansbridge, "Town Meeting Democracy," *Working Papers,* 1 (Summer 1973), 8-9.

49. Center for New Schools, "Strengthening Alternative High Schools," *Harvard Educational Review,* 3 (1972), 319.

50. See Bertrand de Jouvenel, "The Chairman's Problem," *American Political Science Review,* 55 (1961), 368, and Robert A. Dahl and Edward R. Tufte, *Size and Democracy* (Stanford, Calif.: Stanford University Press, 1973), pp. 66-68. Dahl and Tufte's book, published after this essay had been written, takes up several of the same issues.

51. In *Street Corner Society,* William Foote Whyte observes, "Once Doc asked me to do something for him, and I said that he had done so much for me that I welcomed the chance to reciprocate. He objected: 'I don't want it that way. I want you to do this for me because you're my friend. That's all.'" (Whyte, *Street Corner,* p. 257.) George Homans uses this passage to illustrate "a norm that is one of the world's commonest: if a man does a favor for you, you must do a roughly equivalent favor for him in return" (Homans, *Human Group,* p. 285). This "exchange theory" illuminates one aspect of human interaction. But for the purpose of describing friendship it is more important that Doc insisted on acting as if no exchange existed. We generally put our friendships as far as possible out of the realm of equivalence. We try not to treat them like commercial transactions.

52. See Mancur Olson, *The Logic of Collective Action* (Cambridge, Mass.: Harvard University Press, 1971). Olson specifically excludes groups that I would term "friendships" from his analysis (p. 6, n. 6, p. 61, n. 17, pp. 160-162).

53. Dahl and Tufte, *Size,* p. 90.

54. See Verba, *Small Groups,* pp. 22-29; Kurt Lewin, "Group Decision and Social Change," in *Readings in Social Psychology,* eds. Theodore M. Newcomb and Eugene L. Hartley (New York: Henry Holt, 1947), and Edith Bennett, "Discussion, Decision, Commitment and Consensus in 'Group Decision,'" *Human Relations,* 8 (1955), 251-273.

55. Seymour Martin Lipset, Martin A. Trow, and James S. Coleman, *Union Democracy: The Internal Politics of the International Typographical Union* (Glencoe, Ill.: The Free Press, 1956).

56. Robert Redfield, "The Folk Society," *The American Journal of Sociology,* 52 (1947), 301. It was from Redfield's work that Kurt Vonnegut developed his First Law of Life, that "Human beings become increasingly contented as they approach the simpleminded, brotherly conditions of a folk society." (Kurt Vonnegut, Jr., "Fiftieth Annual Address to The American Academy of Arts and Letters and The National Institute of Arts and Letters," reprinted in *Vogue,* 160 [August 15, 1972], 57.) See also Rawls, *Justice,* pp. 441, 442, and Alvin Toffler, *Future Shock* (New York: Bantam Books, 1970), pp. 285, 310, 317.

    The sociologists and anthropologists who in some way distinguish between these two forms of social organization include not only Redfield, but also Tonnïes (*Gemeinschaft* and *Gesellschaft*), Durkheim (organic and mechanical), Weber (communal and associative) and Cooley (primary and secondary groups).

57. Even members of nonpolitical associations develop skills and interests within these associations that subsequently lead them to try to influence decisions in the larger polity. See Herbert Maccoby, "Differential Political Activity of Participants in a Voluntary Association," *American Sociological Review,* 23 (1958), 524, and Sidney Verba and Norman H. Nie, *Participation in America* (New York: Harper & Row, 1972), p. 185.

14

IN DEFENSE OF COMPULSORY VOTING

ALAN WERTHEIMER

The most cursory examination of contemporary political science journals would readily lead to the conclusion that studies of political participation in general, and voting in particular, appear with more frequency than any other specific subfield of the discipline. Despite all this research, or perhaps because of it, there remains marked disagreement over both the normative implications of the studies and even over the empirical findings themselves. For example, there is some question as to just what percentage of those eligible to vote actually do so, when all the de jure and de facto ways in which citizens can be excluded from the polls are considered.[1] Empirical considerations aside, there have always been those who have lamented our failure to reach the

Periclean ideal. From the turnout studies of the 1920s and 1930s to contemporary political scientists whose interests are generally more philosophic and whose ideological leanings less conservative, we have been urged not to resign ourselves to the status quo of political participation, to consider both the causes and cures for the regrettably low level of participation, and to reject a conception of democracy that focuses on competition among elites, striving instead for a democracy that makes citizen participation its primary business.[2] Others, whose interests are generally more quantitative and empirical, or whose philosophical leanings are more conservative, have accepted the existing levels of participation if not with glee, then with the confidence that a considerable amount of apathy is quite compatible with liberal democracy.[3] The arguments put forth in defense of apathy have claimed that high participation is either a source or indication of instability; that high participation is a feature of totalitarian polities; that the apathetic are either ill-informed or authoritarian, so that it is just as well they do not participate; and that voter apathy is even a tribute to the values of freedom and privacy.

Despite these differing perspectives, widespread consensus appears on several points: (1) While some scholars are not overly disturbed by the present levels of participation, that level is, nevertheless, generally described as "low." (2) It is generally assumed, although rarely specifically argued, that the act of voting is the sine qua non of political participation. (3) While those who are satisfied with existing levels of participation would have no reason to do so, even those who would prefer higher levels of participation rarely, if ever, argue for the obvious remedy—making participation in elections a legal obligation of all qualified citizens.[4] Suggestions for increasing turnout regularly include reducing the number of offices to be filled at elections, simplifying the registration process, making registration automatic, making election days a national holiday, and, needless to say, running more educational campaigns designed to instill or appeal to a sense of civic responsibility. It is universally assumed that the decision to vote or not to vote ought, must, or always will be made by the citizen without fear of penalty—that it is less desirable to have citizens participate under the threat of a penalty than not to have them participate at all. Compulsory voting might be consistent with totalitarian values, the argument goes, but it could not be a feature of liberal democracy—"the right of voting is worse than useless, indeed, becomes a gross deception, where its use is not free and unfettered." [5] Our liberal commitment to the minimization of legal coercion is so pervasive that we cannot even contemplate the idea of compulsory voting, much less defend it. To compel someone to vote is, after all, tantamount to "forcing men to be free."

The purpose of this chapter is to offer a defense of compulsory voting for polities in which the manifest function of elections is to select candidates for public office in a competitive framework. [6] In defending compulsory voting, I will argue that a competitive electoral system is a public good, that is, a good from which all citizens derive a benefit regardless of their contribution to it; that, as with many public goods, it is irrational for an individual to contribute voluntarily to maintaining the electoral system; that to assure the continued viability of the electoral system and to prevent unjust "free riding," the obligation to vote should be legally enforced; and that a legal form of compulsion is, in some very important respects, less coercive than our present system of voluntary participation. The support of these claims will constitute the core arguments in defense of compulsory voting. I will, however, go on to suggest, in very speculative terms, that some significant "side payments" may well accompany a system of compulsory voting.

The universal reluctance of American political scientists to consider compulsory voting as a serious and plausible alternative is somewhat surprising in that it has long been a practice in several liberal western democracies. Belgium has had a system of compulsory voting since 1893, the Netherlands since 1917, Australia since 1924, and it has been adopted by several, although not all, Swiss cantons. [7] For the most part, compulsory voting has been integrated into the political culture of these nations and apparently arouses little controversy, although Tingsten reports some evidence of deliberate sabotage in Switzerland; that is, there has been a definite increase of the percentage of blank ballots. [8] While compulsory voting has generally been accompanied by increases in the proportion of blank ballots, there has been a more substantial increase in actual votes cast. While there may be some truth to the old adage about horses and drinking, it seems that if people are motivated to go to the polls by the fear of a fine, they will, most likely, cast a vote for one of the available candidates or parties.

In Belgium, abstentions dropped from 20-30 percent to 5 percent, and Australia's turnout rose from 60 percent to 90 percent. In defending compulsory voting, I have in mind a system similar to those found in these nations, a system in which the citizen must pay a fine if he fails to appear at the polls, unless he can produce a valid excuse. While not a feature of compulsory voting systems in these nations, fines as a function of income would seem to provide a just means of ensuring that the penalty for abstention would weigh as heavily upon the rich as the poor.

Because the specific opportunity to abstain is rarely provided, blank ballots are generally considered to be "invalid," that is, they are lumped together with incorrectly marked ballots. I see no reason to demand that a citizen choose from among a specific set of candidates. Thus, particularly in a compulsory voting system, it would be desirable to make write-in ballots easy to cast and to provide a specific opportunity for abstention. While many may object to the argument of this paper on philosophic grounds, I trust that few will reject compulsory voting on technical grounds. Compulsory voting works in other nations, and there is no technical reason why it could not work here. It is, however, quite possible that in the absence of a constitutional amendment, a system of compulsory voting might be deemed unconstitutional. One experiment with compulsory voting in Kansas City came to an end when Chief Justice Brace of the Missouri Supreme Court ruled it unconstitutional in 1896. In doing so the Justice said: "The ballot of the humblest voter in the land may mould the destiny of the nation for ages. Who can say it will be for weal or woe to the republic? Who that it is better that he should cast, or withhold it? Who dares put a price upon it?"[9] I do not know if this opinion would be upheld today, but it is irrelevant to my argument. I am arguing that compulsory voting makes sense, and it is quite possible that a perfectly reasonable social practice might be deemed inconsistent with the American Constitution.

The argument does rest upon one assumption—that competitive elections are a desirable political practice. While the desirability of such elections is generally not directly questioned, the actual practice of electoral politics in the United States has at least raised the question in many minds. Some have argued that candidates do not keep their campaign pledges, that there is insufficient choice among the candidates or parties, that the candidates are so smartly packaged by the public relations men that one cannot determine who the candidate actually is, or that all of them are evil anyway. Now one could accept all these claims and still maintain that elections are a desirable political practice in that they are the best available mechanism for choosing public officials. Competitive elections do provide for the peaceful replacement of our leaders, and any serious examination of the relevant literature must support the conclusion that, in the long run, the preferences indicated in elections do have at least marginal effects on public policy.[10] While those of us who lead rather comfortable lives are prone to ignore them, marginal differences are differences—especially to those whose lives are on the margins. If the assumption that elections are a desirable political practice is not granted, compulsory voting could not be defended. But if this assumption is not granted, it makes no sense to defend a system of noncompulsory voting either.

Most of the benefits that electoral systems provide are "public goods." A public good is a good which, if it is made available to any member of the community (or subgroup, e.g., a labor union), must be made available to all members of the community (or subgroup), even if the individual does not contribute to providing the benefits. A good is public when it cannot be "feasibly withheld" from any member of the community.[11] Thus, public highways, national defense, and police protection are public goods because they are available to all citizens, in part because there is no feasible way of excluding noncontributors from enjoying those goods. Similarly, the benefits of an electoral system are available to all citizens. Even those who do not vote derive benefits from the fact that elections are conducted, and even those benefits that accrue to a certain subgroup as the result of an election (e.g., a policy favoring labor unions as a result of the victory of a certain candidate) are public goods in that they are available to all members of the subgroup, including those who did not vote for the preferred candidate. Since the benefits made available by the provision of a public good are available to all, the rational individual will receive the benefit of the good but will attempt to avoid incurring the cost of providing it. The rational individual will "free ride," that is, will enjoy the benefit provided by other people's contribution. Were citizens not legally compelled to pay taxes, we would expect them to enjoy the public goods that the government provides but to avoid contributing to their provision. Precisely for this reason, we do not attempt to provide public goods on a voluntary basis. To insure that public goods are provided, we force ourselves to contribute. It remains the case that within the framework of the law, citizen behavior is quite rational; citizens do attempt to minimize their contribution, to "free ride" to the extent possible.

It is irrational for any individual to contribute voluntarily to the provision of a public good since, by definition, the utility of that good to the individual is available regardless of his contribution. It is irrational for A to pay taxes if A could enjoy the benefits provided by the taxes paid by other persons. It is similarly irrational for A to vote if A can enjoy the benefits provided by the votes of his fellow citizens and the votes of the members of particular subgroups to which A belongs. A will receive those benefits regardless of what A does.[12] The reward to A from voting can be represented as an equation in which $R = P_1 \times B_1 + P_2 \times B_2 - C$, where R = total reward, P_1 = the probability that A's vote is necessary to sustain the electoral system, B_1 = the benefit to A of having an electoral system, P_2 = the probability that A's vote will decide the outcome of the election, B_2 = the benefit to A from the victory of his preferred candidate, and C = total cost, a composite of time, energy, money, information, etc.[13] The benefit (B_1) of having an electoral system at all may be considerable, but the probability (P_1) that A's vote is necessary to sustain that system approaches zero. The probability that A will cast a deciding vote in favor of his preferred candidate (P_2) is greater than P_1, but it too approaches zero.[14] More important, the benefit to A (B_2) from the victory of the preferred candidate is quite small, smaller than it is generally thought to be. This benefit is a function of two variables: the difference between the candidates (what Downs terms the "party differential") and the effect that the victory of the preferred candidate will have on the policies that A prefers.[15] While A may prefer the candidate of party X over the candidate of party Y, it may well be that party X has a share of the legislative body which is either so small or so large that the addition or subtraction of one member will make no difference in terms of the policies that A prefers. Thus, even if A had the opportunity of casting the deciding vote in favor of his preferred candidate, the benefit accruing to A from having cast that vote might approach zero. The costs (C) of voting, it may be argued, are not terribly burdensome—it takes little time or energy to cast a ballot. While that is more true for some than for others, the costs of acquiring sufficient information to cast a correct vote (that is, a vote that achieves the individual's own preferences) may be considerable. Whatever the costs, when one calculates the sum total of the benefits times the probability that one's vote is necessary to provide those benefits, the positive element in the equation is so small that the total reward (R) will almost always be negative.

I have been using the concept of rationality in a very narrow sense. In saying that it is irrational to vote, I am saying only that the external rewards from the act are outweighed by the costs involved in performing the act. I am not saying that it is unreasonable, stupid, or meaningless to vote, for if elections are a public good, then it may be morally obligatory for all citizens to share the burden of providing it. While it is perfectly reasonable to do one's share in providing a public good, it is nevertheless also true that one does not improve one's own position by doing so. As Downs puts it, "we do not take into consideration the whole personality of each individual when we discuss what behavior is rational for him. We do not allow for the rich diversity of ends served by each of his acts, the complexity of his motives, the way in which every part of his life is intimately related to his emotional needs." [16]

The objection often made to the claim that it is irrational to vote is to ask: "What if everyone did that? Wouldn't that lead to an irrational result?" The obvious answer is that in considering the costs and benefits of an action, one takes into account what other people are likely to do. Thus, while it is true that "if everyone did that" the result would be irrational, the point is that "not everyone does that." If this line of response sounds a bit too facile, it is because the objection is couched in the wrong terms. It is not that abstention is irrational, but that it is immoral. It is wrong not to do one's share in providing a public good; it is wrong to "free ride" on the burdens carried by other citizens. [17] If the benefits of voting were solely "private," that is, available to A only if A incurred some cost, it would make no sense to assert that there is a duty to vote—we do not generally argue that persons have duties or obligations to advance their own interests. To say that one has a moral obligation to do that which would only benefit oneself is inconsistent with the way in which we discuss obligations. But if the benefits provided by voting are public rather than private goods, it is not at all difficult to claim that there is at least a prima facie duty to do one's fair share. While Morris-Jones is quite correct in stating that "arguments about compulsory voting must include arguments about the duty to vote," his failure to recognize that there is such a duty stems from his failure to see the benefits of electoral systems as public goods.[18] To assert that there is such a duty is, of course, insufficient to support a system of compulsory voting, for a general duty to vote "is naturally compatible with resistance to compulsion."[19] Not all moral duties need be nor should be legally enforced. Thus, I still must show why it makes sense to provide legal enforcement for this particular duty.

The rest of the argument would be easier were it not for the fact that the premises I have just defended have been rejected by political scientists who claim to adopt an "economic" or "rational" approach to the explanation of political behavior. In a recent book, William Mitchell addresses the new generation of student voters by ostensibly appealing to their self-interest. He demonstrates that elections can bring about significant changes in public policy and that therefore those affected by the policies should vote if they have the opportunity of doing so. Unfortunately, he never meets the problem head on. After putting forth several axioms of political behavior (for example, that "citizens prefer to minimize their total and relative shares of the burden" and consequently that "citizens prefer to 'free-load' as much as circumstances allow. . . ."), he curiously avoids the conclusion that these premises entail.[20] He fails to show that the action of any individual will bring about a positive result for him, and his demonstration of the narrow margins of many elections is interesting but irrelevant. Because he is skeptical of the willingness of young voters to be convinced by moral arguments, or perhaps because as a political scientist he is unwilling to make moral arguments at all, Mitchell avoids arguing that the young should vote because they have a duty to do so, and thus ends up putting forth an argument which, because it appeals to self-interest, is necessarily inconsistent.

Even Anthony Downs, who attempts to develop a strictly deductive economic model of politics, smuggles in moral arguments through the back door. In accounting for the fact that many citizens do decide to vote, he says that a rational citizen may be "willing to bear certain short-term costs he could avoid in order to do his share in providing long-run benefits."[21] Now it is, of course, perfectly rational for one to incur short-term costs in order to provide long-run benefits, but it is not rational to do so solely because one was doing one's "share." As Barry suggests, "this may be good ethics, but it is not consistent with the assumptions . . . which require the citizen to compute the advantage that accrues to him from doing x rather than y; not the advantage that would accrue to him from HIMSELF AND OTHERS doing x rather than y. . . ."[22] If one does not wish to rely on moral arguments, the other alternative is to redefine the concept of rationality. In their attempt to develop a calculus of voting, Riker and Ordeshook say that if we say that the decision to vote is irrational, we would be assigning "a sizable part of politics to the mysterious and inexplicable. . . ."[23] To say that an act is "irrational" is not (at least in ordinary discourse) to say that it is "mysterious or inexplicable." If we say that an act of murder is irrational, a "crime of passion," we mean that the costs to the murderer of performing the action outweigh the gains; we certainly do not mean that we cannot (at least potentially) explain the act. If we say that it is irrational for an automobile driver not to buckle the seat belt, we mean that the costs of doing so are outweighed by the gains; we do not mean that we are mystified.

Nevertheless, Riker and Ordeshook have a problem. Although their fear of describing an action as irrational is misplaced, they recognize that the probability that an individual's vote will bring about any external benefits for him is quite low. Since they feel compelled to explain the decision to vote in rational terms, they define rationality so as to include among the rewards of the act all the psychic satisfaction that accompanies the act of voting. Thus in addition to the "B" (benefit) factor, they include a "D" (duty) factor in their equation. The "D" factor is the algebraic representation of all the "positive satisfactions" a citizen feels when voting—feeling good about complying with the ethic of voting; enjoying the affirmation of one's allegiance to the system, party, or candidate; avoiding the feeling of guilt associated with abstention, etc. Riker and Ordeshook are no doubt correct in assuming that these psychic factors are crucial to any explanation of the decision to vote.[24] It is puzzling, however, that they should be called rational considerations. The definition of rationality is, fortunately, of no great import. I have argued that we cannot account for voting in terms of the external rewards of the act, and with that premise Riker and Ordeshook have no disagreement.

Although we know that it is true, we are still disturbed when we discover yet another context in which individuals acting in their own interest cannot provide for their collective interests. Perhaps the reason that political scientists have argued that the decision to vote is rational is that there is a latent but strong belief in anarchism or laissez-faire liberalism at the root of our conception of society. Nevertheless, Adam Smith's invisible hand cannot be seen not because it is invisible, but because it is like the emperor's clothes. As Olson puts it, unless a group is so small that each individual's contribution is necessary, or unless there is "coercion or some other special device to make individuals act in their common interest, rational, self-interested individuals will not act to achieve their common or group interests." [25] The "logic of collective action" requires that when a collectivity deems it essential that a certain public good be provided, it ordinarily uses coercion in order to insure that all citizens do their part. Let us say that the water supply of a community were in danger of becoming contaminated by an excess of algae caused by the extensive use of high phosphate detergents. In the absence of any general prohibition against the use of such detergents it is irrational for an individual citizen to incur the extra cost of low phosphate detergents, and there is no evidence that the voluntary use of such detergents has been sufficiently extensive to have a significant effect. Only those communities whose water supply was genuinely threatened have prohibited the use of high phosphate detergents, and I suspect that not even all of those communities have done so. For moral or prudential reasons, we are generally reluctant to use coercion to provide public goods, the result being that such goods are often not provided, or are provided in insufficient amounts.

As a case study in the ability of communities to provide public goods, voting presents a paradox. There is no legal coercion, there are no "special incentives" (at least, we assume, not generally) to lure people to the polls. Nevertheless, sufficient numbers of citizens do contribute to the provision of this public good to make elections one of our most viable and stable institutions. Free riding is indeed unjust, and it is wrong for the nonvoter not to do his part in providing the public good. But it may be preferable to tolerate this injustice if the alternative is to introduce unnecessary legal coercion, especially when those who do take on the burden of providing the public good do not seem to mind doing so. Before that matter can be resolved, the fact that so many citizens are willing to forgo their rational self-interest and contribute to the public good deserves an explanation.

If we consider the psychology of the decision to vote, we find that citizens are more likely to vote if they feel that their vote makes a difference and/or if they feel that they have an obligation to vote. In terms of motivation, that the act of voting is inefficacious if irrelevant, it is sufficient that the citizen feel efficacious. The relationship between a sense of political efficacy and the propensity to vote is, of course, one of the most well-confirmed propositions about citizen behavior.[26] Although much has been said about the relationship between the sense of political efficacy and political participation, relatively little has been said about the relationship between the sense of political efficacy and political reality or "actual efficacy." The little evidence we do have indicates the absence of a strong relationship between actual efficacy and the feeling of efficacy, at least in the context of voting, although the efficacious are generally the better educated and the more informed. For example, the actual efficacy of a voter is directly related to the expected closeness of an election; the slimmer the margin among the candidates, the greater the probability that an individual's vote will be decisive. Yet when compared with other variables, the perceived closeness of an election has relatively little effect on turnout. In recent American presidential elections, the closest elections (1948, 1960, 1968) had an average turnout lower than the landslide elections (1952, 1956, 1964).[27] The feeling of political efficacy seems to be rooted in the citizen's personality, his sense of self-esteem, his sense of personal efficacy, not in any rational calculations about the political reality within which he operates. Citizens who feel efficacious as persons also tend to feel politically efficacious, and if they feel politically efficacious, the chances are that they will decide to vote.[28]

While helping to explain voting behavior, the sense of political efficacy is considerably less important than the "sense of citizenship duty."[29] In the 1956 election, 52 percent of those with a low sense of political efficacy voted, while 91 percent of those with a high sense of political efficacy did so.[30] Thus, the spread (in terms of percentage voting) between those with a high and low sense of political efficacy is 39 percent, while the spread between those with a high and low sense of citizenship duty is 72 percent. To look at those figures in another way, while citizens who feel inefficacious may well vote (52 percent of them did so), those who do not feel a sense of duty rarely do so (13 percent of them voted). If we examine the content of the "sense of citizenship duty" scale, we find that seven out of eight respondents did not believe that "it isn't so important to vote when you know your party doesn't have a chance to win," and an equal number disagreed with the statement, "so many other people vote in the national elections that it doesn't matter much to me whether I vote or not." [31] While some persons vote because they believe that their vote is significant, others vote simply because they feel that they ought to. As Lane puts it, "One can satisfy his conscience as easily by a non-significant vote as by a significant vote." [32] For example, over half of those who did not care at all about the results of the 1956 election still voted, presumably because they were motivated by a sense of duty.

While the sense of citizenship duty may be quite strong, it appears to be easily satisfied, that is, one can fulfill one's duty by the simple act of voting. One need not participate in other ways.[33] Thus, when citizens are not moved to participate by a sense of duty, they tend to act more rationally—they do not participate. Olson notes that union members expressed the wish for higher attendance at union meetings, presumably because increased attendance would strengthen the union. Nevertheless, the union members rarely attended those meetings themselves. Their actions, according to Olson, "were a model of rationality . . . [they] will get the benefits of the union's achievements whether [they] attend meetings or not," and if they did attend the meetings, they would not "be able to add noticeably to those achievements." [34] The sense of citizenship duty that moves many of them to do their part in providing one public good (elections) does not extend to union meetings, thus, they do not do their part in providing for another public good (a stronger union).

The attempt to inculcate a general sense of loyalty and duty among the citizenry is not, of course, peculiar to the American system. The overwhelming importance of the electoral process within that general sense of duty may be somewhat unique. The importance of elections as a mechanism for making all kinds of decisions is introduced to us at an early age. Schools not only have mock elections in which students go through the motions of voting in a national election, but elections are used to make a multitude of decisions—to choose class officers, team captains, topics for study, games to be played, etc. The centrality of the electoral process in the American conception of politics is introduced early and it persists. A factory worker named De Angelo, who never goes to political meetings, told Robert Lane that "voting is the thing, the right to put in the guy you want—that's the big thing." [35] To paraphrase Vince Lombardi, voting is not only the big thing, for many it is the only thing. Attitudes toward voting and elections are a curious mixture of positive feelings about elections in particular and negative feelings about political participation in general. It is a recognition that voting may be the only opportunity for citizens to express themselves, or as one of Almond and Verba's respondents put it, "outside of voting, there isn't much the average fellow can do. . . ." [36]

If those who vote do so because they feel efficacious or dutiful, those who do not vote are apathetic, cynical, or alienated—or so goes the literature. If my argument is sound, it may well be that those who do not vote are making accurate perceptions of their role in the polity, but do not have their perceptions obscured by a high sense of efficacy (dare we say "false consciousness"?) nor are they compensated by a strong sense of citizenship duty. While there is a strong case for worrying about those who feel efficacious, because the citizen who is socialized into society's dominant values is taken as the norm, the nonvoter is deviant and it is his psyche which is in trouble. Now it may well be that the nonvoter is often apathetic, cynical, and alienated, but he is also often poor, uneducated, and black. The various institutions that socialize the majority into the dominant values of the society do not achieve the same impact on those on the margins. Those who live in marginal conditions are not subject to the same influences of school or the media, and they hear different things at home and from their friends. Since they are not formed into "good citizens," they act rationally and do not vote.

What appeared to be a paradox—that citizens seem voluntarily to act against their own self-interest to provide a public good—should not now seem quite so paradoxical. Olson claims that "rational, self-interested individuals will not act to achieve their common or group interests" without "coercion or some other special device." Nothing that has been advanced here indicates that he is wrong. Quite the opposite, we have shown that in the case of voting his analysis is confirmed. Rather than assume that in the absence of coercion, rational individuals will not provide for a public good, we should not be so quick to assume that individuals are always rational. We should not underestimate the ability of a society to encourage such altruism, although its ability to do so is clearly related to the cost to each individual of providing the public good. It is most likely to occur when the cost of providing the public good is quite small. For example, it would be quite surprising if Americans were prone to contribute voluntarily tax dollars that they were not compelled to pay. And if we were to observe a society in which citizens contributed substantial proportions of their income without legal coercion, we would suspect that rather extensive forms of psychic manipulation were in use. We would hesitate to call such contributions "voluntary." That is, of course, precisely the point. When we observe that individuals in large numbers forgo their self-interest to provide a public good, we must at least raise the question of the "voluntariness" of those contributions. Do we have a system of voluntary participation in elections now?

The answer, clearly, turns on the way in which "voluntary" is defined. The usual conception of a voluntary action is that it is one performed in the absence of either physical coercion or the threat of penalties. In this sense, the decision to vote is generally a voluntary one. But is that an adequate conception of voluntary action? [37] The influence of Freud is too strong for us naively to argue that the absence of external restraints is both the necessary and sufficient condition for a free choice. In describing the phenomenon of psychic compulsion (the way in which the superego—the conscience, the sense of guilt—successfully internalizes social norms and constitutes an extraordinarily powerful form of repression), Freud has added a new and significant dimension to our understanding of freedom and compulsion. The socialization process in which civilized men become socially and morally mature is a process in which coercion, "a threatened external unhappiness—loss of love and punishment on the part of the external authority—has been exchanged for a permanent internal unhappiness, for the tension of the sense of guilt." [38]

To the extent that our actions are the product of society's determination of what we should do and feel and not our own determination of our own ends, it is not appropriate to say that our actions are voluntary. There is, of course, an important sense in which almost all desires are socially determined. The desire for certain kinds of food, for example, is a product of society. What makes a desire or action involuntary is not that it is socially formed but that it is maintained only by constant reinforcement and perhaps even lies. Our society attempts to instill in the average citizen the feeling that *his* political actions do make a difference. Riker and Ordeshook, in commenting on the tendency of citizens to overestimate the probability that their vote will be decisive, state that "the subjectively estimated chance of a tie ... may be as high as the propaganda urges it to be, even though in objective calculations, the chance of a tie may be low." [39] (A rational model indeed!) To the extent, then, that a person votes from a feeling of political efficacy which is, in itself, a feeling based on misunderstandings of political reality, I think it fair to say that such a vote is somewhat less than voluntary. If the citizen performs a certain act out of a sense of duty, the action may certainly be voluntary; it may be the ultimate case of moral autonomy. To the extent that the feeling of duty or obligation derives from the individual's experience, judgment, and understanding of his relationship to others, actions out of a sense of duty are certainly quite voluntary. But such is clearly not the case with voting. We are not allowed to determine whether or not we have a duty to vote and then act upon it. Rather, that sense of duty is created and maintained at great pains and expense to the society. Elections become rituals in which citizens cleanse themselves of guilt. Thus, if we employ a conception of compulsion that includes psychic phenomena, in the face of all the evidence available to us about why people vote, it is rather difficult to claim that the act of voting is, at present, "free and unfettered." [40]

The case for compulsory voting should now be clear. Elections are desirable political mechanisms which we should all help to sustain. Since the rational action for each of us would be "free ride" and allow other citizens to carry the burden, we should force ourselves and our fellow citizens into carrying a fair share of the burden. The alternative to a system of compulsory voting seems not to be a system in which citizens are permitted to decide freely whether or not to cast a vote. The alternative to legal compulsion is a system that encourages us to be irrational, in which we systematically delude ourselves about the extent of our efficacy and in which we need continually to promote and reinforce a strong sense of guilt. The alternative to a system of legal compulsion is not voluntary voting, but psychic compulsion. In adopting a system of legal compulsion we would be able to reduce the extent of psychic compulsion. We would have to vote in order to avoid a fine, but we would not have to endure the massive propaganda efforts needed to "get out the vote."

I have argued that citizens *do* have a duty to vote and that such a duty should be legally enforced. I have also argued that the legal enforcement of that duty will reduce the extent of psychic compulsion, or, to put it in other terms, the feeling of moral responsibility. If it is desirable for a society to promote feelings of moral responsibility, it can be argued that since compulsory voting would reduce such feelings, it is therefore undesirable. This is a strong objection to my defense of compulsory voting. I will, then, sketch an argument by which that objection can be met.

First, it is necessary to draw a distinction between moral *issues* and moral *feelings*. "The fact that there is a law against murder makes it no less a moral issue, nor are tax laws any less morally binding because they have the support of the courts and law enforcement officials."[41] It is true that laws against murder make it no less a moral issue. It is also true that laws against tax evasion make it no less a moral issue. And were nonvoting made illegal, nonvoting would remain no less a moral issue. Moral feelings are another matter. The legal enforcement of the obligation not to murder does not, I assume, significantly reduce feelings of moral responsibility. However, I imagine that the legal enforcement of the obligation to pay taxes is accompanied by a relatively low level of moral feeling. I imagine that relatively few persons are strongly motivated by a feeling of duty to their fellow citizens when they complete IRS Form 1040, nor are they greatly bothered when they search for ways by which they can reduce their taxes. While tax paying remains a moral issue, we make it legally compulsory even though by doing so we reduce feelings of moral responsibility. Why?

A prudential and a moral answer can be advanced. On the prudential level, the society cannot afford to risk tax evasion on a large scale. On the moral level, we must recognize that when we speak of a person's moral obligations, we generally have in mind a relationship of some intimacy, i.e., the persons at least know one another. When we give those obligations legal enforcement, the relationship remains somewhat intimate, thus the persons involved still feel morally responsible. The problem with tax paying and voting is that the moral relationships occur in a context of remoteness. Were we to free ride by refusing to pay taxes, we would be refusing to fulfill our obligations to persons that we neither know nor care about. And although citizens may *be* morally obligated to strangers, we consider it neither feasible nor reasonable to demand that citizens *feel* morally responsible to them. While making voting legally compulsory probably will decrease feelings of moral responsibility, it seems a reasonable response to the problem of promoting such feelings in a context of remoteness. The extent of psychic compulsion necessary to get citizens to feel a moral responsibility to vote makes it undesirable that we continue to do so.

Compulsory voting is not inconsistent with genuine voluntary political participation. And it is not inconsistent with participation that is motivated by a sense of moral responsibility. It is inconsistent with such participation when participation is confined to the electoral arena. If there is a genuine desire for such participation, we would do well to adopt compulsory voting, stop the massive "get out the vote" campaigns, and provide for arenas of participation in which citizens can not only feel efficacious but also feel efficacious without delusion. With the hoopla and ritual removed from the electoral process, citizens might no longer feel that their citizenship duties are fulfilled by a once-a-year vote. They might no longer feel that voting is the "big thing" or the "only thing." Compulsory voting would, in a sense, liberate us from the domination of elections and render us free to contemplate more meaningful forms of political participation. There might be demands for more participation in decision making in places of employment, in educational institutions, and in determining the kinds of products we consume and the services offered to us.

When compulsory voting was first considered in Europe, it was claimed that it would hurt the working class. It was claimed that it was the rich who did not vote. Whether or not this was true at the time or merely a deceptive maneuver to discourage more widespread voting of the poor and working class, I do not know. But we do know that in the United States and most western nations it is the poor, the uneducated, and the powerless who do not vote and whose political clout is reduced by our system of "voluntary" voting. Under a system of compulsory voting, assuming that the poor and uneducated knew which candidates or parties best represented their interests, they would be compelled to act in their common interests and thus achieve more through the electoral process than they presently achieve.[42] Thus, compulsory voting is more consistent with social justice than is our present system.

There are additional side payments that might accompany a shift to compulsory voting. Compulsory voting would make the meaning of a vote clearer. It has been argued that voting constitutes a form of consent; by voting, the citizen is indicating his support of the system and its rules. If one does not wish one's vote to indicate such support, one has (under the present system) a very good reason *not* to vote. While I am not at all sure that it is fair to draw such a conclusion from a vote under the present system, under compulsory voting it would be absurd to make such an inference. We could not conclude that those who voted were in any way indicating their support of the system. Thus, those who feel obliged *not* to vote under the present arrangement, lest their vote be misunderstood, would be free to vote under compulsory voting. Similarly with nonvoting. Does nonvoting indicate contentment or alienation? Under compulsory voting (assuming that one could cast a blank ballot) we would have a precise count of those citizens who refuse to support any of the available candidates. In addition, those who abstain under the present system because they prefer a minor party candidate who has no chance of winning would be more likely to vote. Thus, compulsory voting would more accurately reflect the strength of minor parties. To the extent that we wish election results to reflect the preferences of the entire citizenry, compulsory voting would serve us well.

Compulsory voting is a good idea. It is a good idea whose time is either past or has not yet come. It is certainly not a good idea whose time is at hand. The very reasons that account for the failure of political thinkers to consider compulsory voting also preclude its adoption. Our latent belief in a type of liberal anarchism has made us so resistant to legal coercion, even when such coercion makes sense, that I doubt if this society could even discuss the proposal seriously. If I am right in suspecting that compulsory voting would not be accepted, it is not because it is not a good idea—rather, it would only confirm one of the major premises of the argument, that men are not always rational.[43]

NOTES AND REFERENCES

1. William G. Andrews suggests that turnout is considerably higher than it is commonly thought to be in "American Voting Participation," *Western Political Quarterly*, XIX (1966), 639-652. S. Kelley, Jr., Richard E. Ayers, and Wallace G. Bowen argue that cumbersome registration procedures account for the relatively low turnout in the United States in "Registration and Voting: Putting First Things First," *American Political Science Review*, LXI (1967), 259-279.

2. Among those who have argued for a more participatory conception of democracy are Jack L. Walker, "A Critique of the Elitist Theory of Democracy," *American Political Science Review*, LX (1966), 285-295; Lane Davis, "The Cost of Realism," *Western Political Quarterly*, XVII (1964), 37-46; Graeme Duncan and Steven Lukes, "The New Democracy," *Political Studies*, XI (1963), 156-177; and Peter Bachrach, *The Theory of Democratic Elitism* (Boston: Little, Brown, 1967).

3. Among those who have argued the more conservative or "elitist" position are Bernard Berelson et al., *Voting* (Chicago: University of Chicago Press, 1954), pp. 306ff.; Gabriel Almond and Sidney Verba, *The Civic Culture* (Princeton, N.J.: Princeton University Press, 1963), pp. 473ff.; W. H. Morris-Jones, "In Defense of Apathy," *Political Studies*, II (1954), 25-37; Henry B. Mayo, "A Note on the Alleged Duty to Vote," *Journal of Politics*, XXI (1959), 319-323; and Francis G. Wilson, "The Pragmatic Electorate," *American Political Science Review*, XXIV (1930), 16-37.

4. Whether or not the legal obligation to vote should apply to all or only some elections is a question I have chosen not to answer in this chapter.

5. James Hogan, *Election and Representation* (Cork, Ireland: Cork University Press, 1945), p. 266.

6. The appropriateness of compulsory voting for noncompetitive election systems is not considered here. Even within the framework of competitive election systems, elections do serve other functions. An excellent discussion of the various functions served by elections is contained in R. Rose and H. Mossawir, "Voting and Elections: A Functional Analysis," *Political Studies*, XV (1967), 173-201.

7. Among the few studies of compulsory voting are those from which this information was gathered. See Henry J. Abraham's articles, "One Way To Get Out the Vote," *National Municipal Review*, XXXIX (1950), 395-399, and "What Cure for Voter Apathy," *National Municipal Review*, LXI (1952), 346-350; William Robson, "Compulsory Voting," *Political Science Quarterly*, XXXVIII (1924), 569-577; and Herbert Tingsten, *Political Behavior* (Totowa, N.J.: Bedminster Press, 1962), pp. 183ff. (originally published in 1937 by P. S. King and Sons, London). In my survey of the literature, I was unable to find any defense of compulsory voting in an American journal. Since this manuscript went to press, Malcolm Feeley has published "A Solution to the 'Voting Dilemma' in Modern Democratic Theory," *Ethics*, 84 (April 1974).

8. See Tingsten, *Political Behavior*, p. 197.

9. Henry J. Abraham's argument against compulsory voting includes this quotation from Chief Justice Brace in Kansas City v. Whipple, 136 Mo. 475 (1896), on p. 347 in the above article.

10. See, for example, V. O. Key, Jr., *The Responsible Electorate* (Cambridge, Mass.: Belknap Press, 1966); William C. Mitchell, *Why Vote?*

(Chicago: Markham Press, 1971); and Gerald M. Pomper, *Elections in America* (New York: Dodd, Mead, 1968).

11. I am using the definition of public goods put forth by Mancur Olson, Jr., *The Logic of Collective Action* (New York: Schocken Books, 1965), p. 14. It goes without saying that to say that x is a "public good" is not to make a value judgment about its desirability.

12. I am excluding from my analysis some strictly private goods that are available to A only if A votes. For example, by voting A may keep his job, please his wife, or serve as a good example to his children. The classic argument on the irrationality of voting is made by Anthony Downs, *An Economic Theory of Democracy* (New York: Harper, 1957).

13. A similar equation is offered by William Riker and Peter Ordeshook in "A Theory of the Calculus of Voting," *American Political Science Review*, LXII (1968), 25-42. The estimate of "P" must take into account information about what other persons are likely to do and the impact that A's decision will have on others. If A's decision to vote will cause ten other persons to vote, then A's calculation of the probability that his vote will have an effect on the outcome of the election must include that consideration.

14. A's vote may have an effect on the outcome even if it is not the deciding vote. It may be the case that the size of the winning candidate's majority will have political effects. For the purposes of this paper I have chosen not to consider this issue.

15. See Downs, *Economic Theory,* pp. 139ff.

16. *Ibid.,* p. 7.

17. I have in mind here both types of public goods I have mentioned: one, the public goods (e.g., the existence of the electoral system) which are available to all members of the community; two, the public goods (e.g., policies favoring labor unions) which are available to all members of a particular subgroup of the community. The irrelevance to moral discourse of the response "not everyone does that" is, of course, part of what Kant had in mind in discussing the categorical imperative. For an excellent modern statement of the problems with that argument in moral discourse, see Marcus G. Singer, *Generalization in Ethics* (New York: Knopf, 1961).

18. Morris-Jones, "In Defense," p. 61.

19. *Ibid.,* p. 61.

20. Mitchell, *Why Vote?,* p. 61.

21. *Economic Theory,* p. 270.

22. Brian Barry, *Sociologists, Economists and Democracy* (London: Collier-Macmillan, 1970), p. 20.

23. Riker and Ordeshook, "Calculus," p. 25.

24. There is a sense in which all rewards are psychic, that is, to say that something is a reward implies that the person values it. The distinction that I am making (and Riker and Ordeshook make) between psychic and nonpsychic rewards can be restated in terms of a distinction between internal and external rewards. An action may entail rewards because of the consequences of the action (in which case the rewards are nonpsychic or external) or rewards may accompany the performing of the action itself.

25. Olson, *Logic,* p. 2.

26. See Angus Campbell et al., *The American Voter* (New York: Wiley, 1960), p. 105.

27. The effect of perceived closeness increases with partisanship. For non-

partisans it has almost no effect; for intense partisans it has some effect. See Campbell, *American Voter,* pp. 99-100.

28. See Lester Milbrath, *Political Participation* (Chicago: Rand McNally, 1965), pp. 56-59.
29. For a general discussion of the literature and some new research see George B. Levenson, "The Behavioral Relevance of the Obligation to Participate," a paper delivered at the 1971 Annual Meeting of the American Political Science Association, Chicago, September, 1971.
30. Campbell, *American Voter,* pp. 105-106.
31. Robert E. Lane, *Political Life* (New York: Free Press, 1959), p. 309.
32. *Ibid.*
33. Milbrath, *Political Participation,* pp. 62-63.
34. Olson, *Logic,* p. 86. Although union members are not willing to make attendance at meetings compulsory, most are quite aware of the "logic of collective action," for most union members support closed or union shops and vigorously oppose "right to work" laws.
35. Robert E. Lane, *Political Ideology* (New York: Free Press, 1962), p. 166.
36. Almond and Verba, *Civic Culture, op. cit.* This quotation is taken from the paper edition, p. 131.
37. For an excellent treatment of the inadequacy of the physical-mechanistic model of freedom and the need for a psychological approach, see Benjamin Barber, *Superman and Common Men* (New York: Praeger, 1971).
38. Sigmund Freud, *Civilization and Its Discontents,* trans. James Strachey (New York: Norton, 1961), p. 75.
39. Riker and Ordeshook, "Calculus," pp. 38-39.
40. Hogan, *Election,* p. 266.
41. I wish to thank Professor J. Roland Pennock for pointing out the necessity of dealing with this issue. This quotation is from correspondence with him.
42. In discussing this point with students at the University of Vermont, a surprising number maintained the rather "elitist" position that the poor and uneducated are too ill-informed to vote their own interests. It seems that there is very little evidence to support this position.
43. Political scientists would have their own good reasons for opposing compulsory voting, for it would make an entire field of study irrelevant. We would no longer be able to study the "decision to vote," since presumably almost everyone would be voting.

INDEX